THE WIZARD, THE EGG AND FITCHER'S BIRD

Returning Spiritual Life to Nature in the Individuation of Women

Laurel Howe

CHIRON PUBLICATIONS • ASHEVILLE, NORTH CAROLINA

www.ChironPublications.com

Interior and cover design by Danijela Mijailovic
Printed primarily in the United States of America.

ISBN 978-1-68503-179-4 paperback
ISBN 978-1-68503-180-0 hardcover
ISBN 978-1-68503-181-7 electronic
ISBN 978-1-68503-182-4 limited edition paperback

Library of Congress Cataloging-in-Publication Data

Names: Howe, Laurel, author.
Title: The wizard, the egg and Fitcher's Bird : returning spiritual life to nature in the individuation of women / Laurel Howe.
Description: Asheville, North Carolina : Chiron Publications, [2023] |
Includes bibliographical references. | Summary: "The animus remains a baffling, misunderstood force in women's psychology, but the fairytale "Fitcher's Bird" brings his ambivalent, wizardly power and his psychic aims as the spirit of individuation into view, reaching into rich alchemical symbolism to do so. The tale and its alchemical background are illuminated with dreams and psychic images from several women's lives, whose stories help us understand the profound personal and archetypal value of engaging creatively with the animus. Like the alchemical nature God, Mercurius, the animus is a life force, an archetype with two sides. His negative side is symbolized in "Fitcher's Bird" by a wizard's longtime ability to abduct maidens from their parental homes with barely a touch by dressing as a beggar and appealing to their charity. He displays a perverse dominance over the feminine that has built up in our traditional attitudes over the millennia and takes hold of women through their own participation in those attitudes. Taking them to his great house in the forest, the wizard promises young women riches for their obedience. But the maidens, like the wives of Bluebeard, predictably enter the one forbidden room and end up slaughtered-in "Fitcher's Bird" they are hewn limb from limb. Only one maiden is clever enough to pay attention to the gift the wizard's positive side offers-a simple egg, symbolizing the process of individuation when an ego nurtures a relationship with the unconscious. Switching her focus to the egg, the heroine redeems her sisters and at the end of the tale makes an appearance as the wondrous Fitcher's bird-an image for the archetypal feminine redeemed from dismemberment and disappearance"-- Provided by publisher.
Identifiers: LCCN 2023040044 (print) | LCCN 2023040045 (ebook) | ISBN 9781685031794 (paperback) | ISBN 9781685031800 (hardcover) | ISBN 9781685031817 (ebook)
Subjects: LCSH: Femininity--Psychological aspects. | Women--Identity. | Identity (Psychology)--Religious aspects. | Fairy tales--Psychological aspects.
Classification: LCC BF175.5.F45 H69 2023 (print) | LCC BF175.5.F45 (ebook) | DDC 155.3/33--dc23/eng/20240125
LC record available at https://lccn.loc.gov/2023040044
LC ebook record available at https://lccn.loc.gov/2023040045

Laurel Howe
1955-2023

For my analysands.

"In the absence of a connection to the divine feminine, humanity is lost."
—A woman's dream, 2020

Contents

Illustrations

Style Note

Following the example set by C. G. Jung, the psychological term *self* is not capitalized in this work because it is a term that refers to the psychological equivalent of the god-image rather than a deity per se or a proper name. For the same reason, the term *eros* is not capitalized when referring to the psychological principle but capitalized when referring to a deity.

Acknowledgments

The women who share their lives in this book have devoted themselves to the process of individuation with honesty and courage, each in her genuine way. We owe them a debt of gratitude for their wholehearted work with the psyche and their willingness to be included in this document. Through their dreams and dialogues with the psyche, we witness the profound redemption of the archetypal feminine that may emerge from an encounter with the spirit of the unconscious, also brought forth and redeemed through their work.

I could not have made it through the writing of this book without the support of my husband, my children, and my friends at home and abroad, who have endured my lack of availability through the years of withdrawal needed to finish the work. I thank everyone for their generosity and love, and especially my husband for all the wonderful meals.

My dear colleagues and friends who read drafts of this work helped me unfold the reality and meaning of the "Fitcher's Bird" fairy tale— Denise Rudin, Charlene Henry, Alan Drymala, Matt Christie, Jennifer Phelps, Eva Wertenschlag-Birkhäuser, and Brigitte Jacobs-Frölich. Thanks to the careful work of editor Siobhan Drummond, the book found the steady legs it needed to make its way into the world.

Dr. Ajay Kumar Singh, professor of art history and director of Bharat Kala Bhavan Museum in Varanasi, India, made it possible to secure a photograph of the artist Manaku's painting, *Hiranyagarbha,* displayed on the cover. I appreciate his care for this work and the museum's devotion to preserving the great artwork and iconography of India and the region. The Philadelphia Museum of Art and the Central Zürich Library generously allowed us to share images from their collection without charge. I also want to express gratitude to the Archive for Research into Archetypal Symbolism and www.ARAS.org for making a vast store of digital images available for research and for helping locate original artwork in libraries and museums throughout the world.

If not for the ongoing devotion of members of the Research and Training Centre for Depth Psychology according to C. G. Jung and Marie-Louise von Franz in Zurich, the observations in this book would not be possible. I am eternally grateful for their commitment to empirical research into the reality of the objective psyche and its aim to be known in its wholeness in human consciousness.

Introduction

As a child, Elise was convinced that the parish church in her Swiss Alpine village was enormous. She remembered sitting in her pew under the cathedral arches feeling her soul expand into what seemed like the lofts of heaven. An imposing gold leaf Christ gazed at her from the rotunda, wondering what she was thinking. As young as 4, Elise felt the *tremendum* of God in the quiet magnitude of hand-hewn image and architecture. She cherished the ritual of the Mass and longed to be an altar girl—to ring the ceremonial bell or light the holy candles the way the altar boys did.

But when she was 7 and preparing for her First Communion, Elise found herself troubled, anxiously second-guessing her relationship to God.

"I had to confess my first sin, and I was out of my head with worry," she told me. "I lost sleep for weeks, maybe even months, agonizing over what sin to tell the priest. It had to be the worst sin I ever committed, but I didn't know which one God would choose for that 'honor.' I became frantic as the day approached. This is going to sound so stupid, but here it is: I was terrified that I wouldn't come up with a good enough sin."

Elise knew that God knew her secrets. He would know if she weren't revealing her most important sin. But how would Elise know what that sin was? To be the best girl she could be—and as the eldest of three children, she was always such a good girl—she had to live up to God's expectations. The rules of Communion didn't help her uncover what she felt in her heart, and God, as far as she could tell, was silent on the matter.

Already at the tender age of 7, Elise didn't feel related to God. She didn't know what God would consider unworthy in her, or for that matter, what he would see as virtuous. Worse, she didn't know how to search her own soul for the truth at this religious milestone; she only knew she had to *say* the right thing, to please the priest, and hopefully through him secure God's approval.

God's mysterious perfectionism stuck with Elise throughout her childhood, his numinosity inextricably mixed with judgment in her imagination. Striving always to be good, she took care of her family in a capacity beyond her years, holding everyone in her rattled household together. But her respect for the authority of the church faded as she became an adult and observed certain hypocrisies. She remembered how the parish priest would hear confession from her alcoholic father, for example, and then join the family at table, imbibing freely in drink. There were other disappointments, but the revelation of widespread pedophilia in the church was the last straw.

Elise left the Catholic Church in her 20s, finding it could not meet her ongoing spiritual inquiries. But the powerful, authoritative voice of God stayed in her imagination, stalking her with threats that she could never be good enough to feel his love and validation, that she would never really know what was worthy in herself. As an adult, she kept subjecting herself to relationships and performance standards that her fatigue and her instincts wanted to reject. She vaguely felt those instincts but ignored them, insisting instead on mind over matter. Yet regardless of how hard she worked in school, in her profession, or as a wife and mother, she could never meet the ingrained expectations of that supernatural, perfectionistic voice of God—an overwhelming, judgmental aspect of the great father archetype that permeated her spiritual life. Elise's thoughts and fantasies about the value of her life remained imprisoned in Catholic ideals, even though she sensed since age 7 those ideals did not belong to her as an individual.

In psychological language, Elise was caught in the so-called negative animus, a term that I use with some reluctance. The negative animus is a collective mindset, a judgmental orthodoxy that invisibly drives a woman's mentality according to her culture's one-sidedness, whether she knows it or not. But as a natural psychic phenomenon, the animus per se is not negative or perfectionistic. On the contrary, he is a woman's own, individuating spirit, driving a woman's quest for spiritual meaning—logos—that is unique to her, something we sense at the core of Elise's earliest spiritual yearnings. He fights tooth and nail to help a woman realize the meaning and value of her imperfect life, mediating dreams and images from the unconscious that are meant just for her. At the deepest level, he is a woman's individual experience of the spiritual aspect of the collective unconscious, encouraging her to break the rules and find him. He becomes negative when his wholeness is ignored or degraded, when he is not differentiated from a collective worldview.

The spirit of the unconscious has no place in our collective, Judeo-Christian ideation of the divine, which is strictly masculine and without shadow. A woman who harbors that collective ideal, even in its New Age guises, is cut off from the darker, instinctual, and more feminine aspects of the god-image that she needs in order to feel the natural validity of her life. Wanting to link a woman to new, unique life meaning, the animus must be freed from the cultural prejudices that see the unconscious and its darkness—including the dark personal experiences it imposes on us—as illicit or meaningless. Even a woman who has studied Jungian psychology may need to go through a profound change of consciousness if she is genuinely to relate to the unconscious as the original, reliable source of meaning and development.

As with Elise, if a woman's search for spiritual meaning is identified with an old notion of good versus bad, right versus wrong, any value she may feel for her own life inevitably becomes enslaved to appeasing that one-sided spiritual attitude. Elise studied other religions and delved into psychology, but her mindset adapted every new idea she encountered to the ideals she absorbed in her youth. Meditation, for example, became another exercise in faultlessness rather than a way to encounter shadow or accept what really *is*—to honor matter as much as mind, reality as much as an ideal. The negative, judgmental animus continued to rule her fantasy thinking, cutting her off from her innate value by intimating that at any turn she could fail to meet the expectations of people in her life. She lost her connection to religious life, even though she always felt very religious.

Discovering Transpersonal Eros

Elise entered analysis in her 50s, not for the first time, and soon began to confront the inner dynamics of inner judgement and perfectionism she grew up with. Taking an inventory of her lifelong obedience to being good, Elise saw that she didn't have access to much, if any, merciful feeling for herself or her vulnerabilities as she was growing up. Her mother and father were both caught in the same standards and could not protect Elise or her siblings from any threats to their individuality.

Since childhood, she found the Virgin Mary fascinating, and Elise had always yearned to be loved by her, but in Mary's presence, Elise felt even more guilty for her doubt and uncertainty, ashamed for feeling alienated from God, and she carried this shame into adulthood. Like most girls and women in this predicament, Elise had no genuine access to divine eros—to a transpersonal reality that would affirm her inherent value as an ordinary, flawed individual with an immortal soul.

In analysis and devoted to her dreams, however, Elise's relationship with the symbolic realm over time finally loosened the grip of those punishing ideals. Elise was naturally faithful to individuation and soaked in the meaning that the unconscious brought her. She wrote down her dreams every day, no matter how small or insignificant they seemed, and began to see that they were reflecting the meaning of her struggle back to her, showing her how to honor her life in a new way, and as it really was. She began to uncover the autonomy of the criticizing thought system that had developed so much momentum over the years and to develop ways of mitigating its harm.

At the same time, Elise deepened her experience of the feminine, mirroring capacity of the unconscious. She knew she was being seen and valued for who she really was by a comprehensive eros interested more in her individuality than her conventional goodness. She began to understand and accept the symbolic dimension of her dreams, which in turn accepted her for everything she was.

The Other Side of Life

Elise's dreams connected her with the truth-telling capacities, the eros, and the wisdom of a different spiritual world—the symbolic realm of the objective psyche and its center, the self. Jung described the self as the paradoxical center and totality of the psyche, which is both individual and shared by all. He described how its unity and wholeness, so difficult to imagine, is expressed most efficiently in mandala images:

Their basic motif is the premonition of a centre of the personality, a kind of central point within the psyche, to which everything is related, by which everything is arranged, and which is itself a source of energy. The energy of the central point is manifested in the almost irresistible compulsion and urge to *become what one is*, just as every organism is driven to assume the form that is characteristic of its nature, no matter what the circumstances. This centre is not felt or thought of as the ego but, if one may so express it, as the self. Although the centre is represented by an innermost point, it is surrounded by a periphery containing everything that belongs to the *self*—the paired opposites that make up the total personality. This totality comprises consciousness first of all, then the personal unconscious, and finally an indefinitely large segment of the collective unconscious whose archetypes are common to all mankind.[1]

Elise began to feel the self, the urge to become who she really was, demonstrating to her that her individuality—not her perfection—was innately sacred, even desired by the collective dimension of the psyche to help it transform. For Elise, and any woman suffering from a negative animus, feeling the eros quality of the self—its reflective interest in everything about her—was the main challenge in her development. But slowly, Elise did absorb the healing experience of being truthfully seen and appreciated by the self, healing her habitual expectation of being constantly judged.

At an important point in her life, after she had prioritized her time to focus more on her dreams and creative work, Elise had a long, numinous dream in which her unique religious yearning was seen and treasured. In the dream, she and her husband discovered an unknown village built into the back of the mountain range near her home. It was a combined religious and community center.

> *My husband and I are driving near our home when we find*
> *a unique place to live, a village we didn't know existed. We*
> *are nestled inside and surrounded by breathtaking rocky*
> *mountain crags. It feels as if we should be on the back side*

---

[1] Jung, "Concerning Mandala Symbolism," *CW*, vol. 9i, par. 634.

of our local mountain range, but we would need to be further west for that to be the case. I continue to admire the scenery and realize that this feels like paradise. What a privilege it would be to see this every day.

Then I see that a community center has been built here. People are milling around, perhaps anticipating an event. To the right I notice a chapel built of white clapboard with pale blue trim. There is a gold, orblike decoration where the steeple would be, perched on top of an equilateral cross. Then I look into a room and see three teenagers preparing to take part in a Mass. There are two altar boys and an altar girl. The girl wears a priestlike red-and-white robe that is stunningly beautiful, a heavy brocade stitched like a Hawaiian quilt, with a curvy, organic, flower-looking pattern. She is joking around with the boys in a way that implies she has more experience and knowledge than they do. She seems to be their superior.

My gaze shifts back toward the chapel, where I see a young priest. He has blond hair and is also wearing a red-and-white robe. He is outside, chatting with folks in a lighthearted and familiar manner. I think to myself that he lacks that authoritarian stuffiness that many priests embody. It is clear that he is very connected to the community—familiar and well-liked by the people who live here.

Elise described this setting, hidden in a location near her actual home, as a place where she would love to live—where she could fully live. It was built for her taste, her feeling for spiritual life and community, and her love of nature. Her interactions with people in the dream brought her an immediate sense of belonging. The mandalalike structure of the combined community and religious center is integrated into "the back side" of the local mountain range, an image of wholeness that exists on the other side of life, in the eternal, psychic realm.

In the chapel, a confident altar girl (which the Catholic Church would never allow) dressed in her beautiful, sacred robes, seems to be fulfilling Elise's own early yearnings to honor the divine as a girl. The red and white of her robes symbolize alchemical opposites—masculine and feminine joined in a fabric whose texture and detailed stitching Elise, a skilled seamstress, found "stunningly beautiful."

In psychological terms, the altar girl is a living character in Elise's inner life, in her own myth. She represents a new eros capacity that in the dream has or could become an integral part of religious life—a spiritualized eros in Elise's religious center, a feminine spirit."[2] The young, blond priest represents a new masculine development in that center, one that is less authoritarian and more related than the traditional priests in Elise's experience, suggesting an eros development on the masculine side—a loving logos.

The gold, orblike decoration on top of an equal-armed, pagan cross, located where the steeple normally would be on a Christian church, symbolizes in another way the goal of renewal and reunion of masculine and feminine realms in religious life. A sphere and a cross each symbolizes wholeness and the union of opposites—the sphere an image of boundless heaven and spiritual life, and the cross the earth with its four directions. Together, the sphere and the cross signal the unification of spiritual and earthly life, or psyche and matter. The joined circle and cross also form the sign for copper, Venus, and woman, emphasizing the presence of the feminine (the reality of the psyche and its eros quality) as the overarching, unifying principle of the dream chapel. The fact that the religious center is not separate from nature but structurally integrated into nature is another way the dream expresses a new kind of religious life taking shape in Elise through her work with the unconscious. The dream points to the comprehensive goal of healing the long split between religion and nature, masculine and feminine, in the human psyche.[3] Reaching back into pre-

---

[2] Brigitte Jacobs-Frölich, in her lectures, has long used the term *feminine spirit* to express the creative, animating reality of the feminine principle, which goddesses of antiquity embody but which has been lost in modern consciousness.

[3] The dream motif of a structure being built to accommodate the development of a new religion has been shared by numerous people working in Jungian psychology. In 1949, Max Zeller reported such a dream to Jung, in which he was working with "many others" to build a "temple of vast dimensions . . . as far as I could see." Jung told Zeller he'd heard other dreams describing a structure being built to house a new religion, that it was happening "in India and China and Russia and all over the world," and that it would take 600 years to come together. Zeller said, "There was the answer to my question what we, as analysts, are doing." Zeller, *The Dream*, 2. In other words, practitioners of depth psychology are building a psychic structure in which a new way of experiencing and understanding the divine is taking shape.

Christian symbolism and combining two symbols into one, the dream paradoxically moves the god-image beyond the Christian one and into the future, indicating the reintegration of the feminine principle. Such a transformation requires a collective development in which consciousness itself becomes more feminine, that is, more related to the unconscious and to matter.

Gold "orb-like decoration

Rooted in Elise's individual religious yearnings, the dream helped her feel in a new way the reality of the self as an objective factor that was interested in her deepest aspirations, mediating her own development. She could sense that the self even needed her—as a place in which its feminine side could develop alongside a recovered masculine spirit indigenous to Elise.

"Fitcher's Bird" and the Spirit of Individuation

The fairy tale "Fitcher's Bird" helps us understand how the true spirit of individuation may be redeemed in a woman's relationship with the unconscious, even when that relationship begins badly. The tale begins, "There was once a wizard who used to take the form of a poor man. He went to houses and begged, and caught pretty girls. No one knew whither he carried them, for they were never seen more."[4] The wizard (or sorcerer in some versions of the tale) enchants the girls into the basket on his back and carries them away to his magnificent house in the forest. He

---

[4] Brothers Grimm, *Grimm's Complete Fairy Tales*, 49.

promises each girl comfort and riches, everything her heart can wish for, in exchange for obedience, and gives each maiden two things: the key to a room she is forbidden to enter and an egg that she must promise to carry with her everywhere she goes, on pain of a "great misfortune." This abduction is the setup of the tale and the beginning of every development it expresses. On a psychological level, the kidnapping describes just how easy it is for the negative animus to carry a woman away into a destructive situation that at first seems so innocent. She willingly complies but soon finds herself obeying commands that threaten her very development, following a pattern that has been repeated for a long time.

The fairy tale implies that maidens have been disappearing perhaps even for generations. All that time, the kidnapped maidens in the wizard's house disobey his command to stay out of his forbidden room. But for some reason, they obey his command to carry their eggs everywhere they go, revealing a conflict in the maidens themselves. As a result, when each maiden enters the forbidden room and finds the gruesome remains of girls who have been killed there, hewn to pieces and left in the wizard's "great bloody basin," she panics and drops her egg into the slaughter. Her egg is permanently stained with blood, revealing her disobedience and giving the wizard his reason to murder her too.

The tale focuses on the fates of three sisters, two of whom are the last to be killed this way. Although the third and youngest sister is also abducted, at the wizard's house she does something apparently no other maiden has tried before. Described as "clever and crafty," she disobeys the wizard's command where it matters most, putting her egg away "with great care" before she explores the house and the forbidden room. Because her egg is safe and protected when she sees her dismembered sisters, it remains unstained. Rather than panic, she performs a miracle, putting the pieces of her sisters back together and returning them to life. The crime of protecting her egg changes the whole course of the tale, making the redemption of her sisters possible.

Seeing her pure white egg, the wizard thinks the heroine is innocent and that she will become his bride, but the rest of the tale shows us how she works her way out of that predicament and brings about a further redemption symbolized by her appearance as Fitcher's bird. Simply by tending to her egg, which on a psychological level refers to individuation, the heroine not only transforms a long-standing, murderous pattern but reverses its destructive effects. She reveals how a woman tending the egg of individuation can transform and even reverse the destructive influence of a one-sided masculine energy that abducts her into the deadening prison of innocence and obedience. She also shows us how such an act may help redeem the feminine principle itself in the psychic realm.

The Egg and Individuation

The egg is a symbol with rich mythological history. It appears in many creation myths, representing the unseen, unknowable beginning of the world as well as its ongoing evolution. It is an image for potential life and its mysteries—how life arrives from an invisible source and develops according to uncanny patterns that only nature knows. Psychologically, the egg symbolizes the development of consciousness out of the unconscious through the cultivation of symbolic life, that is, individuation by way of nature. The egg's oval shell represents the individual container of psychological life that develops over time, a personality that can fulfill its own spiritual potential when the opposites inside (represented by the yolk and the white) are united in a unique way in her or his life.

In alchemical symbolism, the egg's development into a bird represents the natural growth of the inner divine being that begins in the unconscious of an individual and, properly tended, emerges into life as a tangible psychic reality. The heroine takes care of her egg, which means she takes care of her individuation process, and she does it according to what the egg needs, not what everyone else has done in obedience to the wizard. In a woman this would mean that finally she is tending to a relationship with the inborn divine factor—even as it has been introduced to her by the wizardly animus. In discovering her own reflective capacity, a way of tending to her life and development according to the symbolic language of the unconscious, her consciousness has already become more feminine.

Taking care of the egg saves the heroine's life and disempowers the wizard's evil momentum. Yet, we must remember, the wizard gave her that egg. He gave her everything she needed to recognize and depotentiate his evil side. Does his right hand know what his left hand is doing? How do we understand these two sides of the wizard?

The Nature Spirit

Like "Fitcher's Bird," many fairy tales harbor a transformational spirit, often a devilish character whose evil activity paradoxically leads to renewal. The wizard represents a psychic figure that we reject in our conventional religious and rational lives, one that we have relegated to the unconscious and so forced into a negative role. He is a spirit of nature, or a spirit of the unconscious and its transformational capacities, an archetypal force of uncontrollable energy.

The true spirit of the unconscious has a very difficult time getting through to a woman when she is caught in an old ideation of the god-image, as happened for Elise. His energy is split between good and evil, dismembering her connection to wholeness. As an autonomous phenomenon, however, the individuating spirit is constantly challenging a woman to realize his very dynamism as an objective reality, an aspect in fact of the suprapersonal feminine realm of the collective unconscious. He actually wants to connect a woman to that realm and to wholeness, helping bring a new god-image to bear in which masculine and feminine are united.

Elise experienced the autonomy of this inner spirit as a negative force for the greater part of her life, its presence colored by her original, imprinting encounter with the patriarchal father-god of the church. Using the judging voice of the old god-image, the spiritual energy of the animus tortured her constantly. But because she did finally pay attention to his dynamism per se with utmost sincerity, differentiating his autonomy from the messages in which he was caught, her inner religious life was renewed, for example, in the beauty and deep symbolism of her dream of a new religious center. The sheer energy of the animus, cast at first in a negative role, paradoxically led to a profound renewal of her spiritual life and reverberated into the god-image.

The wizard is an image for two dimensions of the animus that are in direct conflict with each other, one demanding obedience to convention, the other insisting on individuality. The danger for a woman lies in the fact that both sides of the animus, as well as the conflict itself, are fueled by archetypal, mercurial energy—wizardly energy. As long as this division in the animus remains unconscious, its conflict will torture her, pitting herself against herself. Tending to the conflict head-on, however, she may eventually find that, although the conventional side of the animus torments her with perfectionism, at the same time, and with the same gestures, the individuating side of the animus offers her the egg of her own development.

Alchemical Motifs in "Fitcher's Bird"

Examining the close connection in this fairy tale between the wizard, the egg, and the image of a "wondrous bird," we begin to realize that all three can be seen as aspects of the elusive alchemical spirit of nature, Mercurius. He, like Christ, is a god of death and resurrection, but Mercurius has an openly devilish side, mainly because we see him that way but also because he is asking us psychologically to die and resurrect with him, in order to bring new psychic and religious possibilities into the world. He is sometimes called the "egg of nature" because, according to the alchemists, he personifies nature's mysteries of growth and transformation.[5] In the imagery of the alchemical philosophical egg, we will see how Mercurius is the egg, the bird that hatches out of the egg, and the transformation itself—from bird to egg to bird. Knowing all this, we can hypothesize that "Fitcher's Bird" is a tale about a woman's encounter with Mercurius and, once she pays attention to the unconscious, his encounter with her.

Indeed, the wizard's Mecurius-like attributes, and the fact that so many other motifs in this tale are alchemical, hint that "Fitcher's Bird" could be an alchemical fairy tale about Mercurius, one that is rare, if not unique, for its feminine perspective. Whether or not this version of the so-called sister-rescue tales comes out of an alchemical tradition, the mercurial

---

[5] Jung quotes the "Aurelia occulta" from *Theatrum chemicim* IV (1659): "I am the egg of nature, known only to the wise, who in piety and modesty bring forth from me the microcosm, which was prepared for mankind by Almighty God, but given only to the few, while the many long for it in vain." Jung, "The Spirit Mercurius," *CW*, vol. 13, par. 267.

wizard, the egg, the bird, honey, and fire are alchemical motifs that express the unfolding of the individuation process according to nature's mysteries. The fact that these motifs appear in a fairy tale of feminine redemption, and from the feminine point of view, gives us a rare opportunity to explore the alchemical symbolism in terms of women's psychology.

Organization and Aims

This book strives to depict the empirical encounter of women with the spirit of the unconscious, at first experienced as the "negative animus." A woman beset by the animus is confronting the effects of an old religious attitude that lives in her psyche, animated by unconscious dynamism and collective pressure to conform to a deep split between good and evil, masculine and feminine, spirit and matter. On the collective level, the negative animus is a pervasive problem, appearing differently in every woman, though with the same general outline. He is grueling to analyze because his negativity hides out in the minds of those very women as if he were positive, mimicking collective attitudes. For many women, conventional, punishing patriarchy, including a New Age preference for a higher, light-filled spirituality and the need to always be good and full of bliss, is fueled as much by that inner dynamism and is extremely difficult to catch in consciousness as a punishing phenomenon. I am devoting this book to the innumerable women who suffer from this problem. Although the process of individuation described in these pages is also applicable to men, I discuss the fairy tale primarily for women whose struggle with the animus may, when seen as a spiritual problem, lead to a profoundly meaningful life, if not a perfect one.

In the following pages, we will explore the experiences of several women who have struggled mightily with the problem of the autonomous animus that is trapped in conventional ideals—even the new ideals that don't seem conventional at first glance. These women offer an intimate view of how the collective demeaning of the feminine realm and the unconscious is internalized, and how it can become destructive and even dangerous, cutting women off from their instinct to tend or value their inner life and its natural darkness. What a woman must go through to realize and dismantle her *participation mystique* with a masculine, perfectionistic worldview or a critical, aesthetic, righteous, or intellectual attitude toward life, and the profound transformation she experiences in doing so, is almost impossible to describe without the help of a fairy tale like "Fitcher's Bird." We will explore several women's experiences of the negative animus and identify its personal and archetypal qualities. We will see how a woman's shadow secretly cooperates with the orthodoxy of the animus, making him even more difficult to identify. And we will find out how bringing such a destructive pattern to consciousness can lead to redemption in both feminine and masculine realms.

We will discover how, when one woman turns toward the flow of life in the unconscious for meaning, her relationship to the transpersonal realm is transformed on a fundamental level, and so is the god-image itself. This reverberating transformation is expressed in the tale by the heroine appearing in the unusual image of Fitcher's bird. To transform herself into such a rare, wondrous bird, the heroine dips herself in honey and rolls in feathers—a rather rudimentary image of the opposites but united in a wholly original way and according to the timeless wisdom of the birds and the bees. Symbolically, honey represents the saturating eros quality of the psyche, and feathers the elusive, spiritual quality of the psyche. Fitcher's bird thus is the epitome of a psychic image, an expression of wholeness that can be realized when a woman's spiritual life is informed by the natural language of the unconscious. As a white bird, she is an image for the soul, redeemed from a worldview that for so long has forgotten that the divine aspect of life *is* nature.

Lest we think too poorly of the wizard, we must remember he is not only a kidnapper and a murderer but also the mysterious awakening spirit who provides the heroine with the key and the egg that lead to the exposure of his own evil, and therefore to a profound transformation. His two-sidedness as a spirit of the unconscious is as much a subject of this fairy tale as the heroine's transformation. He, the heroine, and the feminine side of spiritual life are all redeemed together, thanks to the heroine's clever persistence.

Grimm's Fitcher's Bird

from *Grimm's Complete Fairy Tales* (Garden City, NY: Nelson Doubleday)

There was once a wizard who used to take the form of a poor man. He went to houses and begged and caught pretty girls. No one knew whither he carried them, for they were never seen more. One day he appeared before the door of a man who had three pretty daughters. He looked like a poor weak beggar and carried a basket on his back, as if he meant to collect charitable gifts in it. He begged for a little food, and when the eldest daughter came out and was just reaching him a piece of bread, he did but touch her, and she was forced to jump into his basket. Thereupon, he hurried away with long strides and carried her away into a dark forest to his house, which stood in the midst of it.

Everything in the house was magnificent; he gave her whatsoever she could possibly desire, and said, "My darling, thou wilt certainly be happy with me, for thou hast everything thy heart can wish for." This lasted a few days, and then he said, "I must journey forth and leave thee alone for a short time; there are the keys of the house; thou mayst go everywhere and look at everything except into one room, which this little key here opens, and there I forbid thee to go on pain of death." He likewise gave her an egg and said, "Preserve the egg carefully for me and carry it continually about with thee, for a great misfortune would arise from the loss of it."

She took the keys and the egg and promised to obey him in everything. When he was gone, she went all round the house, from the bottom to the top, and examined everything. The rooms shone with silver and gold, and she thought she had never seen such great splendor.

At length, she came to the forbidden door; she wished to pass it by, but curiosity let her have no rest. She examined the key, it looked just like any other; she put it in the keyhole and turned it a little, and the door sprang open. But what did she see when she went in? A great bloody basin stood in the middle of the room, and therein lay human beings, dead and hewn to pieces, and hard by was a block of wood, and a gleaming axe lay upon it. She was so terribly alarmed that the egg which she held in her hand fell into the basin. She got it out and washed the blood off, but in vain, it appeared again in a moment. She washed and scrubbed, but she could not get it out.

It was not long before the man came back from his journey, and the first things which he asked for were the key and the egg. She gave them to him, but she trembled as she did so, and he saw at once by the red spots that she had been in the bloody chamber. "Since thou hast gone into the room against my will," said he, "thou shalt go back into it against thine own. Thy life is ended." He threw her down, dragged her thither by her hair, cut her head off on the block, and hewed her in pieces so that her blood ran on the ground. Then he threw her into the basin with the rest.

"Now I will fetch myself the second," said the wizard, and again he went to the house in the shape of a poor man and begged. Then the second daughter brought him a piece of bread; he caught her like the first, by simply touching her, and carried her away. She did not fare better than her sister. She allowed herself to be led away by her curiosity, opened the door of the bloody chamber, looked in, and had to atone for it with her life on the wizard's return.

Then he went and brought the third sister. But she was clever and crafty. When he had given her the keys and the egg and had left her, she first put the egg away with great care, and then she examined the house and at last went into the forbidden room. Alas, what did she behold! Both her sisters lay there in the basin, cruelly murdered, and cut in pieces. She began to gather their limbs together and put them in order, head, body, arms and legs. And when nothing further was lacking, the limbs began to move and unite themselves together, and both the maidens opened their eyes and were once more alive. Then they rejoiced and kissed and caressed each other.

On his arrival, the man at once demanded the keys and the egg, and as he could perceive no trace of any blood on it, he said, "Thou hast stood the test, thou shalt be my bride." He now had no longer any power over her and was forced to do whatsoever she desired. "Oh, very well," said she, "thou shalt first take a basketful of gold to my father and mother, and carry it thyself on thy back; in the meantime I will prepare for the wedding."

Then she ran to her sisters, whom she had hidden in a little chamber and said, "The moment has come when I can save you. The wretch shall himself carry you home again, but as soon as you are at home send help to me." She put both of them in a basket and covered them quite over with gold, so that nothing of them was to be seen, then she called in the wizard and said to him, "Now carry the basket away, but I shall look through my little window and watch to see if thou stoppest on the way to stand or to rest."

The wizard raised the basket on his back and went away with it, but it weighed him down so heavily that the perspiration streamed from his face. Then he sat down and wanted to rest awhile, but immediately one of the girls in the basket cried, "I am looking through my little window, and I see that thou art resting. Wilt thou go on at once?" He thought his bride was calling that to him; and got up on his legs again. Once more he was going to sit down, but instantly she cried, "I am looking through my little window, and I see that thou art resting. Wilt thou go on directly?"

Whenever he stood still, she cried this, and then he was forced to go onward, until at last, groaning and out of breath, he took the basket with the gold and the two maidens into their parents' house. At home, however, the bride prepared the marriage-feast and sent invitations to the friends of the wizard. Then she took a skull with grinning teeth, put some ornaments on it and a wreath of flowers, carried it upstairs to the garret-window, and let it look out from thence. When all was ready, she got into a barrel of honey and then cut the feather-bed open and rolled herself in it, until she looked like a wondrous bird, and no one could recognize her. Then she went out of the house, and on her way, she met some of the wedding-guests, who asked,

"O, Fitcher's bird, how com'st thou here?"

"I come from Fitcher's house quite near."

"And what may the young bride be doing?"

"From cellar to garret she's swept all clean,

And now from the window she's peeping, I ween."

At last, she met the bridegroom, who was coming slowly back. He, like the others, asked,

"O, Fitcher's bird, how com'st thou here?"

"I come from Fitcher's house quite near."

"And what may the young bride be doing?"

"From cellar to garret she's swept all clean,

And now from the window she's peeping, I ween."

The bridegroom looked up, saw the decked-out skull, thought it was his bride, and nodded to her, greeting her kindly. But when he and his guests had all gone into the house, the brothers and kinsmen of the bride, who had been sent to rescue her, arrived. They locked all the doors of the house, that no one might escape, set fire to it, and the wizard and all his crew were burned.

Part I

The Old God-Image
and the Missing Feminine

1
The Psychological Anatomy of "Fitcher's Bird"

Originally a vital oral tradition, fairy tales have been passed down through the generations for hundreds, perhaps thousands, of years. In her research on fairy tales, Marie-Louise von Franz found that "certain themes go as far back as twenty-five thousand years before Christ, practically unaltered."[6] Until the Grimm brothers recorded European tales in the mid-1800s, each tale-teller added his or her own twist to the tales, contributing to an organic development from one generation to the next. Given the fact that the stories develop locally, it is remarkable that fairy tales with identical motifs, characters, and plots appear in different countries, even different continents, as if they arose from a single source.

Global similarities in fairy tales can only be explained psychologically. Their dramatic elements and motifs express fundamental archetypal patterns of the collective unconscious—psychic dynamics that unfold underneath consciousness, reflecting and influencing human life in similar ways all over the world. The archetypal dimension of fairy tales informs us how the psyche's unifying, worldwide presence is trying to renew itself, and how it needs conscious human help to do so. More specifically, fairy tales show us how the god-image we all share—psychologically identical to the self—is trying to transform and how that urge affects our lives, making demands on us. Fairy tales can lend transpersonal meaning and guidance to individual struggles if understood for their archetypal aims.

Grimm's "Fitcher's Bird" is one of several so-called sister-rescue tales from around the world in which a heroine rescues her two older

---

[6] Von Franz, *The Interpretation of Fairy Tales*, 4. Her source for this statement is Max Schmidt, *The Primitive Races of Mankind*. Von Franz has written comprehensive instructions for fairy tale interpretation and demonstrated the practice in her series of books about fairy tales (see bibliography).

sisters who have been kidnapped and imprisoned or killed by a devilish character.[7] In the Italian version "How the Devil Married Three Sisters" (also retold as "Silver Nose"), the devil dresses as a fine gentleman and marries the sisters, one by one from the eldest to the youngest.[8] Taking each bride to his mansion and leaving her alone one day, he forbids her to open a certain door, which turns out to be the door to hell. When he returns, he can see that his wife has disobeyed him and opened the door, because her corsage has been burned by hellfire. As punishment, he throws her into hell, assuming she will burn to death. Finally, the youngest wife puts her flower into water before opening the door, keeping it unscathed. Convincing the devil that she has obeyed him, she saves her own life and pulls her sisters, who have not died after all, out of hell. In the end, the three sisters dress up a dummy to look like the youngest bride. The devil falls for the dummy and is so humiliated when he realizes his mistake that he flees in embarrassment and loses his taste for marrying.

In the Norwegian tale "The Old Dame and Her Hen," the sisters fall into a deep chute in the ground when out searching for a lost hen.[9] When they refuse to marry the troll who lives down there, he kills them. The youngest tricks the troll by pretending she wants to marry him, giving her the freedom to enter his realm unharmed and rescue her sisters. In the Sicilian tale "The Story about Ohmy," the heroine not only rescues her murdered sisters but also an enchanted prince, emphasizing a redemption in both masculine and feminine realms.[10]

"Fitcher's Bird" is the least Christianized version of these stories. The sisters are not taken underground or into hell but into the forest, a less morally censured image for the collective unconscious. This is the only

---

[7] Aarne/Thompson/Uther Tale Type 311, The Heroine Rescues Herself and Her Sisters, includes, among others, "The Cobbler and His Three Daughters" (Basque), "The Three Sisters Who Were Taken into the Mountain" (Norway), "The Hare's Bride" (Germany), "The Three Chests" (Finland), "The Widow and Her Daughters" and "Peerifool" (Scotland), "Zerendac" (Palestine), and "The Tiger's Bride" (India). See Uther, *The Types of International Folktales*, 191.

[8] Crane, *Italian Popular Tales,* 78–81.

[9] Dasent, *Popular Tales from the Norse*, 16–24.

[10] Zipes, *Beautiful Angiola*, 287–94. My thanks to Charlene Henry for introducing me to this tale.

sister-rescue tale in which they are given not only a key to the forbidden room but also an egg. The motifs of the egg and the bird at the end of the tale and other alchemical symbols give "Fitcher's Bird" a particularly alchemical and feminine atmosphere. Some of its motifs can be traced back to alchemical texts from the beginning of the first millennium B.C.E., when alchemy had already begun to compensate for a patriarchal attitude toward the psyche and the feminine that was becoming prominent in Western religion and philosophy.

From an archetypal perspective, we can see that all the sister-rescue tales are oriented around the redemption of the feminine by the feminine; a sister rescues her sister, and none of the tales end in marriage. These sisters pull themselves up by their own bootstraps, no prince in the wings. In psychological terms, these centuries-old tales still show us how a woman may rescue eros on her own terms. The opus is intimate and personal and yet collective, since an individuating woman is tasked with realizing how eros is trying to develop in the unconscious from an eons-long patriarchal threat whose collective intensity has invisibly penetrated her own being. To be renewed, the archetypal feminine needs her honest help from the most intimate levels of her life where she must honestly confront what she has been denigrating in herself.

In "Fitcher's Bird," compared to the other tales, the heroine participates in a profound transformation that goes beyond the mere rescue of her sisters and involves their resurrection and redemption, connecting her with the powers of the gods. After reassembling her sisters' dismembered bodies, bringing them back to life, and sending them home with a basket of gold, she makes an epiphany as the "wondrous" Fitcher's bird in the forest. The sisters' resurrection symbolizes a redemption of eros in life and Fitcher's bird a new, objective, feminine reality that subsequently appears in the psychic realm. In alchemical terms, the wizard burning in his own fire can also be seen as a redemption, in which his energy is realized for its elemental, amoral archetypal roots. Thus, in the forest, in the deep unconscious realm, we witness an image of wholeness in which the wizardly spirit of the unconscious as well as the feminine side of the self is redeemed, not through heroism, repression, or obedience, but through a genuine human encounter with the dynamism of the underworld.

The Self at the Center of Every Fairy Tale

In all her works about fairy tales, von Franz reminded us that every tale tries to describe the comprehensive reality of the self—the central, organizing phenomenon of the psyche and its drive for wholeness.[11] This is one of the reasons tales from different parts of the world are so similar. The self is the psychological equivalent of the collective god-image as well as its source; the self evolves from one generation to the next and needs human beings to complete that evolution by bringing it consciously into life. We may sense the energy of the self and its urge for transformation in our personal lives but not know what it is or how it relates to us, except through the images and stories it shows us in dreams, fantasy, myth, and fairy tales. Von Franz wrote:

> All fairy tales endeavor to describe one and the same psychic fact, but a fact so complex and far-reaching and so difficult for us to realize in all its different aspects that hundreds of tales and thousands of repetitions with a musician's variations are needed until this unknown fact is delivered into consciousness; and even then the theme is not exhausted. This unknown fact is what Jung calls the Self, which is the psychic totality of an individual and also, paradoxically, the regulating center of the collective unconscious. Every individual and every nation has its own modes of experiencing this psychic reality.[12]

At the beginning of "Fitcher's Bird," the egg symbolizes the original "unknown fact" of the self. At the end of the tale, the image of Fitcher's bird—the heroine in her bird costume—represents a woman's intimate connection with that unknown fact. The development is nothing

---

[11] Von Franz, *The Interpretation of Fairy Tales*, 5.
[12] Ibid., 2.

short of a psychological rebirth that renews the feminine in both personal and transpersonal life.

The egg is primarily a feminine image, representing gestational growth that takes place unseen, as it does in a womb, a seed, or psychologically in the unconscious, according to natural principles. As a symbol for the self or the inner god-image, the egg includes all that our outer god-image excludes: darkness, the feminine, nature, matter, ongoing development, and its presence as an inner divine factor in individual life. We will see that in alchemy the philosophical egg even includes evil as an aspect of the drive for life—something we see in the wizard's paradoxical nature.

For an individual, the egg symbolizes the miracle of a unique life that grows in its own way as from a single cell, that is, from the core of the personality, the incipient monad, the self, and is consciously realized as such. At the same time, the egg symbolizes the psychological vessel that is created with the equally miraculous realization that the unconscious exists. When the unconscious is seen as an objective phenomenon, consciousness and the unconscious can come together for the purpose of mutual development, creating a vessel between them, in the imaginal realm, in which the development may take place. Each individual egg vessel—each personality—is a singular container of the opposites of the self, the yolk and the white symbolizing a particular constellation of consciousness and the unconscious, or masculine and feminine principles, that can bring about new psychological life when their relationship is contained and tended according to nature's guidance, that is, according to the symbolic realm. As we see in alchemical texts, consciousness and the unconscious have to be separated, differentiated from each other, so they can reunite in a new relationship suited to individuation. The resulting transformation, when felt and brought into life, has an effect in personal and archetypal realms.

Jung emphasized throughout his work that the self is a union of opposites, a confounding *complexio oppositorum:*

> Empirically, the self appears in dreams, myths, and fairytales
> in the figure of the "supraordinate personality" (v. ego), such
> as a king, hero, prophet, saviour, etc., or in the form of a
> totality symbol, such as the circle, square, quadratura circuli,
> cross, etc. When it represents a complexio oppositorum, a

union of opposites, it can also appear as a united duality, in the form, for instance, of tao as the interplay of yang and yin, or of the hostile brothers, or of the hero and his adversary (arch-enemy, dragon), Faust and Mephistopheles, etc. Empirically, therefore, the self appears as a play of light and shadow, although conceived as a totality and unity in which the opposites are united. Since such a concept is irrepresentable—*tertium non datur*—it is transcendental on this account also. It would, logically considered, be a vain speculation were it not for the fact that it designates symbols of unity that are found to occur empirically.[13]

The egg with its yolk and albumen symbolizes a united duality of confounding opposites whose potential to transform consciousness is contained in a single personality. By the same token, the heroine and the wizard are a duality, a play of light and shadow that at first fall into a destructive, dynamic pattern that thwarts renewal. Psychologically, they show us how the opposites can be unconsciously and destructively united or dissolved in each other in the beginning of an individuation process, differentiated, and united again in a way that renews life according to the self's transformative mandate, fulfilling the often repeated alchemical motto, *Solve et coagula*. The arc of this transformation will become more evident as we work our way through the amplification of the fairy tale's motifs.

The Heroine: Ego Related to the Self

It is vital to remember that the fairy tale heroine or hero doesn't represent an ego per se, but an archetypal model of an ego related to the self; in this sense, the heroine is an *archetypal ego*, showing us how the ego can help the psyche transform in a particular situation. In "Fitcher's Bird," the heroine's challenge is to follow her instinct to protect her egg in spite of the wizard's edicts. "Clever and crafty," she takes the egg seriously, and her relationship with it soon becomes mutual. She protects the egg from falling into the wizard's evil basin, and the unstained egg protects her from being killed. Symbolically speaking, this mutual protection

---

[13] Jung, *Psychological Types*, *CW*, vol. 6, par. 790.

between a woman and an egg would signal some degree of connection between the ego and even an incipient awareness of the self. For some women a vague, instinctual curiosity about the unconscious may lead her in spite of all reason to knock on an analyst's door, sensing that there is undiscovered meaning in her life. Any new feeling connection between ego and self is by itself a miracle in the face of our collective prejudices against the unconscious, so a woman must be clever and crafty, perhaps defying her family's expectations and even her own worldly goals in order to follow her instinct for individuation.

As a seminal protector of feminine development, the heroine in her transpersonal capacity fulfills the role of the Kore archetype, the image of a young, blooming woman so pervasive in ancient Greek life along with her male counterpart, the Kouros. She represents the mystery of renewal in nature, fertility, love, and human life (fig. 1). As an arche-type, the Kore connects women to the mysteries of the feminine side of the self, and she can inspire the development of spiritual eros in the anima of men. All the maidens in the tale are Kore figures in the sense that they represent potential development in emotion, feeling, and relatedness in life—development that is more natural when humanity and the feminine side of the divine are in relationship with each other.

The easy kidnapping of marriageable maidens into the underworld of the wizard's realm—

Figure 1. Kore, by Aristion from Paros
Found on a grave in Merenda (ancient Myrrhinous), in Attica. Marble, 550–540 BCE. She wears a wreath on her head, jewelry and a dress that was painted red. She is holding an unopened lotus bud. National Archeological Museum, Athens, Greece, #4889. Author's photo.

the way he controls them with barely a touch—tells us that potential eros development is elusive and weak, barely real to consciousness and easily reabsorbed into the unconscious. In our worldview, we don't realize that eros is trying to develop and move into the world, or that it is murdered regularly, because we have no sense of its divinity and are so inured to its absence. We tend to think of eros as an erotic quality, not realizing it has a spiritual dimension that has been trying to come to life for ages. Women face this devastating ignorance of eros, its development, and the fact that it is missing in worldly life and in the most personal aspects of their everyday lives.

The travails of the heroine and her sisters show us not only the challenge of a woman seeking her own life meaning but also the struggles of archetypal eros itself, trying to develop in human consciousness beyond the way it is currently known. All tales of feminine redemption reveal how the divinity of the feminine can be redeemed in a woman's individual connection to the self or a man's connection to the anima, however peculiar it might seem to the outer world. But what does this really mean as a life experience? The heroine's appearance as Fitcher's bird at the end of the tale seems a strange way to depict a woman's realization of something divine in the feminine realm until we look closely at the costume's elements and the psychological and spiritual development they represent. We will see that a union of honey and feathers symbolizes the goal of a profoundly spiritual femininity, yet grounded in natural eros.

The Wizard and the Animus

Just as the heroine does not represent an ego per se, the wizard in "Fitcher's Bird" shows us not an animus per se but an archetypal model of animus influence over a woman, the mercurial spirit of individuation. The wizardly animus appears at her father's door—the way she lives in her father's house or her father's realm, the way she is influenced by traditional mindsets. He appeals as a beggar (an impoverished attitude) to her innocent charity, easily convincing her she can trust him. Enchanting her with barely a touch into a deadly situation, the unconscious side of the animus sweeps her away into a world of destructive fantasy, where he can be murderous toward her development as long as she is unaware of his ravishing power.

In a more detailed example of this dynamism, the wizard's appearance may represent the arrival of what seems to be an ordinary thought but one that is actually beggarly and destructive toward a woman's development, taking hold of her attention and activating a complex. For a woman with an eating disorder, for example, he may knock on her door in the form of a fleeting thought that she has gained weight. Giving innocent charity to that thought, from the point of view of her father-generation attitudes toward the aesthetics of the female form, she is immediately abducted into an activated complex, where her feeling for herself is dismembered and murdered. She doesn't yet recognize the phenomenal power of the animus to abduct her magically into punishment, nor does she realize how she is gripped by standards that are destructive toward her individuality. The ease of her abduction indicates how the power of the orthodox side of the animus works through the ideals already in her mind, appealing effortlessly to her fantasy about herself and how she should fit into the world. She is convinced that she is ugly and therefore worthless, and these assumptions end up destroying her relationship to herself, to others, and to her inner world. Eros—her eros for her own life as well as any objective eros that might be trying to develop in her psyche—is dismembered before she has a chance to notice. In this way, the repeated murders of maidens represent the ongoing murder of eros for the self that is trying to develop in a single woman. These dynamics are personal, but they reflect a deep split in our collective psyche toward the feminine, toward the reality of eros.

When the first two sisters see the murdered girls who came before them, evidence of breathtaking evil, they are immediately killed. On the one hand, we could say they become victims of the wizard's evil through no fault of their own, but on the other hand, it can be argued that they already have a propensity for unconscious evil that makes them vulnerable to the wizard's promise of riches. They are incapable of protecting the eggs he gave them according to the eggs' needs, and instead they obey the stale edicts that allow them to ignore their eggs and that lead to their murders. The maidens show us how a woman may unconsciously sacrifice the development that is trying to come alive in her own psyche, perpetuating the old, anti-feminine evil that insists on perfect innocence, rather than awakening to its grip on her. Her guilt lies in remaining more or less willfully unconscious, in thrall to such riches as power, recognition, or perceived innocence, all built on patriarchal attitudes to which she has long been inured.

The phenomenal force of the animus animates a woman's beliefs about right and wrong, good and bad, with his archetypal power. Ideas about how she is supposed to behave, what she is supposed to think, how innocent she should be, how attractive, how right she is, or how beleaguered, may become inexplicably demanding in her life. The sheer force of the unseen nature spirit rumbling around in judgmental fantasy thinking can make her antsy, anxious, depressed, demanding, controlling, and unfulfilled. Taking up residence in her ideas about what she and her life are supposed to be, his energy may amplify her cogitations about either the inadequacies or the superiorities of her life to an unbearable pitch that probably everyone else in her life can hear, even if she can't. She participates in the dismemberment of eros because such a judgmental attitude makes it impossible for her to relate to herself or anyone else in any real way.

The animus constantly demonstrates his autonomy, if only by proving to a woman that she can't bend her behavior, her thoughts, or her mood to what she considers acceptable, no matter how hard she tries. He lends dynamism to her fantasy world, whether it is highly flattering or devastatingly punitive. In either case, he dismembers her sense of her real value and her eros connection to the self in a magical, wizardly way. In his most destructive guise, he may use all of the force and ammunition of old perfectionistic philosophies to convince a woman that, unless she is perfect or outstanding, she is worthlessly ordinary.

We should remember that the unconscious animus can be dangerous. He can destroy a woman's life by attacking her inherent value, her relationships, even her sanity, quite effectively, all the while remaining invisible, identical with her way of thinking. He can demolish her esteem, cause addictions, and inspire obsessive perfectionism, using her own convictions to do so. Some women experience the negative side of the animus as a death urge, as if she could actually be killed by persistent destructive urges, illnesses and disappointments. Jung discovered a concomitant danger in the anima, saying, "the insinuations of the anima, the mouthpiece of the unconscious, can utterly destroy a man."[14]

However, once a woman can see how the animus archetype magically compels her impulses and her own judging mind, she may

---

[14] Jung, *Memories, Dreams, Reflections,* 187.

become more curious about his dynamism and his symbolic messages. In turn, he may lend himself to the urgent discovery of the high value of her individuality. She may gradually realize that wholeness, including darkness, is the goal, rather than perfection. I don't think we can fathom the depths of paradox that lie beneath individuation in any given individual; in some cases, even death itself can be an arbiter of individuation if a person can accept it as such.

Once animus dynamics are seen and contained in the individuation process, a woman's identification with collective ideals is the thing to be dismembered, and this is the second way we can understand the repeated killing of maidens in the tale. A woman's old relationship to the god-image has to die if a new one is to come alive in her, and this requires an absolutely individual response to a collective problem. She may have to go through many psychological deaths as she keeps finding herself trying to appease old standards over and over, each time getting clearer about what is really wanted of her. Her eros connection with the self gets stronger and stronger, bringing the self more and more into life with each death and resurrection of clarity.

If a woman can engage the spirit of the unconscious in the far-reaching transformation that he is after, she brings female individuation—a woman's encounter with the death and resurrection archetype—into human life in a way that as von Franz pointed out has no official representation in religion.[15] The resurrected sisters are images for eros that seemed to be dead but are brought back into earthly human life, stronger and more visible in life. The surprisingly profound image of the heroine dressed as a marvelous white bird made of honey and feathers symbolizes the corresponding, reborn feminine archetype whose value is newly realized after a long period of disappearance. Our goal is to understand how these renewals are manifest in women's personal experiences with the dynamism of the animus.

---

[15] See Howe, "Redeeming Mary Magdalene: The Feminine Side of the Death and Resurrection Archetype," in Schweizer and Schweizer-Vüllers, *Wisdom Has Built Her House,* 89.

Empirical Interpretation

In order to get to the psychological meaning of a fairy tale, we take certain steps to ensure that we understand its motifs and dramatic elements at the archetypal level. Von Franz suggested we dissect the anatomy of the fairy tale into the four classical elements of drama, just as we do with dreams. These are:

1. exposition (the time and place);
2. dramatis personae (the people involved);
3. peripeteia (the ups and downs of the plot, sometimes called rising and falling action, including a reversal of fortune, and the climax or denouement); and
4. lysis, a solution (or a catastrophe) that brings the tale to a close.

With the dramatic elements identified, we have the framework for the tale's characters and motifs, whose symbolic meanings allow us to explore the tale's psychological goal and the solutions it articulates. For example, in "Fitcher's Bird," the antagonist is a murderous male figure similar to Bluebeard, who in the eponymous fairy tale also murders women in a forbidden room. As an antagonist who paradoxically leads the heroine to redemption, the wizard may be compared to Merlin or Mercurius, both of whom can be devilish in the way they bring about transformation and seek recognition and redemption in human consciousness.[16] The wizard is especially Mercurius-like when considered in connection to the eggs he repeatedly offers the maidens; Mercurius is called the "egg of nature, known only to the wise" in alchemical texts.[17] The wizard as a mercurial figure, the egg motif, the role of the heroine's relationship to the egg in bringing about a dramatic turning point, and the ending with a great fire and the epiphany of a bird all suggest that we are in alchemical territory and will need to take special care in exploring these motifs accordingly.

---

[16] See Jung and von Franz, "Merlin and the Alchemical Mercurius," in *The Grail Legend*, 367ff.

[17] See the quote from "Aurelia occulta" in Jung, "The Spirit Mercurius," *CW*, vol. 13, par. 267

Exposition

The fairy tale exposition refers to time and place, often beginning with the phrase "once upon a time," which in psychological terms refers to the timeless quality of the collective unconscious. In "Fitcher's Bird," most of the action takes place in the never-never land of the wizard's house, but the father's house is where the action begins. The wizard appears three times at the father's house dressed as a beggar. He enchants each sister into his basket and carries her back to his "magnificent" house, located deep in "a dark forest." He goes back and forth between the two houses a total of four times. On the first three trips, he takes a maiden from the father's house to his house, murdering the first two. The fourth trip to the father's house is part of a reversal. This time, the wizard is under the heroine's command, tasked with taking the revived sisters back home. Returning to his own home the final time and expecting a wedding, the wizard instead is locked in his house and burned in a fire.

Exposition

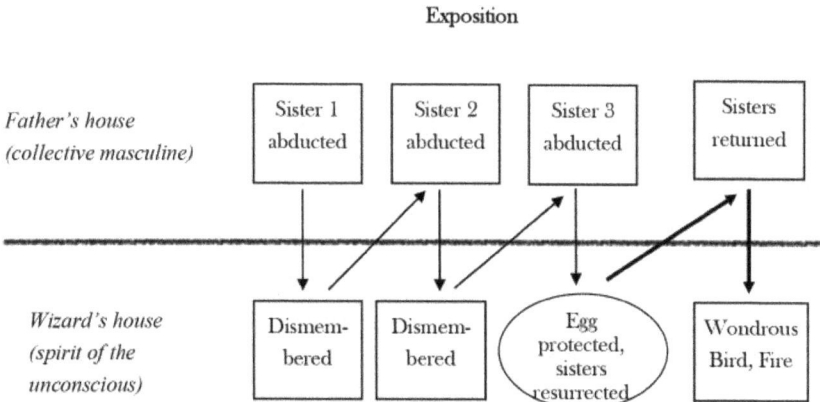

Figure 2. Exposition of the Fairy Tale

The wizard makes four trips back and forth between the father's house and his house in the dark forest. The back-and-forth pattern reveals how everyday unconsciousness may be regularly possessed by the deeper, archetypal level of the collective unconscious. The possession itself, however, may eventually provoke an awakening to the reality and autonomy of the collective unconscious, which in turn changes the pattern. Such an awakening is indicated by the heroine's protection of her egg, which is emphasized in the diagram because it leads to a turning point in which she saves her life and resurrects her sisters from a seeming death. In psychological terms, her actions bring lost eros back to life in both realms.

The rhythmic pattern that takes place between these two locations—the father's house and the wizard's house—represent two realms of psychic life and how they affect each other, but also the subtle in-between reality that connects them. As the wizard goes back and forth between these two realms, their connection seems to strengthen, until finally the heroine can see how they are connected. Her relationship to her egg represents her awareness of that connection—a consciousness of the unconscious.

The father's house shows us a psychological situation in the upper realm of everyday life. Eros (the mother and daughters) is missing or abducted, and logos (the father and brothers) is old, weak, or absent. In a woman's life, a weak father and missing brothers would represent the absence of a living logos, a lack of understanding of her psychological situation relevant to the unconscious. Her worldly animus, her way of thinking, would not be related to new symbolic meaning from the unconscious but would drive her according to conventions she grew up with. In other words, the fact that she lives in a father's house would indicate that she lives in a father complex, in which her conscious attitudes are overrun by the masculine conventions of her father's generation. In the example of a woman with an eating disorder, the father's house would represent a patriarchal attitude toward the body that is partly conscious and partly unconscious, notwithstanding her intellectual powers or her devotion to feminism, which unfortunately can be overrun with masculine values and power motives.

The lower realm of the wizard's house in the forest represents the depths of the collective unconscious, where the true destructive power of the "poor weak beggar" is revealed and carried out—where developing eros is destroyed. The wizard in this respect represents real evil, when he murders the maidens he abducts predictably, rhythmically, as if he needs their deaths to keep him going. In both upper and lower psychological realms of the "Fitcher's Bird" drama, masculine and feminine are locked into a predictable, vile pattern that seems to be happening out of sheer momentum, feeding the overall unconscious situation that keeps eros from developing in either realm. The pattern only changes when the heroine sees what is going on between the two realms, her awareness apparently having built itself up through repetition. Otherwise, her life and the eros development it represents would end in the same nameless calamity as all the others.

In a woman, such a profound change would mean that she has become conscious of the animus and his dynamism, conscious of the unconscious dimension of life, and this ability of one woman to see the dynamics changes everything. Willing to have a relationship with the animus, she attends to a psychological container, an egg, in which the personal and archetypal realms may come together, building up a relationship with the self. In other words, she brings into life the third, in-between realm—the imaginal realm where the relationship between consciousness and the unconscious may slowly evolve. Over time she contemplates her predicament, creating a place in her imagination where she can relate to the animus, understand his appearance in her dreams, and become more and more aware of how she gets abducted. She begins to see how she lives in her father's house with her old opinions and how she is abducted by her own masculine attitudes into a destructive, unconscious dynamic that destroys eros.

Even when we have created a space in which to observe the unconscious, we may be taken in by the archetypal realm many times before we can begin to contain its dynamics rather than act them out. For some women, the animus can appear in "holy convictions" that may seem to defy her father's attitudes but really recycle them—philosophical truths, aesthetic principles, conspiracy theories, or fervent rationality— even a power-oriented conviction to Jungian psychology.[18] It takes time and repeated encounters for her ego to become acquainted with its entanglement in such convictions and to see herself getting abducted by them.

In summary, collective animus opinions and attitudes come from the upper, everyday world, but the wizardly power of the animus drives those opinions from the lower, archetypal world. A woman can only realize this fact as she becomes acquainted with the unconscious—as she recognizes

---

[18] Von Franz used the phrase "holy convictions" to refer to her own experience of the animus in an interview at the C. G. Jung Institute of Chicago, April 5, 1975, recorded by Frances Wright. Unpublished transcript produced by the Research and Training Centre for Depth Psychology according to C. G. Jung and Marie-Louise von Franz, 2020.

the often well-hidden collectivity of her convictions and sees how they are propelled by archetypal energy. The true animus, the spirit of the unconscious, wants to connect a woman to her own thoughts and ideas, her own creative stream. He wants her to realize the unseen wonder of her individuality hidden deeper in the psychic realm, underneath her father-generation belief system. But as long as his dynamism remains identified with opinions that don't really belong to her, the egg of development he offers goes unrecognized.

For example, nearly every night, the animus brings a woman dreams from the depths of her psyche. Each dream contains the key to its symbolic meaning. If she is stuck in conventional thinking about her dreams, she won't be interested in their deeper meaning or inclined to interpret them symbolically. A woman trapped in a conventional animus tends to see dreams as either criticizing her or supporting her in the same old ways, and she doesn't know how to understand the radically different, symbolic wisdom they might be offering. She goes on obeying the old opinions, striving always toward the good. Tragically, she won't feel how the wisdom of the self is trying to connect with her at a lower, even chthonic level through the truth-telling capacity of her dreams. The eros and wisdom from the self are killed by her own critical, naïve, or dismissive mindset—her way of living in her father's house, psychologically speaking. The unconscious spirit constantly offers a woman the egg of individuation, but naturally it takes time for her to develop a feeling, eros connection to its profound reality. The fact that a stubbornly rational system of thought must be trained to the alternate universe of symbolic thinking makes the transformation even more exacting.

Dramatis Personae

Now we give attention to the dramatic characters in "Fitcher's Bird" and what they mean psychologically. Counting the masculine and feminine figures in the beginning and again at the end of the story helps define the specific psychological development the fairy tale expresses. In the beginning of our tale, the wizard appears "before the door of a man who had three pretty daughters." These five characters—wizard, father, and the three daughters—make up the initial dramatis personae (fig. 3). The mother seems not to be mentioned on purpose, indicating an absence of motherly eros, an absence magnified and perpetuated by the maidens being abducted and killed. At the same time, the father is not protecting his daughters from being taken.

Dramatis Personae

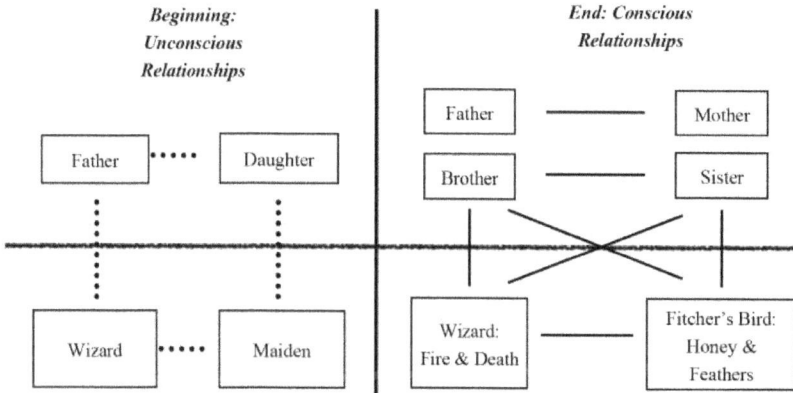

Figure 3. Dramatis Personae
From the beginning to the end of the tale, the heroine has connected the upper and lower realms, which restores balance to two generations of masculine and feminine in the upper realm, and introduces a new feminine image to the lower realm where once the wizard dominated. In psychological terms, this indicates that a connection between consciousness and the unconscious restores balance in life as well as in the unconscious.

We also don't hear anything about the brothers, the younger generation of masculine energy, until the very end of the tale. In the beginning, the older generation (father and wizard) are the only masculine, logos figures in the picture, and the young maidens are the only feminine, eros figures. The father and daughter create an unconscious pairing in the upper realm, reflected by the wizard and the maidens in the lower realm, again emphasizing the mirroring relationship between the two realms.

In symbolic terms, old masculine figures (aging logos) and young feminine figures (new eros) are in a lopsided relationship, the former dominating and destructive toward the latter. Until the heroine changes the pattern, both are caught in a death loop, keeping development shut down in life's upper realm, where eros continues to be abducted, and in the unconscious lower realm, where eros is murdered. The tale emphasizes that when consciousness and the unconscious are not relating to each other in one woman, eros development symbolized by the maidens remains at a standstill in both realms.

This situation, in which the older-generation masculine dominates the younger-generation feminine, is typical of fairy tales of feminine redemption. It reflects our collective situation, in which women and men are still tethered to old attitudes that demean the feminine and don't realize this fact; the problem is much deeper than most of us can imagine. The archetype of the Kore is not visible in life, and so neither is her disappearance when she tries and fails to make her presence known. New eros, new values, new ways of relating that are developing in the unconscious do not find their way into life, largely because we don't have the consciousness to recognize what they are. "Fitcher's Bird" indicates that the abduction and murder of maidens have been going on for a long time, even generations, giving us another clue that the antifeminine pattern represented in the tale is related to enduring cultural and religious attitudes.

At the end of the tale, after the heroine has protected her egg and rescued her sisters, we are told that the sisters arrive at their parents' house rather than their father's house, giving us a hint that indeed there are two parents in the girls' home. At the end, we find out there are brothers as well. We can imagine the homecoming when, after so many maidens have disappeared, the two sisters return alive. Following the heroine's instructions to send aid, the brothers and kinsmen of the bride—the whole of the masculine side of the family—are sent to the heroine's rescue, indicating psychologically a new awareness of the problem. These masculine energies in a woman would represent an activation of new logos energy, a new kind of understanding that can recognize and protect developing eros.

At the wizard's house, the brothers and kinsmen lock the wizard in his house and set it on fire but not before the heroine appears as the wondrous Fitcher's bird, depicting the image of an earthy, feminine spirit that is much more symbolically complex than is immediately apparent.

We will dig into alchemical symbolism to explore the two final images of the wizard in the fire and the heroine as a bird; they express a new balance between masculine and feminine in the archetypal realm that mirrors the balance between brothers and sisters, mother and father, in the realm of earthly life.

Peripeteia

Peripeteia comes from the Greek, meaning "sudden change" or "adventure" or a reversal of circumstances. As a dramatic element, it refers to plot, the tale's ups and downs as well as the transformation of the heroine or hero. "Fitcher's Bird' starts with the two elder sisters, who, like countless other maidens, obey the wizard's instruction to carry their eggs everywhere they go in his house and end up murdered because of it. Changing this pattern, the third sister takes her egg seriously and survives (fig. 4). The number three is often the magic number in fairy tales: The hero or heroine achieves a difficult task after two failed attempts, bringing about a change of circumstances. The motif of three tries indicates a beginning, middle, and end to a process. Psychologically, the three trips (and the time spent between one realm and the other) signal a development between consciousness and the unconscious that has become irreversible in time.[19] In other words, there is no turning back, no regressing, without incurring harm.

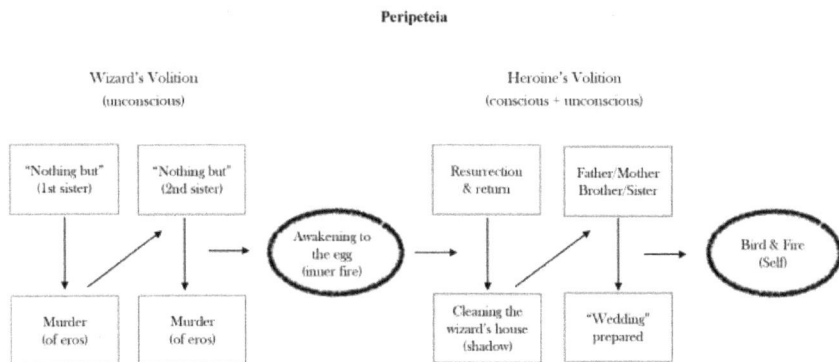

Figure 4. Peripeteia

The two elder sisters and maidens before them display a "nothing but" attitude toward their eggs, which leads to their gruesome demise and the repetition of the same dynamic for what seems like generations. The heroine on the other hand takes her egg seriously and treats it with care. The heroine in relationship to the egg or the self drives the rest of the action, leading to the fire in the wizard's house and her epiphany as Fitcher's bird. Her awakening to her egg and her ensuing work psychologically represent an encounter and containment of the autonomy of the unconscious, wizardly animus, which changes the nature of his volition.

---

[19] See Abt, *Introduction to Picture Interpretation,* 123; and von Franz, *Number and Time,* 109.

In "Fitcher's Bird," there is a fourth journey in which the resurrected sisters are returned to their home. The wizard is no longer in control for this trip back to the family home. He is sent on his way by the heroine, loaded with a supposed dowry of gold and the resurrected sisters. Goaded on and forbidden to rest by the voices of the older sisters he carries on his back, he is under their control without knowing it, unwittingly returning the life he once stole and dismembered in a new, stronger form that is accompanied by gold. Through the concerted effort of all three sisters, the wizard is forcefully oriented toward life instead of death, although the tale's ending will tell us that his taste for death remains an aspect of his nature. Overall, there is a reversal in power between the wizard and the sisters, which signals an enantiodromia, when a psychological dynamic reaches the end of its tether and swings back in the opposite direction. What seems like a sudden change, however, is the result of a strengthening of consciousness that has been in development through the first three journeys.

A fourth repetition does not so often appear in fairy tales, but when it does, it indicates an important psychological step. It means not only that a transformation has taken place but also that its meaning is integrated into life, affecting a living transformation. This final journey when the sisters are taken home represents the integration of redeemed eros into life—the climactic miracle of individuation. The wizard being forced to carry the sisters at their direction tells us that the integration of eros is something that is accomplished at the behest of the feminine realm, yet it is a mutual endeavor between a woman and the animus, once his energy is oriented toward her opus with the psyche. The basketful of gold symbolizes the high value of this development, of eros consciousness returned to life.

The journeys of the three sisters taken together as a single psychological development can be seen as one woman's gradual coming to terms with the unconscious dynamism of the animus. In psychic time, the death of the first two sisters could represent years, or even what feels like lifetimes, in which one woman has obeyed the negative animus and avoided a relationship with the unconscious. In the fullness of time, she finally can see the reality of what has been abducting and torturing her. She can go her own way, according to her own spiritual life, more able to discern destructive impulses and subject them to the transformative fire, knowing full well she is guided by the self. The fourth journey symbolizes an integration of new eros into life, which in a woman means she can feel eros as a reality that is affecting her relationships in a new way. As simple as it may sound, she may realize, for example, that she has become less concerned about appearances and more interested in people as they really are.

As the sisters are returned home, the heroine has created and dressed herself in the image of the wondrous Fitcher's bird at the wizard's house in the forest. We can't underestimate the value of such a startling feminine image appearing in the domain that has belonged exclusively to the wizard. Such an image in a woman's psyche would indicate that her personal work with individuation brings the transpersonal dimension of the feminine principle alive; the tale seems to tell us that the archetypal feminine is strengthened and even healed by such personal effort. We can't necessarily conclude that this outcome is guaranteed as a rule, but the fairy tale hints at the possibility that an individual's receptivity to the unconscious has a healing effect on the whole psychic realm. This idea is reflected in the alchemists' description of Mercurius as a world-redeeming god, as we will see.

The death and resurrection of the sisters in "Fitcher's Bird" has parallels in the other sister-rescue tales. In "Silver Nose," the sisters are rescued from hell, and in "The Old Dame and Her Hen," they are recovered from the underground world of mysteriously deep chutes. The death or disappearance of the sisters into some version of the underworld, followed by their redemption, is the organizing core of all the sister-rescue stories, linking the events to the mythological disappearance and return of deities throughout history. This motif, which appears in nature cults as well as Christian, Greek, Gnostic, Egyptian, and alchemical forms, is an image for the renewal of the god-image from its disappearance into the collective unconscious. Since death and resurrection of the sisters in "Fitcher's Bird" occurs in Kore figures, we may look at the fairy tale's events in terms of the death and resurrection of the feminine side of the god-image that has been trying to develop and make its way into our consciousness for millennia. The fairy tale puts this awesome, eon-defining phenomenon at the core of woman's development, making the redemption of a woman's life value and the redemption of the feminine principle fundamentally mutual.

Lysis

The heroine in her bird garb of honey and feathers uses a decorated skull to lure the wizard and his comrades into his house, knowing he will mistake the skull-bride for herself. The wizard and his crew are locked in his house, and the house is set on fire. This is the end of the tale, the lysis, or solution. We are familiar with fairy tale endings that express a psychological solution through the image of a marriage, indicating that feminine and masculine entities have gone through a mutual renewal and come together in a new way. In "Fitcher's Bird," the heroine instead avoids a disastrous marriage. This doesn't necessarily mean that the opposites have not transformed or that they are not united in a new way, however. In this fairy tale, the opposites are united elementally, in true alchemical terms.

The wizard is united with fire, which doesn't necessarily mean he is killed. The original German versions of the fairy tale emphasize that the wizard and his mob were locked in the house and stuck inside; the tale says simply that they burned.[20] This suggests the alchemical goal of transforming the devil in his own element rather than the Christian goal of casting the devil into hellfire with the naïve idea that he can be eliminated. The wizard has set the whole drama of transformation in motion, including whatever further metamorphosis awaits him in the fire. If he represents Mercurius, then he *is* the fire, as well as the transformation that takes place there. The fact that he has been set on fire in his own house tells us that the heroine has identified his close connection to fire, dynamism, and death, all of which are godlike in their own right.

The image of the heroine in her costume by itself expresses a union of opposites in a way that is true to the tale's alchemical features. Rather than being tarred and feathered as punishment for disobedience, she covers herself in honey and feathers, which seems like a reward for disobedience

---

[20] "Sie schlossen alle Thüren des Hauses zu, dass niemand entfliehen konnte, und steckten es an, dass der Hexenmeister mitsamt seinem Gesindel verbrannte" (Grimm, *Kinder- und Hausmärchen,* 121).

that brings about transformations the psyche has long awaited. She has engaged a completely new moral code in which protecting her egg is the overriding priority rather than following the wizard's rules. Now she is intimate with the opposites, using her own body to unite them. She submerges herself in honey and then rolls in feathers, binding an earthy, eros substance with the universal icon for elusive spirituality.

Covered in honey and feathers, the heroine psychologically represents an archetypal ego assimilated to the self. The alchemical meaning of honey as a pure, unifying substance that is used in the second *coniunctio* will help us understand the profound achievement that is expressed through the heroine's immersion in it, but fundamentally it represents the eros of the psyche, redeemed on an archetypal level through the efforts of a singular woman.

The Egg and the Opposites

The yolk and the white inside the egg represented to the alchemists the basic opposites of life—the sun and moon, fire and water, or masculine and feminine sides of the psyche. The collective understanding of masculine and feminine as opposites is becoming less absolute in our time; we see that gender and sexual orientation exist on a spectrum, as well as discrete opposites. This shift in perspective reflects the fact that women and men today are increasingly aware of their contra-sexual sides and feel less need to suppress them. From a psychological perspective, however, it helps to differentiate between gender identity, which is more or less relative depending on the individual, and the fundamental masculine and feminine principles that exist in archetypes, nature, and science (fig. 5). As the most fundamental of opposites, masculine and feminine principles define each other through contrast and exist as opposites psychically in everyone. The energic, psychological anatomy of masculine and feminine principles is as mutually dependent as the sun and the moon, a fact that will be important in our exploration of the philosophical egg.

Masculine Principle	Feminine Principle
THINKING/LOGOS Understanding, discrimination (separating).	FEELING/EROS Accepting, realizing, relating (unifying).
Creative: generative, penetrating, phallic.	Creative: gestative, receptive, womb.
Sol: steady light, penetrating, direct, clarity, hard shadow, absolute.	Luna: dark/light, reflective, cyclical, diffuse, soft focus, relative, inclusive.
Spirit	Matter
MIND/SPIRIT/ANIMUS	HEART/SOUL/ANIMA
King: dominant *attitude* towards life; ruling consciousness, prevailing logos. God on earth.	Queen: dominant *values* in life; ruling feeling, relatedness, prevailing eros. Goddess on earth.
Conscious knowledge	Wisdom of the unconscious

Figure 5. Masculine and Feminine Principles

Masculine and feminine principles are opposites that depend on each other to be knowable, through contrast.

2
When Good Becomes Evil and Evil Good

Woman and the Devil

At the beginning of World War II, Barbara Hannah dreamt of an encounter with the devil, whom she blamed for starting the war. In *The Animus,* she reported:

> I was in Chichester Cathedral, where there used to be an unfinished chapel with its reserve of building stones and so forth. Here I met the devil and said to him: "What a mess you are making of the world with the war." He said, "Excuse me, this is not my fault, it is yours." I declined that responsibility, and he answered with something like: "Of course, I do not mean you personally, I mean women, because women can deal with the dark side and with evil and, since they don't, it gets into the hands of men who anyway can't deal with the darker sides of life. If the women won't try, then there are bound to be wars."[21]

The fact that this confrontation with the devil takes place in an unfinished chapel suggests that the work of dealing with evil is part of a renovation process in the collective religious container. The devil has approached Hannah to let her know that it is time to take evil into account as a reality, and women are the ones to do it—because women by nature can "deal with the dark side and with evil" better than men; in psychological terms, they are more open to the unconscious. But how are women to take on such a task, when the prevailing worldview has condemned their relationship to darkness for at least two millennia?

According to Christian ideas that evolved over the early centuries of the church, Eve introduced sin into the world when she disobeyed

---

[21] Hannah, *The Animus*, 1:78.

God's command not to eat the fruit of the tree of knowledge. Instead, she took the serpent's dare, ate the fruit, and convinced Adam to do the same. Unable to contain her desire, exegetes declared, Eve committed the original sin and introduced evil into what otherwise could have been paradise forever.[22] Humanity inherited the taint of concupiscence and is doomed to live with death, desire, and pain, forever carrying the burden of the first mother's transgression. In this way of understanding the Garden of Eden story as a morality tale, obedience and innocence are the highest value. The serpent and his instigation of desire or curiosity in a woman are the lowest.

But while Eve has been blamed for evil all this time, alchemy and fairy tales have safeguarded a different, psychological wisdom, which depth psychology has made visible in our era: while an encounter with what we consider to be evil may wrench us out of the paradise of innocence, by the same token it widens our consciousness, opening our eyes to the opposites and even revealing ambivalence in our god-image. In fact, Jung felt that through Eve's disobedience, Christianity revealed what could have been an openness to its own development. Eve shows us that it is possible for human beings to help God know Himself, and vice versa:

> What is remarkable about Christianity is that in its system of dogma it anticipates a metamorphosis in the divinity, a process of historic change on the "other side." It does this in the form of the new myth of dissension in heaven, first alluded to in the creation myth in which a serpent-like antagonist of the Creator appears, and lures man to disobedience by the promise of increased conscious knowledge (*scientes bonum et malum*).[23]

---

[22] The idea of original sin stems in part from Paul's statement: "Therefore, just as through one man sin entered the world, and death through sin, and thus death spread to all men, because all sinned" (Rom. 5:12 NKJV). The phrase and the doctrine of original sin were formulated by Augustine of Hippo (354–430) and made official during the councils of Carthage (411-418) and Orange (529).

[23] Jung, *Memories, Dreams, Reflections,* 327. Jung went on to describe other ways that Christianity seems to anticipate transformation and how the survival of humanity depends on our ability to deal with objective evil.

The serpent easily enticed our first parents to sacrifice their innocence for the sake of increased knowledge, but it pitted them against the creator. Not only did they become conscious of the opposites—life and death, good and evil—but they could also see God's inner conflict in tempting them to do something he claimed he did not want them to do. If the serpent represents the left hand or unintentional side of God, his goal seems to be to awaken human beings to God's two-sidedness. If the serpent is not the left-hand side of God but instead his own independent force, then he seems to have enough power to influence humanity on his own. In either case, the serpent represents an autonomy, a deific force whose wily reality humanity and God must deal with together, bringing ample opportunity for mutual development.

The serpent's presence in this drama also tells us that God is of two minds concerning his children's obedience. He showed Eve and Adam the tree of the knowledge of good and evil, commanded them not to taste its delicious fruit, and if that wasn't enough temptation, He allowed the serpent to tip the scales. What did He really want Eve to do? We asked the same question of the wizard: What did he really want the heroine to do with her key and her egg?

From a psychological perspective, the serpent is one of many images for the autonomous spirit of the unconscious that drives us irrevocably toward greater consciousness, whether we acknowledge him as an aspect of the god-image or not. He represents a dynamism in nature and in the psyche whose unpredictable aims are forever uncanny and fascinating to consciousness. Jung had the vision to realize that this spirit, condemned for two to three millennia, wants to be recognized for his vital role in the development of consciousness—for the fact that, among other things, he is that aspect of the god-image that pushes for renewal any way it can.[24] As impossible as it may seem, this spirit seems to want us to integrate him into our understanding of the divine, along with his curious, feminine partner and mother of all living, Eve. The devil in Hannah's dream expresses a similar yearning, hoping that women finally will be the ones to acknowledge his reality.

---

[24] See, in particular, Jung, "Answer to Job" and "A Psychological Approach to the Dogma of the Trinity," *CW*, vol. 11.

Eve instinctively chose the psychological imperative when confronted with the choice between ignoring evil and having a relationship with it. Adam in most accounts needed to be persuaded, though not by much. Psychologically this means that it is the feminine (in a woman or a man), the unifying urge, that naturally wants to connect with something new, even if it means treading into forbidden territory. Eve represents a comprehensive relatedness that prefers to include darkness and the unknown and try to understand them, rather than leave them out of the picture—a willingness that the devil in Hannah's dream seems to acknowledge. Eve and the serpent, woman and the devil, show us a natural partnership that promotes a development of consciousness, but one that remains stubbornly illegitimate in the Christian view.

The Shadow of the Garden of Eden

Walter Odajnyk pointed out in his interpretation of "Bluebeard" that fairy tales in which a heroine ostensibly is forbidden from seeing a dark truth are shadow versions of the Garden of Eden story.[25] Like the wizard in "Fitcher's Bird," Bluebeard forbids his wives to enter a certain room, and yet he gives them the key that will open its lock (fig. 6). Presumably, Bluebeard wants each wife to be a good girl and remain ignorant of his evil deeds, to remain a naïve maiden, virginal at least in her obedience. Either she obeys him, or he will have to kill her like all the others. Likewise, the wizard in "Fitcher's Bird" supposedly wants his abducted maidens to stay out of his room, to remain ignorant of his evil, and to keep their eggs unstained. To this day, these tales are interpreted by moralists as a warning to women about the dangers of being too curious.

Psychologically, these pseudo challenges in the fairy tales are identical to God showing Adam and Eve the beautiful tree that could bestow secret knowledge and telling them they should never eat the sweet fruit from that tree. The wizard shows the sisters a key to a mysterious room and tells them not to use it. He gives each one an egg that could hatch into who knows what and tells them to carry it everywhere, knowing they will probably obey him and expose their eggs to danger and themselves

---

[25] Odajnyk, "The Archetypal Interpretation of Fairy Tales: Bluebeard."

Figure 6. Bluebeard Tempting the Heroine

Bluebeard's command not to seek the hidden truth calls to mind God's command not to eat the fruit of the tree of knowledge. The commands paradoxically evoke the unavoidable temptation to do the opposite, and thus to increase consciousness. Illustration by Gustave Doré, from Charles Perrault, *Stories or Tales from Past Times, with Morals* (1864).

to destruction. The reward he offers her for obedience is "everything thy heart can wish for," just as God offers Adam and Eve a life of ease and innocence for renouncing their curiosity. In every fairy tale with a forbidden door, the hero or heroine opens it, verifying that the instinct for greater consciousness is stronger by far than any mandate for obedience.

By the time Hannah in the middle of the 20th century dreamt of the devil challenging women to "deal with the darker sides of life," women were almost inextricably caught in the opposite, Christian conviction not to deal with darkness—on pain of death, as expressed in the fairy tale and the myth. For at least 2,000, years they have been carrying the blame of the first mother, Eve, for doing just what Hannah's devil suggests.

The hell of the matter is that women destined to deal with the darker sides of life on a psychological level—those whose fate is to individuate—must confront evil outside and in. To individuate, they accept the temptation to work with the trickster spirit of the unconscious that the world has condemned, and they confront the false innocence that has been building up in themselves, telling them that either they are perfectly innocent or they hardly deserve to live.

Like the serpent, the wizard in "Fitcher's Bird" is a spiritual provocateur. He is an image for the hidden spirit in each of us, a spirit the church could never imagine—a devilish energy that promotes new logos and new eros, new consciousness. Perhaps most offensive to the church, such a spirit could lead us to a renewal of the god-image. Yet in the domain of the psyche, the wizard and the serpent simply *are* aspects of the god-image, or in psychological terms, the self. They represent the life principle itself in all its ambivalence, its conflicts, and its autonomy, including the way it drives our intellectual and religious understanding in sometimes dubious ways.

In women and in men, consciousness is so inured to our religious attitudes that awakening with genuine open-mindedness to the spirit of nature, an unmitigated, serpentine power requires an enormous transformation in assumptions. To see the spirit of the unconscious for what it is and to understand its aims, a person must confront inherited ideals, including an almost inevitable identification with a divine imperative that can only be seen as good.

As a schoolboy of 12, Jung was already confronted with this conflict when, after a great struggle, he allowed God to show him a "forbidden thought," a blasphemous image in which God revealed quite graphically what He thought of the church's ideas about Him. The image involved the cathedral in Basel, which had just been renovated with shining new roof tiles. After resisting as long as possible, Jung coaxed himself into thinking the thought through.

> I gathered all my courage, as though I were about to leap forthwith into hell-fire, and let the thought come. I saw before me the cathedral, the blue sky. God sits on His golden throne, high above the world—and from under the

throne an enormous turd falls upon the sparkling new roof, shatters it, and breaks the walls of the cathedral asunder.[26]

In that moment, Jung realized that the living god was not the god of the church and that his vision had shown him

> the immediate living God who stands, omnipotent and free, above His Bible and His Church, who calls upon man to partake of His freedom, and can force him to renounce his own views and convictions in order to fulfill without reserve the command of God. In His trial of human courage God refuses to abide by traditions, no matter how sacred.[27]

This early vision opened Jung's mind to God as a living phenomenon prone to unpredictable ideas, rather than the ideal that lives in the church's grand, idealistic architecture and doctrine. Had Jung not allowed such an irreverent image to come forward, he might not have made one of his greatest discoveries—that the living God exists not in the church, but in the psyche, and wants to evolve beyond exegetes' understanding of what God is. This insight later gave Jung the perspective he needed to follow the alchemists' irrepressible desire to discover the true nature of the divine.

Women and the God-Image

For contemporary Western women, innocence according to the church may seem irrelevant. Women have achieved sexual liberation and are building careers and gaining political power. But, as we will see in the lives of women shared in this book, innocence and perfectionism are secretly alive and well in the psyches of women, demanding from a deep, emotional stream a perfect life, perfect appearance, perfect relationships, and perfect recognition. They still must be seen as correct, or as causing no trouble, or having impeccable motives. Perfectionism and innocence may have a very long reach into a woman's most intimate thoughts about herself, her life, and the people in her world, and reveal a deep split in the

---

[26] Jung, *Memories, Dreams, Reflections,* 39.

[27] Ibid., 40.

feminine psyche. A woman who has fallen into this split is easily be taken in by either-or thinking: Either her life provides her with all she thinks it should, proving her value, or it is not worth living. Either she is perfectly blameless or she is worthless.

The spirit of the unconscious on the other hand would see things differently, finding a woman's individuality to be of the highest value, no matter how much she sins or how humble a life she lives. The lowly spirit of the unconscious wants to help her realize the eternal meaning of her life as it is, rather than insist on impossible guiltlessness.

In fact, according to Hannah's dream and these shadow versions of the Garden of Eden story, women in our day have a particular responsibility to confront the shadow of the Christian worldview as it haunts them in their personal lives. Women are needed to face the hidden, dismembering evil in spiritual ideals of innocence and perfectionism that affect them, their families, and their world. Fundamentally, the old standards prohibit a relationship to the unconscious.

"Fitcher's Bird" goes a step further than "Bluebeard" or the other sister-rescue tales in defining this conflict between old and new god-images. Its redemption motifs—the resurrected sisters and the epiphany of Fitcher's bird as an image for the feminine side of the self—indicate that a woman who defies conventional commands for innocence and instead dares to take care of her own egg of individuation redeems not only her own psychological life, but she also helps redeem the feminine archetype itself, along with the wizardly spirit of the unconscious, from languishing in condemnation. The image of the heroine dressed as Fitcher's bird, covered in honey and feathers, emphasizes above all a woman's profound capacity to feel the saturating eros of the feminine side of the self. Such a unique, healing image as Fitcher's bird tells us that when a woman answers the call to deal with the dark side and with evil as it exists in her own psyche, she finds herself engaged in the redemption of the transpersonal feminine that is trying to emerge from the collective unconscious not only in her own life but also collectively. This is the crucial, eon-changing goal that "Fitcher's Bird" shows us.

Enduring God's Opposites

Our collective identification with perfection and reason is so automatic and ingrained, it is almost impossible to identify consciously. We keep expecting perfection, rather than wholeness, to be the goal of psychological development. When an innovative Westerner gets hold of an Eastern meditation practice, more often than not, he or she turns it into another puritanical version of an ever-ascending, bliss- and perfection-seeking exercise in which the effects of the unconscious are suppressed rather than engaged, and the opposites are left still isolated from each other. Such approaches are new only in technique; they leave us without a valid experience of darkness that so clearly exists in ourselves and in the god-image.

Jung poignantly addressed the problem of manifest evil when discussing another of God's dastardly temptations—the one he inflicted on Job. In "Answer to Job," Jung explored Yahweh's own vulnerability to temptation when he accepted the devil's dare and subjected Job to horrific torture in order to test his faith. Having lost his wealth, his well-being, and his family, Job still had the integrity to reject the accusations of his neighbors, who assumed he had done something wrong to deserve such horrific punishment. It was Yahweh, not Job, who fell to the devil, willing to make a wager on the limits of a good man's faith. The biblical story reveals that God didn't know the reality of human suffering or how He imposes misery on His own creatures. For this reason, Jung said, God had to send His son (a new version of himself) to experience what human suffering is. By being more morally conscious than God, Job forced God to transform. Job shows us how to stand up to the dark side of God, forcing Him to become more related to human reality.

We can find it difficult, if not impossible, to accept that the transpersonal actually does have a dark side because the very idea goes against the grain of our earliest understanding of God. Most of us were taught from the first day of Sunday school that, according to the doctrine of *privatio boni,* God is only good.[28] Evil is only the absence of good and

---

[28] Jung discussed this doctrine and its dangerous effect on human consciousness in several places; see, for example, "Late Thoughts" in *Memories, Dreams, Reflections,* 327–54. In "A Psychological Approach to the Dogma of the Trinity," he writes, "How can one speak

not a real phenomenon except as a human weakness. But psychologically understood, Job's story puts an end to this ideation, or the notion that God rewards us for being good and punishes us for being bad. Instead, Job's predicament shows us that God—or, psychologically speaking, the self—is manifestly autonomous and unpredictable. We all see this in the inexplicable ups and downs of our own lives. If we understand the autonomy of the objective psyche, we realize that our suffering of the particular opposites in our lives is related to our psychological fate, our potential development, and has little to do with what we deserve. The dark side of the psyche and its presence in our lives are not our fault. But Jung points out that, like Job, we are tasked with enduring the conflicting sides of the god-image that appear to us intimately, because through us they can transform. Jung said:

> All opposites are of God, therefore man must bend to this
> burden; and in so doing he finds that God in his "oppositeness"
> has taken possession of him, incarnated himself in him. He
> becomes a vessel filled with divine conflict.[29]

Jung is suggesting that if we awaken to the two sides of God, or God's image as it appears in the self as a *complexio oppositorum,* we face the burden of carrying the opposites and their irreconcilability as they manifest in our own lives. We then could see our imperfections and our dark urges as meaningful encounters with transpersonal autonomy, an enormously difficult experience as shown to us among others by Eve, Job, and then Christ.

In symbolic terms, Christ the son of God shows us through His life and death that when God's opposites fall into the human vessel, they can be nearly impossible to endure. Accepting the divine conflict is not just a conceptual problem, as difficult as that already is, but one that forces us to face the psychological fact that Christ's agony cannot save us from our own, as the church promises. Rather, Christ gives us an image for the torment that we inevitably endure as vessels for archetypal conflict.

---

of 'good' at all if there is no 'evil'? Or of 'light' if there is no 'darkness,' or of 'above' if there is no 'below'? There is no getting round the fact that if you allow substantiality to good, you must also allow it to be evil" (par. 247).

[29] Jung, "Answer to Job," *CW*, vol. 11, par. 659.

Like Jesus, we are pinned down by the opposites in a way that can be mortifying to our egocentricity, killing what we thought we were and at the same time introducing a new understanding of what we could be, what our spiritual life is asking of us. Suffering the opposites brings us into intimate contact with the phenomenology of the archetypal or transhuman realm and its continual imperative to transform. Nothing is spared from the transformation, not even our ideas of good and evil—another lesson Jung learned early from his vision of God shitting on the church.

Our inability to take in the reality of the opposites or acknowledge the dark side of our god-image has been tragic for humankind, mainly because we remain identified with goodness. We are left defending our version of the so-called one true God at all costs, along with the evil that we do—including the wars that we start and the resources we consume— in the name of goodness as we see it. Without a connection to evil or the shadow, our egocentricity has the God-given right not to reflect on its own hubris.

"Fitcher's Bird" shows us what the shadow of our dominant worldview destroys in the background when we don't see this dark side. Our insistence on innocence murders feminine development. Potential new eros that could connect us legitimately to darkness, the shadow, matter, nature, the inner world, and each other in a new way is killed through the sheer momentum of a destructive pattern in which innocence, especially righteous innocence, is maintained at all costs and used to legitimize the most egregious evils of power. The emergency resonates in our very beings, women and men alike. New eros—the principle of relatedness and inclusiveness, and a concomitant awareness of the holy quality of our material lives—is desperately needed to renew our psychological and religious lives and our relationship with nature, yet it keeps getting killed off by our enlightened attitude toward darkness as something that can be meditated away.

The Negative Animus and the Shadow

The problem of false innocence is a particular emergency for women, because it so effectively keeps them away from the darkness which they can deal with better than men, as the devil in Hannah's dream suggested. Women psychologically tend to be closer to darkness, but the need to appear innocent scares them away from that darkness more than we can comfortably fathom. One analysand told me, "I've been trying to be 'good' for as long as I can remember. I can't imagine myself without trying desperately to be good, and only good." Another said, "I have fought every minute of my life not to be obsolete. If I stop that fight, what else am I supposed to do?" And another who grew up in a strict Christian sect lamented, "The message I got growing up was that if I am not perfect, I don't deserve to live."

The wizard in the beginning of "Fitcher's Bird" has all the bewildering power of the Old Testament God when he threatens to punish women severely for disobedience. His instruction to "preserve the egg carefully . . . and carry it continually about with thee, for a great misfortune would arise from the loss of it" echoes the spine-chilling threat a woman carries in her ears, convincing her that she must be completely without blame, correct, or pleasing in order to be liked, to be valid, or even to survive. She must take care of the egg of her soul not as her own but as something that belongs to an old man who loves girlhood innocence. The voice that she hears in her mind echoes that of the ambivalent Yahweh, but as a modern woman she may not recognize the similarity.

The desperate need to remain unblemished in the eyes of others casts a long shadow, especially when we don't realize where it comes from.[30] Innocence splits a woman away from her inherent value as an ordinary human being, offering no alternative to perfection. She only knows that if she isn't perfect, correct, righteous, or highly virtuous, she is corrupt and even contemptible. The negative animus whispers either/or thinking into her ears constantly. No matter how hard she tries, she is never sufficiently without sin, not smart enough, not thin enough, not happy enough, not successful enough, not admired enough, and therefore, it seems evident to her that she is a failure or pathetic and undeserving. One analysand told me she was afraid she could "individuate wrong," revealing how far away she felt from her genuine core. A woman may feel as if she has been working and working, trying and trying, and somehow

---

[30] Von Franz tells the story of a woman who destroyed her children by smothering them with good intentions, creating dependency and killing their motivation; see *Shadow and Evil in Fairy Tales,* 178.

a sense of validation eludes her, as if it were a great secret the world has kept hidden from her. As we explore the psychological work of several women, we will see how deflation and inflation are almost identical in these yearnings.

One of the saddest manifestations of the negative animus complex can be seen in a woman's inability to know what she really feels because she is trying to figure out what she *should* feel, as we saw when Elise tried to predict what her First Communion sin should be. A woman may constantly second-guess herself to the extent that she can't love what life has given her to love because she thinks it might be illegitimate. On an inner level, she may find it impossible to take in the healing reality or meaning of the images that the self pours out to her in dreams. I cannot begin to convey the tragic loss of soul that I have seen in such ruthless self-effacement. Reflecting even the smallest appreciation to such a woman can bring enormous relief—if she can feel it.

The Power Shadow

A woman tortured by perfectionism inevitably finds herself lacking, either in the value she can feel for herself or the attention she is receiving from others. She may try to compensate for her feared inadequacies by proving to the world how worthy or faultless she really is. She simply cannot be wrong or found lacking. To camouflage her insecurity, she may hide behind feminism, intellectual prowess, prestige, cold beauty, bombastic righteousness, sweetness, or martyrdom. She may become ruthlessly opinionated, controlling, or oppositional, seeking to fulfill a personal sense of goodness or power, even using other people in her life for this purpose. When a woman needs to prove her life virtuous, highly interesting, or without stain, she may be incapable of showing genuine interest in other people, possibly crossing into outright narcissism.

An animus-possessed woman may be under the illusion that she isn't supposed to suffer or that her suffering proves she is unworthy, and she may be crushed by the fear that people can probably see that something is wrong. To make matters worse, she fears that God hasn't made a clear effort to comfort her or show His approval. He hasn't shown her how she can make a contribution according to the norms of the collective. Why doesn't God just tell her exactly what He wants her to do? In every case, inflation and deflation are chillingly close.[31] Whether she considers herself wonderful or worthless, the only way an animus-possessed woman sees herself is through the eyes of other people—through the projection of her own impeccable moral standards or the superior blessings of her life, which she may be constantly compelled to share. If she is extraverted, her need for approval may be more obvious than she realizes. If she is introverted, her torment may be invisible to others, except that she looks as if she is carrying the burden of the world.

Another version of animus possession appears in the woman who, perceiving her life to be substandard, becomes the bitter victim of stifling martyrdom, plagued with overbearing self-pity, convinced that the world is against her and that she will never be properly seen. Catastrophic thinking leads her to imagine every possible worst-case scenario that could appear in her life, keeping her from pursuing her goals for fear of failure and thereby intensifying her bitterness. She inflicts on herself the very power shadow that plagues her and unwittingly infects others' lives with her misery.[32]

If ever there was an answer to Freud's desperate question about what women want, it would have to be that women want to be seen and valued for who they are—who they really are. The soul recognition a woman truly wants, however, cannot be gotten from the outer world or even the outer God; she will only find it in a relationship with the psychic realm, where wholeness rather than perfection is the highest value.[33]

A Healing Connection to the Self

As the fairy tale suggests, the antidote that breaks the spell of a mesmerizing, dismembering command for blamelessness is a devoted relationship to the symbolic egg—the hidden inner reality of the self.

---

[31] See von Franz's interpretation of "The Handless Maiden" in *The Feminine in Fairy Tales,* 70ff.

[32] An example of such a woman is Susan Traherne in the play *Plenty* by David Hare, made into a film by Fred Schepisi in 1985, featuring Meryl Streep and Charles Dance.

[33] A poignant example of this predicament is expressed by Mother Teresa in Kolodiejchuk, ed., *Mother Teresa: Come Be My Light: The Private Writings of the Saint of Calcutta.*

There, a woman may find that a new god-image lies hidden, one in which the feminine has a crucial role to play and individual life is highly valued. This is the point of the fairy tale, and of the heroine's actions to protect her egg. I will repeat it over and over again: *the heroine and her egg represent an eros connection between ego and self*—between personal and archetypal life. The achievement of this relationship is expressed in the symbolic honey in which the heroine drenches herself at the end of the tale and the fact that it anchors the feathery reality of the psychic realm.

In every case, a woman in the possession of a negative animus is unknowingly desperate for an inner connection to her own value, validity, and meaning—including her own darkness, if only because it is hers. Such a depth of recognition can only be mediated through a relationship with the self, which reflects and accepts all aspects of her individuality. Tending to her dreams, a woman builds up her feeling for the reality of that accepting wisdom. She protects her individual connection to the divine, not as instructed by protocol but according to her instincts and her relationship to the unconscious, gradually understanding with certainty what life really wants from her. This is where the positive side of the animus—the awakening side that is related to the self instead of the old religion—tries to lead her. The true animus wants her to realize the divine mandate of her individuality. For this he leads her to his mother and spouse, the psyche, the soul of the world. She learns slowly that the eros of the self does not bring her bliss or guiltless sainthood, but it allows her to be everything that she is.

A New Paradigm

The most unusual motifs in "Fitcher's Bird" compared to other sister-rescue tales are the egg the wizard gives to each maiden in the beginning and the strange image of a woman in a bird costume at the end. The heroine's wherewithal to disobey the wizard's command and to put her egg away before exploring his house tells us that apparently she has moved out of the wizard's enchantment, at least enough to protect her egg in her own way. The mutual protection between the heroine and her egg leads to every development and redemption in the fairy tale; it is a small but miraculous event that in symbolic terms marks the arrival of a new paradigm, emerging in the fullness of time after generations of trial and error. The fulfillment of the heroine's relationship to the egg is expressed in the image of a rare and wondrous bird, a creature that seems divine and yet is unmistakably down to earth.

Psychologically speaking, if a woman is taking her egg of development seriously, it means that, miraculously, she has emerged from the unconscious enough for individuation to take hold. The opposites have come into view, at least in terms of consciousness and the unconscious. She embarks on a spiritual life that has been returned to nature's images and processes. Eventually, she can acknowledge the autonomy of the animus thought system instead of pretending it isn't a problem. She finds freedom on the one hand and a mandate on the other to investigate the areas of her psychological life that have always seemed to be illegitimate.

When the heroine enters the forbidden room and looks directly at the tragic destruction that the wizard and her sisters' obedience to him have wrought, she reveals a critical psychological moment. In a woman, this moment is the one in which she realizes how eros has been destroyed in her own life by an evil dynamic. The dismembered sisters represent earlier manifestations of eros development if we consider all three sisters together as depicting a single, developing eros relationship to the self. In a woman, the heroine's courage of heart represents a development that would have been strengthening for some time. An ability to look at the darkness in her own unconscious animus complex, to see how she has been under the influence of a murderous power, and to realize this fact under the auspices of her relationship to the self means a woman has built up a protective connection to the egg of her own development, no matter how difficult it may seem at times to bear her own shadow. As in the fairy tale, the lead-up to such a feeling realization may require a long process through a repetitive pattern, as old values obedient to old attitudes are dismembered and a new kind of eros for the self slowly builds itself up until she feels protected enough to see the truth.

On a personal level, a woman who has developed a relationship with the unconscious and thus can see what has been going on in her animus complex may over time be freed from meaningless, neurotic suffering oriented around being good or feeling accepted by certain worldly perspectives. She can without hesitation defy an antediluvian edict with 2,500-year-old roots in the collective religious psyche—as soon as she sees it operating in herself. She may be freed from the need to be obedient, talented, bright, sublime, or strictly pleasing in order to serve her divine purpose in life. She can see the evil that lies coiled in the pretense of innocence. Further, when a woman sees her own involvement with a system of thought that destroys eros, she suddenly knows that she is connected to—and part of—the suffering of the feminine principle itself, so long relegated to the dark corners of the psyche along with the spirit of the unconscious.

Women and the Suffering Soul

Psychologically speaking, the repeated murders of young women in "Fitcher's Bird" represent how a woman's potential eros connections to the self are snatched away and destroyed by the negative animus before they have a chance to develop in life, over and over again. I have already alluded to an implicit paradox in this destruction that is difficult to accept. On the one hand, the murder of eros is destructive to the whole psyche and morally wrong in human and transhuman terms. Eros on personal and objective levels needs to develop, to connect us to the unconscious and to each other if we are going to survive the effects of our natural selfishness. We are reminded of the historic tragedies of war and genocide that are only possible when we are disconnected from eros, or when eros in us is too weak to change our ways.

On the other hand, the fact that the heroine's survival comes only after so many have died also tells us that over time a certain, immature eros has not been strong enough to survive or to help reverse the momentum of destructive, antifeminine dynamics. The dismemberment of the immature feminine is evil on the one hand, and yet on the other hand it is a just-so phenomenon, a dying that must reach its own turning point, one individual at a time. The maidens' repeated murders are related to the death and resurrection of the eros principle itself as it tries to build itself up in strength over an unendurably long period of time.

The turning point illustrated in the fairy tale when the heroine takes care of her egg leads to her bringing her sisters back to life and sending them home on the wizard's back. In psychological terms, what seemed to be dead is resurrected and returned visibly to life. In a woman, this would mean that a hard-won, strong-enough eros connection to the self finally puts a profound renewal into motion. Eros that seemed to be dead is renewed, brought back to life in a stronger iteration of itself. Since this happens at the archetypal level as well as the personal, the death and resurrection archetype is fulfilled—a very difficult event to articulate, especially as it is so intimately tied to a woman's personal life. The following dream is from a woman named Sandra, as she was going through a profound experience of redeemed eros in her marriage and for herself:

> *It is time to plant some things in preparation for spring. I know that now is the moment to dig up yellow green growth that develops under the earth during the winter. I dig into some soil behind a fence in an area that seems to be a part of our yard. I find lots of beautiful, glowing yellow-green leafy branches and pull them out of the soil. These we can weave through fences for a bit of color, and they slowly grow roots that take root in the spring. I look at the hole that I have dug and am amazed at how big it is, and as deep as a grave. The earth is so soft that it was easy to dig. It is quite deep, almost a perfect square with clean corners.*

The dream expresses a miraculous resurrection of vegetative growth that happens completely underground and is dug out of the earth as if it were in a grave, connecting it symbolically to the miraculous resurrection of wheat from the body of Osiris. The bright green leaves were a color Sandra truly loved, and she associated them with the renewed love she felt for her husband and her own life after a long period in which she doubted that love. Eros here is connected with the life principle that survives death.

We can only fully appreciate the dismemberment of eros in the fairy tale on the collective level as representing great suffering in the soul of humanity, as that soul (the psyche) struggles to make its presence known, over and over again in individual lives. How many people will dismiss as meaningless the miraculous new growth brought to them in dreams? When we consider how many millions of dreams daily are dismissed out of hand as nothing but images for what we already know or strange impressions brought on by a bad meal, we begin to realize just how common and destructive ignorance of the unconscious really is—how new psychic life is routinely murdered because, as a culture, we don't follow the instinct to brood over the meaning of our dreams or fantasies. It truly is tragic that humanity is missing the nourishing meaning of all those forgotten dreams. Yet such murder is a common, ordinary event that will change only in the fullness of time, as one individual at a time realizes the problem in his or her own life. The gold of new consciousness really does come out of the darkest material.

The fact that the murders in the tale go on for so long tells us that awareness of an unconscious pattern, even a horrendous one, may take many generations of one person's psychological life to achieve. Even as individuation begins, aspects of eros development may continue to be lost. Awareness and then real acceptance of the unconscious on a personal level is gradual, on a collective level secular, and in both cases fraught with mistakes and failures. The old god-image is more powerful psychologically than we can possibly imagine. As individuals, we are forced to examine ethical mores time and time again to find what is truly new. And yet, mysteriously, breakthroughs do occur. In the fairy tale, eventually one maiden becomes conscious enough to disobey the command that so many others have mindlessly obeyed and take up her egg in her own way. In a woman this would mean that the renewal of life in the divine feminine is activated.

The fact that the heroine exercises archetypal powers in resurrecting her sisters and putting the wizard under her control shows us too that tending to life in the psychic realm initiates a mutual redemption between human and archetypal worlds. Likewise, each woman in this book realizes to some degree that she is needed to help the feminine side of the divine incarnate, to become real in the world, because she is the only one who can bring her particular experience of the psyche to bear—to redeem the matter of her own life.

In the end, the renewal of the self is depicted not in the image of a new queen or bride, as in many fairy tales, but rather as an earthy kind of water bird. The appearance of the heroine dressed as a bird made of honey and feathers signals a unique transformation achieved through a woman's long-term engagement with the nature world of the psyche. The heroine in her bird form represents an individual woman and her singular realization of the self. Fitcher's bird is a novel image, one that conveys a woman's unique, visceral, eros connection with the self as a mystery and a miracle that is worn, lived. The self becomes for such a woman a distinct psychic reality so strange and so inspiring that it finally can be felt as unmistakably real.

Von Franz described how a felt connection to the self can heal instinctual life in a woman and visa versa:

> It is a normal process in life too when the ego is not in union with the deeper layers of the instinctive personality, for then it gets torn between the opposites. If the ego could relate directly to the Self, which is a unifying symbol, the conflict would fade and the ego would function again in wholeness. That is the normal way in which the opposites function, and the main impulse is again the flow of life, the ego serving or moving along the flow of life which comes from the totality.[34]

We can think of the heroine in her Fitcher's bird costume as symbolizing an ego immersed in a relationship with the self. As such, she can "function again in wholeness . . . moving along the flow of life which comes from the totality." The image of the heroine covered in honey and feathers reminds us that a woman's healing relationship with the self is not primarily intellectual. Closest to her skin is the feeling and sensory experience of the self, that is, the honey of its natural eros; this is what binds her to the feathery, symbolic fact that otherwise might vanish into conceptual ether. Honey as an eros substance, a "golden glue" in alchemical symbolism, binds in a way that is pure and strong, symbolizing the unmitigated strength of a feeling connection to the self, one that has evolved through the hard work and wonders of individuation.

In other words, the image of a woman's body drenched in honey shows us how a woman's most intimate reality may be joined to the self

---

[34] Von Franz, *Shadow and Evil in Fairy Tales,* 38.

in a bond of eros both natural and spiritual, one that cannot be broken. *It takes eros to feel eros; on the deepest level this is what it means for a sister to rescue her sister or for a woman to rescue a relationship with the feminine side of the self.* The bond must be understood for what it is, and for this reason, beyond all else, the bond is felt. A woman may have to go through a profound transformation to feel the eros that is trying to reach her, but once she can, the honey saturation is permanent, bringing about a new and unique iteration of the feminine principle through her experience.

The women who have generously shared their lives with us in this book will show us how slippery and agonizing an animus confrontation can be and yet how it may slowly lead to a world-changing transformation. A woman who engages in a long-term opus with the unconscious inevitably deals with darkness, as Hannah's dream devil implores, and goes through the painful process of accepting it as a reality in her own life. But her work also redeems a facet of the feminine self that has been waiting just for her, through all the centuries that the psyche has been ignored and diminished, because she is the only one who can realize the feminine side of the self as it appears in her own life.

3
Animus Development in Childhood

The animus is an inborn, spiritual instinct that guides a woman's urge to understand herself and the world. She may remember as a young girl experiencing the animus as an inner companion with a unique voice and distinct capacities to explore meaning, truth, nature, science, spirituality, and her own creativity. As a mediator to the outer world, the animus helps her see what she has to contribute to the world and urges her to achieve her goals. On an inner level, the animus stands at the threshold of the unconscious and at first may personify the whole experience of the unconscious. He produces fantasies and other inner images, urging a woman to be curious about them, to find meaning in the symbolic realm and realize her unique connection to the self. He is the driving force in the psyche that urges a woman toward individuation, although to do so he needs to be seen as such. As von Franz beautifully expressed, "The positive animus is an innermost instinctive awareness of the inner truth, a basic inner truthfulness which guides the spiritual woman in her individuation, toward becoming her own self."[35]

Formation of the Positive Animus

Both parents contribute to a girl's attitudes toward religious and intellectual life. If her parents have active spiritual lives and explore ideas in unconventional ways, their daughter will probably reflect a similar tendency to search for meaning according to her own interests. She may feel the animus quite distinctly and can naturally follow her intellectual curiosity wherever it leads her. If her parents are very rational, aesthetic, or philosophical, she most likely will mimic this preference. In both cases,

---

[35] Von Franz and Boa, *The Way of the Dream,* 269.

as long as she is born with a strong mental capacity, she will develop a strong, curious animus.

The father tends to make the most powerful imprint on a girl's animus development, but her mother's animus may also have a strong, if not stronger, presence, especially if the father is missing, passive, or unengaged. Very often the mother and father have a combined mental attitude, more or less unconsciously enmeshed, in which case their children likely will mimic those attitudes until they separate enough from their parents to discover their own inclinations toward meaning, spirituality and philosophy.

Both girls and boys naturally imitate the religious and intellectual attitudes that surround them in daily life, but some children with strong intuition have the natural capacity to differentiate between conventional ideas and those that lead to innovation and new attitudes toward life. We see this clearly in Jung's childhood as he struggled to understand the difference between his own experience of God as a paradoxical phenomenon above and beyond the church, and the God of his father's dogmatic belief.[36] Like Jung, such a child may face a profound inner conflict that anticipates a conscious process of individuation.

Logos Needs Eros

To help their children connect to their own spiritual lives, parents also need strong eros—an ability to value what their children individually deem interesting and meaningful. Although the mother tends to make the strongest eros imprint, eros is not limited to mothers; it is present in any parent who can relate to his or her children and certainly can be more present in the father than the mother. Parents with strong eros model for their children a connection to the spiritual world not by dictating creed or insisting on their own way of thinking but by accepting and relating to original ideas and predilections. Children who grow up with that kind of acceptance sense that their unique inner reality, their own truth, is something that the world anticipates. They can conduct their inner search

---

[36] See Jung, "School Years" in *Memories, Dreams, Reflections*, especially p. 52 ff.

for meaning unreservedly. Such child-centered parenting requires an inordinate level of conscious relatedness.

To develop a positive animus, to trust her spiritual and creative pursuits in the world, a girl needs loving acceptance at home if only because the world is not necessarily ready for her to have her own thoughts. Even just a glimmer of related parenting can help a girl build confidence in her spiritual, academic, or intellectual capacity (logos) and enter the world with a confident sense of self-value (eros). In this way, parents with independent spirituality and loving acceptance of a daughter's ideas and curiosity help build up her connection to her unique spiritual life. As a result, she has a chance to develop a relationship to the unconscious and the animus that is basically positive. Such a girl knows that her God-given individuality and her ideas are valued and protected.

A spiritually inclined girl who is lucky enough to grow up in an accepting household in which her intellect is appreciated may naturally experience the animus supporting her throughout her life without having to become conscious about it. Her thinking and her ability to love herself and others are not isolated from each other, nor are they dependent on each other. She feels the unique value of her own masculine and feminine traits, which are not at odds. She may care for dolls or feel protective toward younger siblings, friends, or pets and have a vital connection to her inner life and her emotional life, and to her instinct to care for others without neglecting herself. At the same time, she may love to explore the mountains and learn history, math, or science or set up an art studio, theater, or laboratory in the garage—all signs of a strong connection to her thinking life, to logos, meaning, and worldly adventure. She will not be susceptible to the intellectual charms of those in authority because she can think for herself. She may thus enter the world with a confident balance between heart and head, based on a naturally formed eros connection to her unique explorations of life and meaning.

Formation of the Negative Animus

In the fairy tale, we see a father who doesn't protect his daughters from abduction, and the mother seems to be absent. Without fatherly protection or motherly love at home, the maidens are vulnerable to the wizard's charming and magical powers. In a woman, the weak father would represent worn-out, conventional spiritual attitudes that can't appreciate new ideas and has no connection to the flow of meaning in the unconscious. The missing mother reveals a concomitant lack of a living relatedness, which allows worn-out masculine attitudes to survive and prevail. Both of these qualities necessarily exist in one person if dogmatic standards are in control. Again, this is a typical fairy-tale pairing that reflects our long-standing cultural reality in which eros is needed to renew spiritual life but is not allowed to develop.

Stilting conventionality exists in mothers and fathers alike and can invisibly insinuate itself into a child's psyche. Strict religious piety or rigid ideals in a household typically eclipse the value of individuality, in which case the whole family suffers from a lack of empathy. Personal idiosyncrasies or new ideas tend to be frowned upon. Such an atmosphere—in which developing eros is regularly killed—can have an obliterating effect on the singularity of a girl or a boy if it keeps them from feeling the legitimacy of their unique ideas or the value of their individual lives.

The film star Frances Farmer was a victim of her family's debilitating system of expectations. Her animus-possessed mother, unable to see Frances as anything but a mirror for herself, had her locked up in psychiatric hospitals as a way to control her rebellion against demeaning experiences and stereotypical expectations in the film industry. Frances returned to her punishing mother for comfort, over and over, unable to take the escape routes that life presented to her. Frances was caught between an outer world that punished her for her individuality and an inner one that demanded individuality at all costs.[37]

If a girl's parents think collectively or have restrictive attitudes toward spirituality or the rules of engagement in life, most likely she will either absorb their conventionality and accept it or find herself in conflict. The conflict may be outward, with her parents, or inward, her inner originality challenged or even tortured by the convention that is being demanded of her. A girl who finds herself sacrificing her own spiritual capacities in order to get along or garner acceptance is almost certain to develop a negative animus complex that continues tormenting

---

[37] See Shelley, *Frances Farmer: The Life and Films of a Troubled Star.*

her with the idea that there is something inherently wrong with her. It seems she just does not fit into her own life. Some girls are hypersensitive to expectation and want to adapt. Others seem fated to challenge the conventions they find themselves confronted with. It is difficult to say in the long run which scenario is harder on a girl's ability to connect with her innate, inner value.

Children with strong empathy and keen intuition can absorb expectations as if through the airwaves, intuiting that they should not challenge unspoken attitudes if they want approval. Their inborn sense of value for themselves goes underground as they try to hang onto familial acceptance. The relationship between fathers and daughters is especially fraught because it mimics the collective psychological situation in which old masculine convention resists and degrades the new feminine development it needs in order to be renewed. The collective psychological dynamic of old masculine standards dominating the developing feminine intensify a girl's struggle to feel valued for who and what she is. It is just as damaging, perhaps even more so, when a girl's mother is animus-possessed, overrun by puritanical or intellectual restrictions and unable to see or appreciate who her daughter really is. She may even carry the archetype of the evil stepmother who, devoid of eros, is incapable of accepting anything new.

If children don't feel valued for who they are naturally, and the situation becomes threatening, they may begin to lose a sense of their own reality. Some may build a compensatory fantasy world in which they can survive psychologically, picturing their lives in a way that explains their sense of feeling unreal or absent in their own home. For example, one 8-year-old girl in my practice revealed to me under pain of secrecy that she wasn't a real girl at all but an experiment. Her mother was a witch, setting up the girl's life as a series of tests—just to evaluate how she would react. This girl's parents weren't conventional, but they held conflicting intellectual views and values that eventually led them to divorce. Each unconsciously tried to win over their daughter to their own way of thinking. She absorbed that conflict and felt split between them. She couldn't access her own thoughts or feel her own reality, except as an object of her parents' examination.

Parents naturally tend to be identified with their own ideals and try, consciously or unconsciously, to turn their children into extensions of themselves. This is a substitute for relating to children as discrete beings, which, based on my clinical experience, is what most parents consciously want to do. But many with the best intentions don't realize they are also insisting subtly or unconsciously that their children be like them. It is just a fact of life, unfortunately, that most parents are unable to fathom what newness their children might bring to the world unless they themselves have a relationship with the unconscious.

Even on an everyday level, a girl's experience of her individuality is strained by our cultural inclination toward spiritual perfectionism and our devaluing of individuality. Families tend to prioritize convention over individuality, even if they don't mean to, by emphasizing the development of thinking, rationality, and perfectionism in children and belittling the value of emotion and imagination or relatedness toward each other. These preferences strike at the core of a girl's basic instinct to be who she is. An emphasis on appearance can be especially damaging to girls, causing them to equate their value with certain standards of beauty and body-image.

Performing for Approval

Any of us may remember a moment in childhood when we realized the possibility or even the necessity to impress others with a performance of what we knew they wanted to see from us. On the one hand, performing for approval is a normal adaptation for girls and boys as they break from immersion in the inner world and enter the outer world.[38] On the other hand, if children using performance to compensate for what they suspect is inadequate or unacceptable in themselves, or as a way to prove they are real, the youths may develop a performance

---

[38] This development is known in Erich Neumann's developmental model and in Kalffian sandplay as moving from the mother world into the father world. See Kalff, *Sandplay*, and Weinrib, *Images of the Self*, for Kalffian theory of childhood development. Kalff's theories are related to those of Neumann in *The Child* and *The Origins and History of Consciousness*.

complex.[39] When such a complex is active, children can hardly tell the difference between performing for approval and their genuine impulses. In the case of Elise, she knew that for her First Communion she only had to say the right thing; the fact that she couldn't feel what was right became secondary. Performance can become a substitute for a missing sense of basic goodness and belonging in the world. Children may be performing but unconscious that they are performing, assuming that this is how everyone garners love and acceptance.

I see the motif of performance appear in many women's dreams when they are psychologically ready to confront the way they may be pretending, acting, or otherwise effacing themselves in order to gain approval or success. This is a delicate topic and must be handled carefully, because performing may have been active since childhood as a survival mechanism and so thoroughly ingrained that facing it may feel like a violation. Some women (and men) may feel that their very existence depends on their secret ability to manufacture their identity. This can be a profound form of identification with the persona, and yet, for some people, even the persona consists of smoke and mirrors. Someone in this predicament is trying to hold on to a baseline, primal feeling for their own existence by performing as if they were real.

The tipping of the balance toward excessive self-consciousness and possession by a performance complex can develop through trauma, relentless experiences of being judged, examined, or unwanted, or a series of life setbacks. Just the fact of life in a rational world may be enough to shock children into second-guessing their self-value as they go to school and begin to compare themselves to others based on intelligence, beauty, or talent. If children realize they are intelligent and can use it to gain approval, they may become overly identified with their giftedness, which

---

[39] Others have referred to this problem as the development of a false self. For various views on this topic of development, see John Allan, *Inscapes of the Child's World*; Robert Coles, *The Spiritual Life of Children*; Michael Fordham, *Children as Individuals*; M. Esther Harding, *The Parental Image*; Linda Schierse Leonard, *The Wounded Woman*; Alice Miller, *The Drama of the Gifted Child*; Violet Oaklander, *Windows to Our Children*; Audrey Punnett, ed., *Jungian Child Analysis*; Lynda Shirar, *Dissociative Children*; Frances G. Wickes, *The Inner World of Childhood*; and D. W. Winnicott, "Ego Distortion in Terms of True and False Self," in *The Maturational Process and the Facilitating Environment*.

contributes to any insecurity they already feel about their innate value as a person, smart or not.[40] Children may become identified with the one trait that garners the most approval, narrowing their development in other areas.

Likewise, a girl with a positive father complex may find herself so identified with her adoring father that she will be blindsided by the fact that others don't see her the way he does, as God's gift to humanity. Although her effort is invisible to most, she has to work very hard to make herself appear as she imagines her father sees her. Later in life, she may have to go through the long process of rediscovering her native truth in the same way a woman with a negative father complex does, though with less existential angst.

A girl with little self-confidence performing for a masculine world quite easily loses her inner sense of herself, her own way of thinking, and the vitality of her instincts. This is one way to understand the situation portrayed in the fairy tale when the wizard so easily charms girls into his basket; the maidens' enchantment represents a girl's eager willingness to conform to powerful demands, invisible because of their everyday, collective and unconscious presence. They abduct her from her inner truth before she knows what has happened. For any child with strong empathy and a will to please, this dynamic may form quite early in childhood.

If a woman in her 30s or 40s is still trying to uphold attitudes and standards that don't belong to her, she may begin to feel the heaviness of an inner conflict between who she really is, which she may barely intuit, and who the conventional animus with his holy standards keeps telling her she is supposed to be. Expressing the conflict creatively can be enormously helpful. But if the hidden, repressed inner life builds up too much energy without coming into consciousness, she may begin to develop neurotic symptoms. Eating disorders are an especially widespread expression of this problem; they cooperate with a woman's sense of isolation, attacking her basic physical identity, her experience of her own body and reality. Depression, usually charged with anxiety, is the

---

[40] Mary Pipher and Sara Gilliam's *Reviving Ophelia* has many practical examples of how to support girls' sense of inner value as they approach adolescence and begin more actively comparing themselves to others. Rachel Simmons's *Odd Girl Out* documents the shocking psychological violence between girls who are willing to ostracize each other using the weapons of collective ideals.

most frequent complaint for such women at the beginning of analysis, and it often becomes debilitating. Intense anger may also be a symptom, as we will see in more than one woman in this book. Many women who grow up with such deep insecurity develop the skill to convincingly pretend that their lives are very positive, even when the facts blatantly contradict them. In private they suffer intensely, or else their pain recedes into such depths that they hardly know it exists.[41] The more introverted she is, the less obvious her painful situation will be to the outer world.

Feeling Unreal

In my work with children, I have seen a profound disconnection from reality from as early as age 4, when a child should be moving toward unabashed and confident embodiment. A child who is struggling to feel real may, for example, revert to baby talk in order to get the attention he or she needs or may become willfully mute or oppositional, throwing tantrums to provoke a reaction that will get noticed (though the child can't consciously express such intentions). Children are forcing the world to notice them, demanding that their existence be mirrored back to them, even if the feedback is negative.[42] They can't verbalize their experience of feeling disconnected from their inner core, but they act it out, and they can express such emptiness in nonverbal forms of therapy.

Often it seems that disobedience is the goal no matter what, and this can gain a child an unfortunate oppositional diagnosis. The analyst must be on the lookout in adult analysands, too, for manifestations of these intense attempts to be seen. The analyst's job is to accept without hesitation any description of the painful experience of being unseen and to help link the suffering inner child to a new possibility of being recognized through the mirroring and reparenting capacities of the self, slowly helping those capacities emerge from the unconscious and become integrated.

---

[41] In her "Rumpelstiltskin" essay, von Franz describes this problem as spinning straw into gold—holding up a fantasy world in which a woman remains infantile and innocent; in Schweizer and Schweizer-Vüllers, eds., *Wisdom Has Built Her House,* 143ff.

[42] See Miller, *The Drama of the Gifted Child.*

The experience of not feeling real is more prevalent in girls than in boys, in my clinical experience. In terms of depth psychology, we are talking about the loss of a feeling connection to inner life, to the self, the a priori core of a child's identity. If children lose a connection to their center, they also lose a sense of themselves as real beings. They can become untethered from reality and abducted into the head-world of fantasy thinking, which further cuts them off from even a basic, cellular experience of their existence and value. For a girl, a disconnection from her identity can be exacerbated by the fact that the world has presented her with no divine feminine image with whom to identify.

For example, I treated a 5-year-old girl named Mia, who had witnessed violence between her parents and was subjected to a cultlike atmosphere. She became oppositional, refusing to dress herself and incessantly using grating baby talk. On an inner level, Mia had retreated completely out of reality and into fantasy. She presented herself in therapy as a princess from another planet, trying to decide if and when she would descend to Earth, what she would look like, and what her name would be. Week after week she brought new fantasies about her identity and expressed them in the sand tray or drew them in crayon. She spelled out definitively the unusual, otherworldly, multisyllabic name she had chosen for herself that day. She strictly corrected me if I even slightly mispronounced her complicated fantasy name, which told me that somewhere in the psyche, her individuality was taking shape and that she could begin to feel its reality.

During many sessions, she sewed clothing for herself, expressing the urge to become materially real. In several sandplay sessions, she got right into the sand tray and bathed herself, pouring sand over her arms and legs as if she were trying to incarnate through contact with her own psychic substance, projected into the medium of the sand. Mia's inner world was trying to help her heal, and eventually, she was allowed to move through her imaginal world as its own reality. As part of this process, Mia had an experience of a planetary goddess whom she trusted to advise her about her identity and her eventual descent to Earth (fig. 7). There was nothing that I needed to do to intervene in this process as the self hidden in this goddess gradually accomplished its own goal.

Figure 7. Mia Standing in the Sand Tray

Mia is standing in the sand tray, her feet submerged in the sand. She wears a costume she made and reverently addresses the figure of a blond woman—for Mia, a cosmic goddess. The goddess is helping Mia decide if and when she would descend to Earth and become recognizable to her parents. Psychologically speaking, she is conversing with the self, discussing how and when they will enter reality together. Author's photo.

Eventually, Mia expressed the experience of connection with inner wholeness in several ways, including a beautiful sandplay image involving a Christmas scene and a map she made of clay depicting all eight planets she had visited, oriented around the sun (fig. 8). She went through a profound healing process that began with an expression of utter chaos. But by the end of her therapy, a felt experience of the inner world granted her the strength to be a real, earthly being, even though at times she needed to visit another cosmic location for replenishment. In other words, she and the self brought each other into the world.

Figure 8. Mia's Initial Tray and Rendering of the Solar System.

Mia's initial sand tray (left) reveals profound inner chaos. At the end of her therapy, the planetary realm of her imaginal life (right) had become organized around a center. She remembered living on eight different planets, some from our solar system and some from other galaxies. The number eight expresses an experience of differentiated wholeness, the sun a central solar consciousness. Author's photos.

Demonic Animus Possession

Severe trauma in a girl's life or acute sensitivity to being rejected may lead to the development of a possessive negative animus of another, demonic intensity. Parents who are overly critical, controlling, possessive, abusive, or actively blind to their children's realities can traumatize children, convincing them that they shouldn't exist or that they are to blame for any family trouble. A possessive animus stemming from such trauma can lead to serious mental illnesses, including major depression, borderline personality disorder, paranoia, or psychosis.

Barbara Hannah conveyed the poignant story of a French nun, Jeanne Fery, whose possession by demons was recorded in 1585.[43] Jeanne reported that the devil appeared to her when she was 4 years old in the shape of a handsome young man who offered to become her substitute father. Hannah understood that this fantasy brought compensation for Jeanne's critical, probably abusive, father; she had lost her mother. Jeanne's fantasy life became quite elaborate, and over the years she became obsessive about her other, inner father. He was charming and seductive, criticizing the priests and nuns she lived with and demanding she secretly do the same. Her imaginal world was full of similarly aggressive spirits who eventually convinced her to privately renounce her religion, even as she became a nun. Jeanne was living a hidden inner life that was completely hostile to her outer Catholic commitments. As her behavior became more erratic and eventually psychotic, people around her saw that she was tormented, and a two-year, intensely difficult exorcism began.

Mary Magdalene appeared to Jeanne during the long ordeal as the only inner figure she could trust to tell her the truth about the devilish plots and voices trying to destroy her. Jeanne considered Mary to be trustworthy because she too had demons cast out from her (Luke 8:2). After the exorcism, Mary stayed with Jeanne throughout her life as an ongoing source of respite and a voice of wisdom—a divine figure for the feminine side of the self, as Hannah pointed out, in which Jeanne could take refuge. Like Mia, Jeanne needed a savior who came from the feminine realm. Mary Magdalene felt more ethically comprehensive,

---

[43] Hannah, *The Animus*, 2:57ff.

more real, and more trustworthy than the illusive masculine phantoms insisting on complete loyalty and obedience.

Hannah recognized that today we would call the nun's possession a psychosis and that we may also recognize such a complete takeover of the personality as a devilish animus possession—evidence of "the existence of the invisible aspect of life and of the inexorable reality of compelling forces which motivate us—with or without our knowledge."[44] Further, Hannah explored how the unavoidable experience of such forces as they exist in the anima and animus—living forces—can be at odds with even the strongest religious convictions, as if they were trying fervently to renew our relationship with the divine.

Summary

Even in cases of animus possession that are not as serious as Jeanne Fery's, a girl may grow into in early adulthood with little or no access to her sense of herself, living in an isolating, inner bubble. As she grows older, she may only be able to find herself through the performances she puts on in order to seek approval in academic or professional life, trying hard to be seen and recognized as valid by imitating the standards she observes and intuits in the outer world. Such animus possession is more prevalent than most of us want to admit, and very difficult to identify as a problem. Collectively, we can hardly see unconscious standards of puritanical perfectionism that continue to permeate our cultural atmosphere and strike at the core of a girl's identity unless the unconscious provides us with an image that helps us out of our blindness.

In the following pages we will explore the dynamics through which a strong negative animus may be brought to consciousness as an autonomous spirit, an "inexorable reality" whose aim is at once more challenging and more positive than we expect. [45] We will see how the

---

[44] Ibid., 2:40.

[45] In addition to analytic work, unconscious dynamics may be accessed through various forms of therapy. When trauma is involved, Pat Ogden's work in sensorimotor processing may be helpful; in Ogden, Minton, and Pain, *Trauma and the Body*, she describes working with the unconscious but doesn't name it as such. Sylvia Brinton Perera, *The Scapegoat*

negative animus is devastating and yet, when divested of his orthodoxy and realized as the spirit of individuation, may lead a woman to the depths of love and a genuine experience of transpersonal life—to the "innermost instinctive awareness of the inner truth." Though individuation may be slow, it is dappled through the years with moments of light and grace that would not be possible if a deep transformation were not taking shape.

Complex, and Judith Lewis Herman, *Father-Daughter Incest,* are helpful books for women with a negative animus complex that is based around the father. Also see Donald Kalsched, *The Inner World of Trauma,* and Nora Swan-Foster, *Jungian Art Therapy,* for ideas and techniques in approaching traumatic family complexes through the unconscious.

Part II

The Wizardly Animus in Women's Lives

If a woman hasn't gone through the experience of being trapped in the demon animus, she has only unconscious thoughts.

—Marie-Louise von Franz

4
The Dynamics of the Inner Spirit

Projection of the Negative Animus

Pearl was in her mid-30s when she began analysis. An educated, intelligent, and capable woman, she was happily married with two young children, developing a private medical practice and successfully negotiating graduate school. But Pearl was struggling emotionally. She was riddled with self-doubt and fearful of haunting anger that in certain, infrequent episodes, she couldn't control. She exploded in front of her children—shouting, throwing things in the house, blaming her husband. She was never physically violent toward her family members, but she knew she was frightening them, and she felt ashamed of herself.

At the same time Pearl found herself in a baffling relationship with a charismatic male professor in her graduate school program. When she first met this man, Pearl was enchanted by his brilliant theories. She wanted to show him that she was intelligent enough to deserve his attention and approval. In other words, at first, she experienced a positive transference, seeing her own spiritual potential in him. But during some difficult exchanges in which she honestly questioned his ideas, the professor's unconscious motivations became apparent, revealing a discrepancy between the outer man as he really was and what the animus projected onto him. Eventually, Pearl could see too that he was fostering cultish admiration from his students, especially the women. Perhaps because he sensed her doubts about his motivations, or because she was especially sensitive and attractive, the professor seemed to treat Pearl differently from the other students, making strangely critical remarks that cut close to the bone. Still, even with her suspicions, she found herself craving his favor. When she didn't get it, she could become convinced that he saw something inherently inept in her and fell into emotional turmoil.

When Pearl began analysis, we were able to untangle some of the dynamics with the professor. We realized that he was the victim of a "mana personality," unconsciously identified with the power he had over his students.[46] Pearl soon took steps to withdraw from his influence, realizing at least on a cognitive level that he could never give her the validation she yearned for. But the following dream made it clear that from the point of view of the psyche, it wasn't the professor, but a demonic animus that was at the heart of her troubles:

I'm all alone in a residential neighborhood in the Midwest. My children are alive, but I can't be with them because I'm cursed forever to be stalked by this devil-man. I'm constantly trying to escape him, running from house to house seeking refuge. It's light out, and then night. I can't find my car to escape, and he's getting closer. He is superhuman and can't be killed. The dream is anxious and hopeless, like this is the rest of my life away from my family. There is a freshness to the landscape, though. A lot of luscious green grass and moisture all around me. That part of the dream has more beauty and hope.

In clinical practice and friendships, I have seen that most women dream of male stalkers or intruders at some point in their lives. Such dreams reveal intrusive, sometimes haunting masculine energy in a woman's own psychology—what von Franz called the "demon animus," whose repetitive, judgmental opinions must be faced in order to uncover a woman's genuine thinking capacity.[47]

On a personal level, we could hypothesize in partial accuracy that the "devil-man" in Pearl's dream represented overwhelming emotional intensity—the anxiety, fear, rage, or self-doubt that hounded her. Another possibility would be that the devil-man represented the professor himself, in the outer world, and his unconscious aggression toward Pearl. Both of these interpretations are true to some extent but reductive, meaning they trace the problem back to what was already known. Interpreting the devil-

---

[46] For a description of the mana personality, see Jung, "The Relations between the Ego and the Unconscious," *CW*, vol. 7, par. 374ff.

[47] Von Franz, *Animus and Anima in Fairy Tales*, 21.

man as a problematic emotion or an outer figure would have left an active projection in place, and the problem would eventually be transferred with equal intensity to another person in authority. Pearl wouldn't have been so triggered by her professor if the inner animus weren't also pursuing her with demonic energy.

Especially when a dream figure is "superhuman and can't be killed," it must be taken seriously as a psychic reality with a goal, a living phenomenon that we may rightly call a deity. On the one hand, the dream revealed a frightening inner dynamic trapping Pearl's freedom to live her own way. But on the other hand, the dream suggested a "freshness to the landscape," pointing toward a renewal.

Father Complex as the Basis of the Negative Animus

Pearl was born into an upper-class, conservative American family. Her mother and father both valued rationality at the expense of emotional realities or individuality. Pearl compared her family's country club social circle to that of the fictional Stepford wives, Stepford being a place to which women are abducted and programmed through brain manipulation into a pleasing, patriarchal conventionality where they desire nothing more than to give birth, cook and clean house, give delightful parties, and agree with their husbands.

But as a child, Pearl found herself constantly at odds with the family ethos. She was creative and individualistic, with strong intuition and feeling functions, personality traits that held little value in the household and ruffled her parents' conventional attitudes. They simply had no framework for the reality or the validity of a creative child like Pearl, whose imaginative spirit was incapable of conforming to their conventionality. Pearl was labeled a troublemaker early on and incorrectly diagnosed with learning disabilities. Although as a child she couldn't express her experience consciously, Pearl felt caged, imprisoned in an alien world. She rebelled instinctively with frequent temper tantrums, driven by an inner imperative for individuation that she could barely intuit. Unconsciously, she encountered the fact that the people around her had no capacity to see, much less appreciate, who she really was. She was meant to develop differently from, and beyond, the family system she was born into, but because no reliable adult could see that, she was deemed a learning-disordered misfit and learned to think of herself as a freak.

As a child, Pearl did feel herself to be simpatico with her father because both of them were introverts in a family of extraverts. She felt that they could naturally connect with each other spiritually or philosophically, but he remained distant and dependent on alcohol for most of her childhood. He never showed direct interest in Pearl, puzzling her and exacerbating the ideation that there was something inherently wrong with her. Her experience of her father as remote and uninterested in her formed the basis of a negative father complex.

Compared to her father, Pearl's professor at first seemed to offer a new authority with updated ideas that were in sync with her developing intellectual life. His modern philosophies seemed to give him a new power to validate Pearl's individualistic nature, until she found him out. When she thought about the professor in the context of her relationship with her father, Pearl realized that he too never showed any more interest in her original ideas than her father did. Rather, he insisted that she and all his students believe in his impressive new truth as if it were gospel. He was parading another form of convention dressed up in new clothes.

Eventually, Pearl could see that her professor's narcissistic indifference toward her was identical to her father's. Lacking relatedness, he passively ignored who she really was, uninterested in any thought that didn't validate what he considered his genius. When she could see the similarity with her father's apathy toward her, Pearl realized on a more visceral level how she was caught in a projection. She was subjecting her innate value to the approval of an outer authority who seemed new but turned out to be as conventional as her father. She had to face the fact that, even with his charming personality and modern ideas, the professor didn't have the capacity to even imagine who or what she was. The psychological predicament was murderous and dismembering to Pearl's sense of her own value. Even so, the demon was not the professor himself. The dismembering demon was in Pearl's psyche, suffering the same split between a conventional worldview and spiritual originality.

Pearl's genuine urge to understand life in a new way—her own spirit of individuation—was projected onto the professor, just as it had been projected onto her father. Realizing this was very painful for Pearl and required a huge adjustment in her expectations. As is typical in the slow withdrawal of projection, even when Pearl could see the projection and know she was chasing an illusion, like many other women in her predicament, she still yearned to be seen and valued by that "damn professor," as she called him. She couldn't help but want his approval. She wanted him to be something he couldn't be, to have empathy he just didn't have. She went to great lengths to impress him but was never rewarded the way she hoped. In fact, he eventually made some particularly spiteful remarks about her during an important public event, which told us that his anima was triggered by Pearl seeing his unconsciousness. Witnessing his overt cruelty and knowing it was morally wrong helped Pearl stop hoping for any empathy or genuine interest from this man.

The strength of such a projection is intense and confounding, propelled by the archetypal energy of the animus. He energizes a woman's fantasies about being seen, recognized, honored, and treasured from the outside in part because he too wants to be recognized and treasured. Until a woman pays attention to him directly, he will suffer anonymity. His suffering as a rejected spirit within she will feel as her own.

Animus Two-Sidedness

In her dream of the devil-man, Pearl runs from house to house, but none of them is her own. Motherly eros and shelter are nowhere to be found. She can't get to her children, which is critical because they symbolize her own inner development; she is cut off from any eros connection to the self.

In blocking development, such a demonic animus has a truly evil effect. It can be difficult for a woman to accept that such aggressive energy is coming from within, as part of her own personality. She may feel ashamed as a natural response to this fact, but the analyst must allay that shame immediately, because it employs yet another layer of judgmental animus torture. No woman is to blame for the destructive energy in the animus that she inherited, that has built up over her developmental years, driving her fantasy thinking; it is autonomous and out of proportion.

Recognizing and mitigating such shame is often the first step toward objectifying the destructive thought system itself. Eventually, it may be possible to accept that negative animus energy itself has a paradoxical, positive aim to help her awaken to its own negativity—to the judgmental thoughts that are blocking individuation. For example, Pearl's animus from the threshold of the unconscious—the positive side of the animus—brought Pearl her dream, giving her a scrupulously accurate account of his demonic side. He could keep her exiled from any place in herself that felt like home through ongoing critical thoughts about herself. The panic she experienced in the dream jolted her enough to register his autonomy; she could see and feel his ability to abduct her from herself. Yet the overall aim of the dream, symbolized mainly by the color green, was to reawaken her natural sense of herself, the instinct for individuation that von Franz described as "becoming her own self."[48] In her connecting with that instinct, both she and the animus could be released from the prison of judgmental one-sidedness.

In summary, with this dream the animus openly revealed his two paradoxical sides. The positive side brought her the dream, and in the dream, he revealed his destructive side. The fact that the animus can be so fundamentally and openly bipolar is the main stumbling block that women face when trying to understand him; he is the devil when locked in one-sidedness, and he is an individuating spirit when his paradoxical truth can be seen and felt. Seeing this two-sidedness, Pearl could begin the long work of observing his effect on her life when he was destructive, yet also how he showed her a meaningful path forward. Dream by dream, the unconscious revealed in unmitigated detail how her fear of being rejected haunted her relentlessly as she sought approval from others. At the same time, with the same dreams, she could begin to feel the positive side of the animus that through truth was compelling her toward individuation. She was being seen for exactly who she was. The more Pearl could feel herself being seen by the animus, the more she could relate to the unconscious as a reflecting phenomenon that saw and accepted every iota of her personality. In this process, an eros connection to the self was building

---

[48] Von Franz and Boa, *The Way of the Dream*, 269.

itself up. Such eros is not coddling but supportive, oriented completely and sometimes ruthlessly toward individuation.

Eventually, Pearl could accept the fact that she was born to the lonely journey of growing out of her family's conventionality and connecting to a deeper core of psychological wisdom that they could neither recognize nor understand. Further, she could see that the devil-man in her dream was not after Pearl herself but targeted her naïve attempts to participate in familial attitudes that were regressive and restricted her potential. The animus opened the way through which both he and she could be freed from imprisonment in a worldview that was too narrow for both of them. Years later, revisiting her experience with her father after a visit home, Pearl realized that "yearning for my father's attention, imagining that he would approve of me if I could just say or do the right thing, kept me infantile. It made me dependent." In such moments of felt realization, the arduous yet meaningful journey out of the father complex could be integrated.

One of Pearl's strongest motivations for entering analysis was her desire for her children to connect with their individuality in life because she didn't want them to suffer the constrictions that she experienced as a child. Through empathy for her children, Pearl could feel love for her symbolic, inner children in her many dreams about them; they represented the indisputable validity of her own burgeoning individuality. I am convinced that women dream about their children so much because their unconditional love for their individuality is so strong that it finally helps them feel a similar devotion for their own inner development. Through her wishes for her children, Pearl could see the positive, even sacred aspect of her rebellious nature that had caused so much trouble growing up, insisting on her individuality despite all odds. She saw that her eldest daughter inherited the same demanding insistence on individuality, and this realization helped Pearl accept her daughter's very strong will with more tolerance.

Feeling more strongly her developing independence from the father complex, Pearl experienced a turning point when she could feel and accept individuation as having high transpersonal value. She could accept dream images like the devil-man not as "weird" or "creepy," but as illuminating support from the self for her psychic healing and development. Over time, such inner support became more central to her than approval from the outside. Her self-confidence grew from the inside out as her connection to the inner world deepened. Although this is always a slow process, the strong feeling of validity that she experienced from her connection to the inner world—an eros connection to the self—brought a healing transformation that she knew was permanent, a foundation for ongoing growth.

Pearl's strengthened connection to her inner world slowly built itself up, a connection represented in the fairy tale by the heroine protecting her egg. She could begin to see how, through a difficult truth, the self by way of the animus reflected her individuality back to her with much more depth and honesty than any human being could. Such a strong new feeling for the genuine authority of the inner world arises in the critical moment a woman begins to look to dream images, rather than outer influences, for the reliable truth about herself. This is the moment the symbolic egg of the self begins to make an appearance in consciousness. The opposites come into view: Consciousness and the unconscious have a chance to become genuinely related to each other, which is the real, underlying goal of the animus.

The Projection of Value in Literature

Numerous examples in literature depict how a wizardly animus may separate a woman from feeling value for her own life or keep her locked in a cage of performance. The animus may trick a woman into isolation by convincing her that she is extra special, as happens to Elizabeth Bennet at the beginning of Jane Austen's *Pride and Prejudice*. He may dupe her into a sterile marriage that flatters her spiritual materialism, such as Dorothea Brooke experiences in her marriage to Mr. Casaubon in George Eliot's *Middlemarch,* a remarkable novel that describes a woman's redemption out of a worn-out, Faustlike, scholar animus through a real experience of love.

If she has a positive father complex, as does Isabel Archer in Henry James's *The Portrait of a Lady* or Lucy Honeychurch in E. M. Forster's *A Room with a View*, a woman may, for a long time, fail to recognize how a lover who treasures her as a pristine possession is actually destructive toward her soul. However, Margaret Schlegel, in Forster's *Howards End*, is an example of an intelligent woman supported by a positive father with strong eros, which allows her to connect confidently to her intellect on the one hand and her inner sense of herself, her own instincts, on the other. She has a naturally positive connection to life in which she can accept the humanity of her imperfect husband, uniting his positive and negative aspects with a natural relatedness that her wounded and more judgmental sister Helen slowly develops.

The projection of inner value or potential onto an outer person is not necessarily all bad, and it seems that not everyone is meant to withdraw those projections. The outer person can be legitimately inspiring, leading a woman through spiritual or intellectual growth and development, never losing their fascination or charm, but remain a motivating influence. This seems to be the case in the relationship between Dora Carrington and Lytton Strachey.[49] It may be that the animus doesn't need to be integrated into consciousness but can instead remain a relatively unconscious aspect of a woman's inspiration.

Projection of the Positive Animus: Mary Magdalene and Jesus Christ

In Pearl's experience, the unconscious animus, in part projected onto her professor, revealed himself as a devil-man. On an inner level he is a deific force bringing the psyche's reality to bear. He is powerful and wily, a real trickster in his capacity to project himself wherever a woman looks. The damnable fact is that the positive, individuating side of the animus can overwhelm a woman just as effectively as the negative side, leading her to the same realization—that she is driven by an elusive, powerful phenomenon that she experiences partly in projection. In both cases, a woman's psychological fate is tied to her ability to separate herself from the projection and develop a conscious relationship with her inner spiritual drive—a process that may unfold over the course of a lifetime. In contrast to Pearl's experience in which her professor did not offer any new ideas or real eros, Mary Magdalene's experience of Jesus of Nazareth offers an example from religious history in which the outer man

---

[49] See Holroyd, *Lytton Strachey*; the film *Carrington* (1995) was based on this biography.

really does propose a new spiritual worldview, with and including love. Mary's feeling for Jesus, though difficult in its own way, was reliable.

In his time, Jesus introduced a profound new experience of God.[50] He was the son of an invisible, purely spiritual father and a human mother. He was God incarnated in the earth of a human being. In symbolic terms, he introduced a new understanding of the divine factor that exists within humanity. Some Gnostics and alchemists saw him this way, as the Anthropos or original human, the god that is infused into the soul of every individual; in some sects, he is hermaphroditic. Some early Christians considered Mary Magdalene to have a critical role in recognizing Christ as that inner, divine reality.[51] Psychologically, we can understand Mary's experience of Jesus in life, and then Christ in death as representing the fact that the divine factor is experienced at first in projection, and how this projection must die for the divine factor to be realized as an inner reality. She shows us how the realization of the inner god is experienced once the projection onto the outer god dies—but this is not something the church could or would acknowledge.

According to the New Testament and legend, Mary Magdalene loved Jesus as a man and followed his teachings over her lifetime.[52] She mourned his death deeply, more deeply than the male disciples. She was the only disciple to remain at his empty tomb, weeping and wondering where his body was laid, and through this genuine feeling reaction, she became the first person to see him resurrected in the garden as a living spirit. We could even say that her persistent emotional reaction was the

---

[50] We can see that in the Hebrew Bible the god-image became completely spiritual, invisible, and male. At that time, the psyche was separating itself from matter and the body so it could become known as a separate entity; the god-image of the Hebrew Bible reflects that differentiation. In our age, the psyche is trying to unite again with the body, to be known as a divine factor in the individual. Some Gnostics saw Jesus Christ as that divine factor and Mary Magdalene as the realizing partner who brings the divine factor into reality.

[51] See Howe, "Redeeming Mary Magdalene: The Feminine Side of the Death and Resurrection Archetype," in Schweizer and Schweizer-Vüllers, *Wisdom Has Built Her House.*

[52] See Cynthia Bourgeault, *The Meaning of Mary Magdalene*; Susan Haskins, *Mary Magdalene*; Kathrine L. Jansen, *The Making of the Magdalen*; Karen L. King, *The Gospel of Mary of Magdala*; and Elaine Pagels, *The Gnostic Gospels.*

very thing that provoked Christ to appear, revealing himself as the divided and undivided God, a spiritual reality that had died in one form and now appeared in another to the one person who loved him enough to see him. In this sense, she redeemed Christ as much as he redeemed her.

If we understand Christ symbolically as equivalent to the Anthropos, he represented the divine not only in Jesus and Mary, but in everyone—the inner divine human who can recognize the inner divine human in others, just as Mercurius in one person seeks Mercurius in others. We can understand Mary to be the first in the Christian religion to come to this symbolic understanding, and so Christ asked her to spread the word.

Psychologically, we can understand Mary's deep feeling experience of Jesus's death, and then her realization of Christ as a living spirit, to represent a withdrawal of her own god-projection and then the healing of a profound transference. Mary's insistent, emotional questioning and yearning to see the missing body of Jesus Christ can be seen as the gradual, mortifying realization of that projection. Not only does the god-projection onto the outer man die, but Mary shows us that the ego, too, goes through a mortifying experience in the withdrawal of projection.

When a projection dies, whether it is positive or negative, one is left with the realization of the inner projecting reality. As a matter of fact the autonomous projection-making factor has been there all along, and further, it wants to be known for its incredible power over consciousness. Mary is the human being who brings that realization to humanity. She is the earth in which the inner god-image is fathomed. Mary had her own divine imperative to fulfill; she had to realize Christ in herself and bring that experience to others. In other words, she, too, went through a death and resurrection experience in which she and the inner god were both renewed.

On a psychological level, Jesus Christ and Mary Magdalene represent a holy couple who are also human. Together they experience the eon-changing realization that God is incarnate in the human realm—that the eternal aspect exists "in here" rather than "out there," projected.

Mary also shows us the feeling capacity needed to realize the inner divine. Like our heroine in "Fitcher's Bird," she is the one among many who realizes where and what the objective spirit really is, though in her case that spirit begins as negative. Perhaps we can see that for Pearl, or for any woman trying to understand what is driving her relationships, the task is identical. When Pearl's projection onto her professor died, it was mortifying because the man she thought could validate her turned out to be a sham, and yet she had a chance to realize this by confronting it on a symbolic level. She eventually saw that the objective spirit of the psyche had been goading her to turn inward and see him as an inner phenomenon, freeing him from his unconscious role and helping him function as a spirit of individuation. The projection itself awakened her to the autonomy of the psychic realm. The fact that the experience is negative for one person and positive for the other is immaterial psychologically speaking, yet we cannot ignore the critical role of love in an individual life. Is one's love reliable? Whether the answer is yes or no, the ongoing renewal of love remains the driving, motivating force underneath the desire to understand one's fate.

As a woman, Mary has a special meaning to women who can relate to the experience of transference, which normally has all the strength of a god-projection, whether that projection hooks itself onto a man or another woman. Women's experiences of transference haven't been discussed in psychological research as much as men's. As with a man, once a woman becomes conscious of her capacity to project, she is no longer one—she realizes that she is two, fulfilling the first step in the Axiom of Maria: "Out of the one comes two." She is the human being and she is the psychic reality that projects itself outward. In her psyche lives a spirit that no longer can survive in *participation mystique* with the outer person and asks for its actuality to be integrated into conscious life. As a woman, Mary's love naturally clung as long as possible to the concrete outer man, Jesus, onto whom the spirit of truth was projected. But insisting that he appear to her after death and seeing his resurrected form, she shows us how a woman must conclude that what she saw in the outer person is a spiritual reality from her own psyche—an aspect of the "hidden immortal within the mortal [person]."[53]

In some Gnostic texts, Christ after his death lives on as such an inner guide for Mary. In the Gospel of Mary, for example, Mary has a

---

[53] Jung, "Concerning Rebirth," in *CW*, vol. 9i, par. 218.

vision of Christ after his resurrection. In the vision, she asks Christ how she is seeing him:

> I said to him, "Lord, how does a person see a vision, through the soul or through the spirit?" The savior answered, saying, "A person sees neither through the soul nor the spirit. The mind [Greek νoγς, *nous*], which lives between the two, sees the vision."[54]

Christ responds to Mary in the vision and tells her she is seeing him via *nous*. Although this word is usually translated as "mind," its more comprehensive meaning is "psyche," especially in its transhuman dimension. In the antique world, *nous* was considered a cosmic phenomenon of mind or intelligence, created by God and shared by human beings. For example in the Hermetic tradition, the krater of Hermes filled with *nous* was said to be sent to earth as a place where people might baptize themselves and be reminded that they contain the divine nous and live by it.[55] Nous is the god-substance in the world, another form of the Anthropos, recognizable by the human being. Nous may remain unconscious until something profound such as a death and resurrection experience occurs and we become aware, we have *gnosis*, of a supraordinate reality living in our own psyches.

Christ in the Gospel of Mary is saying that Mary has this cosmic nous, just as he does, and this means that she, too, has a divine nature that has been recovered through their mutual experience of his death and resurrection. If indeed Mary and Jesus had a love experience, then both would have been in the grip of an eros phenomenon much larger than themselves, and this might have led them to realize a divine quality was incarnated in their experience of each other.[56] Each woman who discovers the archetypal dimension of the animus and each man who discovers the archetypal dimension of the anima participates in the paradigm shift in

---

[54] Gospel of Mary, based on the Berlin Codex 8502, p. 7, line 1, through p. 19, line 5; Robinson, ed., *The Nag Hammadi Library in English*, 525.

[55] See Salaman et al., trans., *The Way of Hermes,* 31ff.

[56] Howe, "Redeeming Mary Magdalene," in Schweizer and Schweizer-Vüllers, *Wisdom Has Built Her House*, 139.

which the psyche is realized as nous, the divine stuff of humanity and the wellspring of spiritual life.

Mary Magdalene's Evolution in the Church

Mary's role in recognizing the reality of Christ, whether as an inner god or an outer one, was ignored by the Catholic Church and even degraded. After five centuries of reflecting on her mysterious role and why Christ would choose a woman to be the first apostle, exegetes finally explained her legitimacy away by landing on the idea that she must have been a prostitute.[57] They simply could not imagine her love for Jesus Christ as having a spiritual dimension, and so her love and its role in the resurrection was sidelined. For them, a woman's love could only be concrete and based in concupiscence, dealing a fatal blow to the role of the feminine in religious life. However, if we read the words exegetes wrote over the centuries from a psychological point of view before and after Mary was deemed a prostitute, we can see into the unconscious side of their thinking, in which the archetypal feminine played an active role unbeknownst to them. Although priests and popes dismissed Mary, the feminine, and anything sexual, at the same time they projected the anima onto Mary as the lover of Jesus Christ, even to the extent that in the background, she became his unofficial wife—and even by extension a kind of love goddess of the church.[58]

In an earlier capitulation to concretism that contributed to the fate of Mary Magdalene in the church, Tertullian (155–220 B.C.E.) decided that Christ's resurrected body was not a spiritual or psychic reality, but that it must have been flesh and blood.[59] Further, the church established rules

---

[57] Nowhere in the New Testament does it say that Mary is a prostitute. The fact that she had seven devils cast out from her (Luke 8:2) was used by Gregory the Great in the sixth century to declare that she must have been a prostitute (St. Gregory's Homily 33, *Patrologia Latina* 76:1239).

[58] This line of clerical fantasy is traced in Howe, "Redeeming Mary Magdalene," in Schweizer and Schweizer-Vüllers, *Wisdom Has Built Her House*.

[59] For example, in his essay "On the Flesh of Christ," Tertullian argued against any conception that Christ's reality could be symbolic or cosmic (as suggested by Marcion and Valentinus). In his way of thinking, either Christ's body was "flesh suffused with blood, built up with bones, interwoven with nerves, entwined with veins, a flesh which

about how Christ as an outer mystery could and should be experienced. As a result of these and other materialistic mandates, the individual nature of the experience of Jesus Christ as nous, clearly expressed in the early Christian point of view, was lost in the official Christian doctrine. *Mary's role in expressing the feminine experience of feeling realization, the eros experience of the inner god, was sent underground for women and men.* The god-image was removed from the mother world of the shared psyche, and the psyche was barred from having anything to do with religious life, forcing the living development of the archetypal feminine and the Anthropos underground, into the collective unconscious, where it was picked up by alchemy and fairy tales.

There is some comfort in the fact that in 2016, Pope Francis issued a decree entitled Apostolorum Apostola, in which he officially named Mary Magdalene the Apostle to the Apostles, honoring her officially as the first person to see the risen Christ. He acknowledged that Christ chose her to be his first witness and to spread the word of his resurrection. The papal decree, following by 66 years the 1950 declaration that the Virgin Mary had been assumed into heaven, indicates that in spite of official exclusion, some aspects of the divine role of the feminine principle are making their way into collective consciousness, as slow as it may be.[60] Mary represents symbolically the anima, a differentiation from the mother, and as such was often unconsciously compared to the Song of Songs Bride. She shows us the feminine, individual feeling experience of the psyche—the eros that is needed if its transhuman dimension is ever to be realized.

Redeeming the Rejected Spirit

The tragedy in not realizing that a divinelike entity lives within the psyche is that we are constantly searching for it in the outside world, actively participating in projection and transference. We yearn for a lover,

---

knew how to be born, and how to die, human without doubt, as born of a human being," or else he is a "phantom" or a "lie" and was never born, never died, and never really resurrected—a complete denial of the psychic dimension that the Gnostics recognized. See Roberts, Donaldson, and Coxe, *The Ante-Nicene Fathers,* 3:525–26. Elaine Pagels traced this line of thinking in *The Gnostic Gospels*, 3ff.

[60] Jung made this point regarding mother Mary in "Answer to Job," *CW*, vol. 11, par. 748ff.

a teacher, a spiritual guide, a parent, or a new outer deity to reflect our value back to us and legitimize our life and talents. We feel isolated from the world because something vital in us remains unrealized. What we really seek is a connection to the unconscious and the eros of the self. But unless we are introduced to depth psychology, the unconscious for most of us remains a suspicious, disreputable concept, or something we should not admit to having. We don't have access to the very thing that can heal us.

While in college and experiencing the intense loneliness of feeling unseen and unreal, Pearl felt that she was living in a bubble, separate from the rest of the world. After an especially painful experience in which a family member betrayed her, she expressed her intense loneliness in a performance art project, in which she sewed a heart onto her chest using needle and thread (fig. 9).

We begin to sense what an existential predicament it is if the soul is calling for a woman's attention, but she has no access to it. The last thing a woman thinks she should be investigating is the darkness of her own thoughts, and yet that is the very path toward redeeming her soul. The animus at his root is her own creative spirit, yearning just as much

Figure 9. Pearl's Heart
Pearl sewed a heart onto her chest with needle and thread, a profound expression of the yearning to feel her own value. Artist's photo.

for recognition as she. He wants to be seen for what he is, and he is the only viable force that can lead her to discover who and what she really is.

The wizard in "Fitcher's Bird" is a fitting image for the animus who keeps torturing a woman until she pays attention to his deific, motivating power and begins to ask it about itself. A woman with a powerful negative animus is always unknowingly in touch with his other, positive side—the dynamic energy that is striving for spiritual meaning through all of her misadventures. She may feel that some faraway entity needs her to bring something creative into the world as only she can, yet as we sense in Pearl's sewn heart, she doesn't know how to focus that teeming creative energy in a meaningful way.

We tend to expect spiritual life to come out of the heavens, to bless us, protect us, and guide us always away from suffering and toward happiness. But according to "Fitcher's Bird," spiritual life may come out of the dark psychological forest and ask us to help in a transformation that at first feels more like a curse than a blessing. It can help a woman suffering from creative frustration to know that an inner divinity shares her experience of being unseen and even rejected by a collective viewpoint. If they could find each other, they could redeem each other, and through relating to each other, redeem the divine dimension of eros. I know of a woman's active imagination of a forest creature, a kind of creative nature animus, with whom she locked arms when she was writing. In her vision, they sat side by side with their arms entwined, and as she wrote with her right hand, he wrote in tandem with his left.

In most tales of feminine redemption, the heroine at an important transitional point finds herself alone in a forest, asleep in a hollow tree, or lost in the wilderness of a foreign kingdom. She is between worlds. Although this may seem like a desperate situation, the heroine has escaped the real threat, whether it's her father wanting to marry her, as in "Allerleirauh" and similar father-daughter tales, or a stepmother trying to do her in. The forest of a different kingdom, not her father's kingdom, is actually her refuge. Psychologically, this would mean that a woman has escaped her identification with a threatening, fatherly experience of the unconscious and now finds herself in the unconscious in a new way. She is in the world of her own solitude, not as punishment, but newly realized as sanctuary. In solitude, she may enter a genuine, introverted experience of the depths. She may be able to accept her loneliness rather than reject it. She may realize that the baffling experience of feeling like an orphan is not her fault but rather that the world has not been prepared for her individuality. Finally finding the unconscious and accepting the wisdom it offers is a miracle in so many ways, not the least because it introduces a woman to the transhuman reality of her uniqueness.

Redemption Begins as Soon as the Animus Is Seen

After some hesitation to get close to her nightmare of the devil-man chasing her, Pearl drew a picture of the scene (fig. 10). She depicted the devil-man's evil side by giving him threatening red eyes and a cobralike demeanor. As she drew, she found herself adding features to the picture that she didn't expect. She gave the devil-man wings and said they were

Figure 10. Pearl's Devil-man.

As she drew this picture of the devil-man in her dream chasing her from house to house, Pearl found herself adorning him with wings of "glittering stone." Her unintentional embellishment tells us that the animus had an influence on her drawing that hinted at his archetypal dimension and his potential role as the spirit of individuation. This image could appear as Pearl made the effort to contain the devil-man's energy. Author's photo.

made of "glittering stone, like opal or quartz." She also found herself emphasizing the "luscious green grass and moisture" that surrounded her in the dream. These surprising details suggest that the spirit of the unconscious participated in the creation of the picture. His glittering wings of stone convey an enduring spirituality. The springlike green surrounding the picture anticipates that the struggle with the devil-man may be circumscribed with the promise of renewal.[61] Taking the time to make a picture, Pearl demonstrated to the devil-man that she could take him seriously, and this made all the difference. Containing his turbulent energy in the form of an image and contemplating its meaning, she was immediately engaged in his redemption as well as her own. She could feel a healing energy emerge from the process as this frightening inner figure was finally allowed a place in the world.

Interestingly, Pearl drew the dream scene enclosed in the shape of an egg, another motif that was not suggested by the dream but which made its way into the picture as she drew (long before I began working on "Fitcher's Bird"). The egg shape points toward an incipient wholeness that the dark experience of the animus was engendering, in the very moment that Pearl consciously grappled with his image. Such a moment when the self appears *in potentia* is expressed in "Fitcher's Bird" when the heroine protects her egg.

In fact, for Pearl the egg image had already appeared in a sandplay image a year before the devil-man dream. The tray contained simple round and oval mounds in wet sand, indicating that wholeness was trying to take shape in the unconscious as she engaged with it objectively (fig. 11). A year after the devil-man dream, similar shapes appeared in another sandplay image in almost identical locations, this time surrounded by green grass and images of home (fig. 12). On top of one of the mounds, she placed a pregnant woman, another image for nascent development, including in psychological terms, the gestation of the self. We can see that the image and experience of home, for which Pearl searched so desperately in the devil-man dream, is being created in this tray, showing

---

[61] Jung's description of the meaning of green in the context of an alchemical text by Abraham Eleazar can bring great comfort in amplifying dreams in which green appears as a dawning realization of the self, and the reality of the animus or anima as an inner companion. See Jung, *Mysterium Coniunctionis, CW*, vol. 14, par. 623.

Figure 11. Pearl's Sand Tray a Year before Her Devil-man Dream

Pearl created a sandplay image early in her analysis, a year before her devil-man dream, of bare oval and circular mounds that symbolize an incubating experience of wholeness. She used a stick to create holes in the wet sand, indicating an urge to penetrate into psychic material. Author's photo.

Figure 12. Pearl's Sand Tray a Year after Her Devil-man Dream

A year after the devil-man dream, Pearl made another sandplay image of egg and oval shapes, this time decorated with a sense of living green grass. A pregnant woman sits in the foreground with a baby behind her. All of these images indicate development that has been taking place in the unconscious and is making its way into Pearl's life. Author's photo.

us that the inner experience of a psychological, inner home was forming itself as Pearl deepened her connection with the unconscious.

The sandplay images that arrived a year before and a year after the dream show us a relationship with the self that was taking shape in the depths of the unconscious. Although she may not have consciously articulated this experience as a growing connectedness with the self, Pearl could feel its development having an effect on her life. She was more confident in her work and as a parent. She had become clear about her relationship with her professor and ended it. Her rage attacks had dwindled, all as she gradually felt more at home in herself.

As we can see in Pearl's work, once the unconscious is engaged, a connection to the self begins to develop as a reality the same way an egg or seed germinates in the dark. As soon as the unknown center is tended, new life begins taking shape there, with the potential to heal the conscious attitude. Pearl came to know that although a daimon, an archetypal power in her psyche, had her in a possession for a long time, once she paid attention to him, he showed her the hidden goal of a psychological development that could bring new meaning to her life. He sparked a development that without her attention would have remained buried in the unconscious. But Pearl would need to continue devoting herself to his world of the psyche for that development to be fulfilled. The picture of the devil-man is one of many Pearl created, one that had a profound effect on her, helping her see that his spellbinding energy was seeking containment in her life—in consciousness and in creative work with the psyche.

Pearl had begun to treasure her dreams, writing them down and drawing pictures in a large, beloved sketchbook. She realized with a new certainty that she was the only one who would give herself permission to pay attention to her own soul images. She was thrilled one day to tell me that while drawing in her journal, she suddenly remembered childhood fantasies of a gorilla companion, an imaginary friend with whom she had secret adventures. She also had recurring dreams about him. Around age 7, she had the following dream:

A giant gorilla comes into my town about the same time every month. The gorilla is ferocious and evil and is hunting for people to kill. My town has a safety procedure. Every month, right before the gorilla comes to terrorize people, the whole town shuts down and transforms into some sort of military barricade. Every home and business has a secret, secured basement protected with steel walls and doors, and we retreat to these places for safety until the gorilla returns to his home in the forest. But I hide from my family when the town sirens resound as a warning of the gorilla's arrival. I refuse to take shelter, feeling determined to befriend this scary beast and discover that he is not the horrible, angry monster everyone assumes he is. Every dream ends with me hugging the gorilla under a shrub, resembling a shaded cave, outside my parent's house.

The dream depicts a secret, loving relationship between Pearl and the gorilla. Psychologically, he is the archaic, animal level of the inner spirit, which the townspeople (the collective) in the dream feared. The young dream-ego chose to relate to the gorilla rather than lock herself away from him like everyone else. The singular relationship between the girl and the gorilla emphasizes the loneliness they each experienced on their own, isolated and misunderstood among the collective. The gorilla belonged to Pearl as an inner childhood companion, but at some point, she lost touch with him.

Now in adulthood, the memory of the gorilla returned, offering a lifesaving connection to the deep, primal layer of the psyche. There were echoes of "Beauty and the Beast" in Pearl's relationship to the gorilla: she was the misfit and he the outcast who could redeem each other through relationship, by valuing each other. Pearl could relate to the gorilla as he was—a primordial aspect of the animus, a creature that longs to be recognized, representing the whole of nature. She made a series of pictures that show him evolving over time into a more and more relatable creature, a result of her curiosity and attention to him (fig. 13). Eventually, his face became almost human, in one picture tenderly gazing at Pearl with soulful eyes, perhaps grateful to be brought into the world with so much care (fig. 14).

Figure 13. The Gorilla from Pearl's Childhood Fantasies

Over the years, Pearl dreamt and drew pictures of her imaginary gorilla friend from childhood. As she worked with him over time (left to right), he emerged from the dark and from anger, reunited with natural life and growth. His development reflects a transformation at the primordial level of the animus archetype, a result of Pearl relating to him. The use of color indicates a development in Pearl's feeling connection to the gorilla and a new sense of him as a reality. Artist's photos.

Figure 14. Pearl's Gorilla Picture Showing Humanization

Pearl's gorilla here has a more human face, especially his eyes, revealing the fact that he has been accepted as an aspect of Pearl's inner life. Artist's photo.

The Beggar: Withholding Value

Another image for the rejected inner spirit is the beggar, which is how the wizard in "Fitcher's Bird" presents himself. According to von Franz, the beggar in fairy tales symbolizes the willful withholding of psychic treasure. The beggar image in a woman's psyche reflects her own, impoverished attitude toward the unconscious:

> The animus appears to be poor and often never reveals the great treasures of the unconscious which are at his disposal. In the role of a poor man or a beggar, he induces the woman to believe that she herself has nothing. This is the penalty for a prejudice against the unconscious—a lasting poverty in conscious life, resulting in endless criticism and self-criticism.[62]

As long a woman doesn't realize the animus as an aspect of the collective unconscious with all the power of a pagan god, he will continue to charm her and infuse her with "endless criticism and self-criticism," that is, with the torturous collective attitudes and judgments that exist in her, working against her in the outer world and causing her to ignore the inner world or not sufficiently value it. The word "should" typically shows up in these dynamics when a woman is working against herself: she should be more beautiful, or smarter, or richer, or more innocent; she should never be wrong.

A prejudice against the unconscious on a personal level often appears as an attitude of entitlement toward the unconscious. It shows up honestly enough, in the desperate need for aid in times of loneliness and despair, when we need more attention from the psyche than we can give back to it. Or it appears in an ignorant, "nothing but" attitude, in which images from the unconscious are seen as nothing new (see fig. 4 in chapter 1). It is typical at the beginning of analysis to hear analysands say "it was only a small dream," or "it was just a fragment of a dream and didn't make sense, so I didn't write it down," or "its meaning was obvious." When dreams are seen as weird or unworthy of attention, this is an indication that the animus remains beggarly, mired in the dreamer's impoverished attitude toward the unconscious. Such an attitude, in which we want the unconscious to be easily understandable or available to us without reciprocation, is common and insidious. We may think a relationship with the unconscious sounds intriguing and we want to know what it has to offer, but we aren't quite prepared for the fact that the

---

[62] Von Franz, *The Interpretation of Fairy Tales,* 173.

unconscious demands as much as it gives. The relationship is mutual in every respect.

One of the most difficult prejudices to overcome is that deplorable, beggarly, or frightening figures from the unconscious have little of importance to convey. Lucy, a woman in her 50s, had many such figures in her dreams over decades. She was plagued with unspoken feelings that one of her biggest life decisions to leave a prestigious job and live a more introverted life was a mistake, that it had cut her off from worldly recognition. She kept sabotaging her introversion by accepting speaking engagements and temporary positions that promised to bolster her reputation but exhausted her. In several of her dreams, some version of a disgusting man appeared, sometimes out of nowhere, obviously wanting to annoy her. She thought these figures reflected her own failure, and she did not want to engage with them. But the following dream helped us understand what these figures really symbolized:

> There is a creepy guy in my bed (or is it a hotel bed?). He
> is lying there, and I don't know who he is. But then he pulls
> back the sheets and reveals himself to me. His legs are spread
> wide so I can see his genitals. He is smiling a sinister smile.
> I think I scream, and he jumps out of the window, looking
> back at me, smiling. My husband comes into the room, and
> I tell him about the man. He looks for the man, but I am not
> sure if my husband fully believes that he exists.

The "creepy guy" reminded Lucy of a meth addict, and she found him repulsive. Symbolically speaking, he is a dark spirit that is trying to reveal himself to her completely, including his creative (phallic) potential and how it sometimes shows up in a disgusting way. He is mercurial in the way he appears and disappears, and in his "sinister smile." His shocking, sudden presence is serpentlike. Lucy's husband, an image for the positive animus, does not quite believe the repulsive one exists, revealing a division in the animus yet to be bridged.

In earlier dreams over a period of decades, similar dream figures wanted to negotiate with Lucy or play board games with her. Finally, with this dream, she realized that the repulsive man was the same one who had shown up in a dream years before, inspiring an important creative work. In fact, she realized with a jolt that he probably inspired her creative writing throughout her life. This was the very spirit that could help her fully engage her creative, introverted life. His repulsiveness reflected her failure to recognize him as a creative spirit or to devote herself to a more introverted, creative life. He showed her the face that she showed to the unconscious. Secretly, she considered an introverted life to be subpar.

A woman may deny the ugly inner man if his presence threatens her view of herself, if she just cannot understand how such an ugly creature would show up in her dreams because, after all, she already has done so much work on herself. But if she can't or won't see the inner spirit for what he is, a phenomenon of nature that is sometimes disagreeable to her ego preferences, he too continues to live a wounded life.

The Divine Nature Spirit

Pearl's gorilla and Lucy's homeless man, like the wizard in "Fitcher's Bird," symbolize an aspect of the psyche that is rejected by the collective and yet longs to be realized in human consciousness. Another poignant image depicting the woundedness of the rejected unconscious spirit was painted by Swiss artist Peter Birkhäuser from a dream and titled *The Outcast* (fig. 15). The artist's daughter, Jungian analyst Eva Wertenschlag-Birkhäuser, explained that this spirit exists as an outcast because he has "no place in the collective," misunderstood and unseen.[63] His blue and green divided face expresses a split between spirit and nature, a wound that he must assume because of our inability to see him as a whole (as nature and spirit) and to "holistically . . . accept nature as it operates in the unconscious, or the light it contains, which is often greater than consciousness."[64] Our rejection of the legitimacy of this spirit (as happens with the serpent in the Garden of Eden) creates an ambivalence in him toward human life.

---

[63] Wertenschlag-Birkhäuser, *Windows on Eternity*, 31.
[64] Ibid., 32.

Figure 15. The Outcast, by Peter Birkhäuser

The green and blue split in the spirit of the objective psyche reflects the human inability to see him as a whole, a being that unites nature and spirit. From Eva Wertenschlag-Birkhäuser, Windows on Eternity: The Paintings of Peter Birkhäuser. Peter and Sibylle Birkhäuser-Oeri Foundation, www.birkhaeser-oeri.ch.

The Devil as Light-Bringer

The wizard in "Fitcher's Bird" is murderous, but he also gives each girl he kidnaps a key to seeing his secret violent side and an egg that has the potential to protect her from that violence. The wizard has been providing what the maidens needed to uncover the murderous situation and survive it. Like the serpent in the Garden of Eden, he is devil and light-bringer in one. The following dream from a woman called Sandra who worked for many years with a negative animus conveys the depths of the transformed animus and how he finally may appear as an inner partner who connects a woman to the archetypal framework of her individuality:

> *I am with a man, a love. Sometimes we are in a group situation, other times we are on our own. In one scene he embraces me from behind, both arms around me, holding me firmly and gently. He tells me he loves me, and I tell him I love him, and we just stay that way for a long time. We feel so connected, it's hard to describe. It's as if we are with the stars or even made of stars, a kind of cosmic constellation of love. I am tingling with love for him. I never want this moment to end, and yet I know, even if it does end in time, it goes on in eternity.*

A "cosmic constellation of love" reminds us of Jung's referral to love as "a *kosmogonos*, a creator and father-mother of all higher consciousness," which "bears all things and endures all things" (1 Cor. 13:7).[65] Such an experience of cosmic love becomes manifest, even in the most difficult of times, when we are connected to the symbolic meaning of inner life. It may seem like a paradox that sometimes we begin with the torturous dynamism of the animus, but a feeling connection is what the animus is after in a woman. He wants love as much as she does, but his means are not of the human realm. When the positive animus is constellated, a woman may have many dreams of an unknown man or even an animal wanting to connect with her.

---

[65] Jung, *Memories, Dreams, Reflections*, 353.

5
The Animus-Enslaved Shadow:
Pleasing, Innocence, and Rage

A difficult but vital part of the work with the animus is to sustain a thorough confrontation with the shadow that has long been in cahoots with his conventional attitudes. Jung in "Psychology of the Transference" describes this process using language and analogies from alchemy to describe how tedious it can be to bring the shadow (anything unconscious, rejected or denied in ourselves) to consciousness:

> The process of psychological differentiation is no light work; it needs the tenacity and patience of the alchemist, who must purify the body from all superfluities in the fiercest heat of the furnace, and pursue Mercurius 'from one bride chamber to the next.'[66]

In psychological terms, Jung refers to the imaginal container as an alchemical furnace on the one hand and a bride chamber on the other, taking his cues from Gnostic and alchemical texts. The fiercest heat of the furnace refers to the emotional heat in which we stew with our dark material, the way Pearl did when she confronted the devil-man in her picture, and then gradually realized through ongoing pictures, dreams, and active imagination, how she was propelled by an inner thought system critical toward her individuality. In that realization, instead of being dismembered herself, Pearl could subject the dismembering dynamic of criticism to its own heat, keeping it in the furnace where it could sweat itself out. For anyone, such containment results in a mutually transforming encounter with the unconscious that eventually can be felt and understood, in which case the furnace has become the bride chamber, where a new union has taken place. In transforming and in building a relationship,

---

[66] Jung, "Psychology of the Transference," *CW*, vol. 16, par. 503.

consciousness and the unconscious go from one bride chamber to the next, transforming each other step by step. The "body" in the quote above represents the personality as a whole, purified "from all superfluities," not by eliminating shadow in the Christian sense but by knowing it and integrating what is possible to integrate. Mercurius represents the wholeness of that integration and the fact that it is continuously changing.

For a woman, the fiercest heat of the furnace refers to the way the unconscious animus fuels relentless fantasy. But if consciousness sees this happening and is able to sweat in the furnace of that realization, the dynamism of fantasy thinking is contained, not acted out, as we saw when Pearl created a picture of her devil-man. When he is contained in a creative vessel, the ability of the animus to demand obedience from a woman or murder her connection to eros for herself or others becomes less and less effective. The more familiar a woman becomes with the way her own fantasy thinking abducts her, the more clearly she can see its stale repetitiveness and become less vulnerable to its fiery energy. The mutual transformation of consciousness and the unconscious—animus and ego—thus moves from one state of development to the next, one new union to the next.

In the fairy tale, the thoroughness of this work is emphasized when the heroine describes her work at the wizard's house as cleaning it "from cellar to garret," repeating the refrain twice. She may have gotten out of the wizard's control and sent him home with her sisters, but he still intends to marry her. Her work cleaning the wizard's house from bottom to top leads to a realization of his archetypal, fiery nature, which ultimately is expressed by his housefire. We can only imagine how hard she must work to clean that house, given the slaughter that has been going on there for so long. In a woman this would mean that seeing animus dynamism is only the first step; now she needs the "tenacity and patience of the alchemist" to transform her relationship to that dynamism. The wizard's house fire is an indication that he is contained in the fire of his own dynamism, thanks to her hard work.

Such a thorough cleaning of the animus complex involves a reckoning not only with the animus but with the shadow—the naïve obedience and willful ignorance that keep a woman vulnerable to conventional attitudes and thus ethically compromised. Pearl had to face the shadow aspect in which she needed to be seen as normal or smart, even willing to manipulate others' perceptions to do so. Lucy's desire to protect an appearance of success is a version of the performance shadow that goes along with orthodox animus demands, binding a woman to the pressures of being accepted and acceptable, even according to a worldview that has lost its validity for her. Working with the shadow is no light work; it takes humility, diligence, persistence, and the openness to consider ethical challenges that the world doesn't necessarily acknowledge. For some, facing the shadow is too much to bear, in which case individuation simply cannot move forward. Without shadow work, a woman may end up unconsciously married to the orthodox animus, forever working against herself and addicted to power, performance, or the approval of others.

Building Awareness

The heroine sees the reality of the wizard's evil when she enters his forbidden room and finds her sisters dismembered in his "great bloody basin." Psychologically, this discovery represents a profound moment when, thanks to her individuation so far, a woman sees how very destructive the unconscious animus has been. Through a relationship with her own symbolic life, she has been given the key she needed to see into the dynamism of the complex, and now comes the moment of truth: her own feeling life has been secretly feeding the destruction. If she can face the truth, she is in the furnace with it—the whole bloody mess of eros destruction. But in the context of individuation, she can hold herself together.

The forbidden room overall represents the place where an unconscious complex has been locked away from consciousness. In some fairy tales involving forbidden rooms, the hero or heroine stands outside the door and sees what is happening inside through a narrow opening (such as in "The Black Woman's Castle"), because it is too dangerous to enter.[67] But in "Fitcher's Bird," each girl enters the room completely and

---

[67] Von Franz discusses the forbidden chamber in "The Black Woman's Castle," in *Archetypal Dimensions of the Psyche,* 174ff, and throughout *Shadow and Evil in Fairy Tales,* where she notes the ambivalence of the archetype's desire to be seen—especially to be seen transforming.

stands over the gruesome dismemberment of past maidens, immediately becoming the next victim. Psychologically speaking, such a complete entry into a split-off animus complex occurs when a woman is taken in by the archetypal power of the animus and becomes identified with it. She may find herself caught in a power drive, or in addictive behavior, or convinced her life is horribly wrong. Even after a lot of practice observing herself getting carried away and dismembered by the negative animus complex, a woman is still susceptible to its dynamism; she has to keep reminding herself that it is archetypal and ambivalent. Even if she has felt nourished by individuation for years, a vulnerable moment may arise when all of her progress seems to vanish and she suddenly becomes the victim of negative, inner commentary telling her that her individuation isn't real, or that it's taking too long, and this latest bloody mess is proof that analysis isn't doing any good. Or, she finds herself in an emotional upheaval with the world, having lost her eros connection to her inherent value.

It seems to be necessary for a woman to see herself in the act of cooperating with destructive animus thoughts repeatedly in order to build her awareness of the dynamism that takes her in so completely. She must watch herself get abducted enough times that finally she can catch hold of the murder consciously, if not in the moment, then in retrospect, and then hopefully enter the furnace of contemplation in which the truth can be realized and the drivenness a bit more transformed.

The unconscious animus abduction is very difficult to bring to consciousness, remaining so powerful for so long because it adheres to conventional ideals of right and wrong that seem perfectly valid when left unexamined, yet they work against eros. Through every new level of awareness, each visit to the furnace, a woman resurrects a bit more of the eros for her life or for relationships that could have been killed by the old standards of perfection. She connects a bit more with the self.

Acting Out against Others

Everyone knows the feeling of wanting to suck nasty comments back into our mouths, even as they are emitted. We say things we regret when, in the throes of the negative animus or anima, we feel insecure and become critical or demeaning of others who threaten us, consciously or unconsciously. If we are reflective enough, such incidents help us become more conscious of shadowy power motives. But some women with strong animus impulses, especially if joined with envy or jealousy, can in a kind of semiconscious state destroy someone else's experience without the least remorse. (This also happens with anima-possessed men.) Such a woman may not put down a person directly but craftily work around them, parading criticism toward this or that aspect of their situation, assuming everyone shares her ideals. She may fall into gossiping, poisoning one person's perception of another, to stack up her own importance in comparison. The sleight of hand is amazing when you see it in action. A woman in a murderous possession can't help herself, and she leaves a trail of blood behind her, perhaps dimly aware of what she is doing. A group of animus-oriented women can behave like a police state, destroying eros for the sake of whatever flag of idealism they choose to fly that day, completely oblivious to the harm they are doing to the psyche.

If one is awake enough (and not in the animus oneself) to see such an attack in action, the least destructive thing to do in most cases is to remain silent, perhaps slightly raising a proverbial eyebrow. It is impossible to argue with the animus. If a critical innuendo is given any emotional energy at all, the massacre only grows. To see the destruction but not take part in it is the only chance that eros may be saved, resurrected from the situation itself somewhere down the road.

Caught in the Act

One of Sandra's dreams helps us see how we might catch ourselves in the act of believing and inflicting animus opinions on others. Sandra had been married to the same man for more than 25 years. Difficulties in their marriage were more apparent when they became empty nesters, and eventually the following dream helped identify part of the problem:

I go out the back door and see to my amazement that there are lilies and daffodils blooming—on March 1! Other flowers have also grown along the fence—plants I might have pulled in previous years, thinking they were weeds. I am amazed, especially at the lilies. They arrived out of nowhere! But then my husband comes along. He goes to the daffodils, which are not quite open, and is very excited to see them. He sits on the ground in awe. I know this is what I love about him, but I just cannot respond. He has intruded into my space, and this immediately puts me in a bad mood. In my heart I can feel a very faint reaction of appreciation for him, and I try to stay with it and keep the critical opinion out. But it still influences my feeling for him and even destroys my ability to appreciate the flowers myself.

In this dream, Sandra's husband is doing something he naturally did in life—appreciating beauty. It is one of the traits that she originally fell in love with and that they shared, but a critical animus thought comes over her in the dream: "He has intruded into my space." This is an example of an unconscious fantasy thought that can abduct a woman's feeling life with barely a touch: The thought is immediately followed by a thoroughly bad mood. Because she doesn't even realize the thought has appeared and is magically convinced of its truth, it destroys her feeling for her dream-husband, as well as her own experience of the miraculous spring flowers, which symbolize the balsam of life. We can see how thoughts themselves carry the wizardly power of the animus, abducting a woman into an unconscious dismemberment about her life.

The dream reflected so clearly how this happened in waking life, Sandra didn't know whether to laugh or cry. She could see how the critical animus in her head had the potential to ruin her marriage. She could observe how her thoughts and her mood worked together, pulling her out of her own feeling for her husband, for life, and her connection to beauty. The dream showed her exactly how her fantasy thinking destroyed love. She had been aware of such dynamics before, but at this point in her analysis, she could really soak it in.

If a woman becomes conscious enough of negative thoughts to see them coming toward her, she may be able to evade them before they have a chance to separate her from her connection to eros. She may be able to put a negative animus thought in neutral gear—just allow it to be—but insist on a feeling level to remain connected to the love she knows she feels. As von Franz declared, "To overcome possession by an unconscious content by slipping out of its grasp is as meritorious as a heroic victory."[68] Simple imaginary tactics can bring some relief, even though they may seem trivial. Pearl would use an imaginary, powerful flyswatter to slap away negative animus thoughts that she could hear buzzing around her ears. Giving her critical fantasy thinking the name Bruno, Elise could begin to recognize the personality behind the orthodoxy that was haunting her. When she felt the buildup of that personality forming, she could tell Bruno to keep his thoughts to himself until she had a chance to listen. Other times she just told him to shut up and mind his own business.

The techniques of the Shambhala meditation practice called "touch and go" can be helpful too.[69] In this practice, one catches a thought as it happens, touches it consciously, and then purposely lets it go, observing how one's emotional state changes with the thought's coming and going. In acknowledging the thought, one isn't rejecting it but touching it with conscious feeling, even with compassion. Letting it go, one observes that it hasn't invoked a mood or convinced one of its truth. Over time this technique can help reveal the dynamic workings of a complex, as well as the sanity that surrounds it. It is also a good precondition to active imagination.

Other times, one must confront the destructive energy more directly. I once dreamt that I was in a cabin in the mountains and could see that a very large man was rolling down a hill toward me. I shut the windows and locked myself in the cabin to keep myself safe. I thought that this was the thing to do until my analyst suggested that I might have let this threatening man in and confronted him in active imagination. I think my analyst was right, because in retrospect I could see that the dream forewarned of a long struggle with debilitating self-criticism. There are times when the animus needs to be handled with wit, or even gaslighted— told, for example, that his ideas will be considered later. But then there are times when he has to be confronted directly in an *Auseinandersetzung*—a deep confrontation. The more familiar a woman becomes with animus

---

[68] Von Franz, *The Interpretation of Fairy Tales*, 177.

[69] Touch and go is a meditation practice that is an aspect of the four foundations of mindfulness, from the Tibetan Hinayana tradition; see Chögyam Trungpa, *The Profound Treasury of the Ocean of Dharma* and *Mindfulness in Action*.

dynamism, the better she knows when to avoid and when to confront. Sandra knew that she absolutely had to confront the system of thought that destroyed her love for her husband, which eventually led to a deep encounter with the positive side of the animus and the dream of eternal cosmic love we read in chapter 4.

The Unconscious Sacrifice of Eros

As discussed in chapter 3, a performance complex can take hold of a girl early in life if she clings too strongly to her ability to please others in order to feel accepted or real. Performing for acceptance can be a productive strategy that helps strengthen the ego in childhood, but it may lose its integrity if it stops a woman from taking a step toward individuation. In extreme cases, pleasing behavior can become destructive to a woman's core identity and lead to mood disorders.

This is what happened to a woman named Sarah. She had a memory from as early as 18 months of age in which she used comedic flattery to stop her father from slapping her from across the room with the force of his extended arm. Even that young, she was aware that she could protect herself from being physically hurt by using flattery or subservience. Over time, she naturally learned to please others the same way, no matter what the sacrifice. Well into adulthood, in part mimicking what her mother did, Sarah used her considerable extraverted skills in hospitality, hosting parties and organizing big family events, and further, making sure they were "perfect," to bring happiness to her friends and family. This was how she expressed love, she thought.

In her 70s, Sarah realized she was exhausted by all the pleasing performances. She knew that something was wrong with the habitual and unremitting giving that still dominated her life. A dream with an image strikingly similar to the dismembered sisters in the fairy tale showed her in no uncertain terms how performance had become destructive, especially to eros:

> *I see a woman who has been tortured. She is lying on the ground, singing. Her legs are twisted around each other like a pretzel several times. I realize this is contorted and unnatural and must be very painful. I look down at what should be her feet, only there I see her vagina, open and*

bleeding. She has been cut at the waist and her womb and genitals are now where her feet should be. Her head and torso are separate from her body, but she is still alive. How can she still be alive, and singing?

The pathos of this dream is stunning. The dream-woman's womb and genitals—symbols for her instinctive feminine nature—are cut away, butchered in the most gruesome way. She is left without legs to stand on, and yet somehow, she is still performing, still singing.

Sarah could accept and feel the graphic psychological reality that this dream image expressed. She knew that the butchered woman revealed a deeply personal experience—how she herself was tortured by her relentless urge to please and how her true instinct for love was disembodied in the process. Sarah's ability to see and feel that fact meant that the pleasing, performing tendency itself then could become an object of analysis—submitted to conscious dismemberment. The dream in this way anticipates the fact that she was in for a bloody opus—a dismembering experience in which the need to be accepted itself would be analyzed and transformed.

The dream image represented not only a personal reality that needed healing but also an archetypal wounding that was calling for Sarah's attention. The dismembered woman in her dream, like the dismembered sisters in the tale, on the deepest level is an image for the natural eros that becomes lost in any woman's need to perform in order to survive her collective situation. There may also be a positive aspect to the image if dismemberment can be seen as the painful process through which eros is being taken apart and put back together in a more mature way.

The Maid to Innocence

A surprisingly stubborn aspect of the cooperative animus shadow is a woman's need to be perceived as innocent, or never wrong, or someone who doesn't cause any trouble. An "innocent" woman is under the illusion that she isn't supposed to have a shadow, and yet she is in constant fear that she might and that someone might notice. Her libido gets tied up in the idea that she must meet certain perceived standards of intelligence and accomplishment, not to mention virtue, patience, and cooperation. She should be in control of her life. She should be too smart or too educated to have a shadow and too enlightened to get angry. If she is caught being disagreeable or wrong, she fears she may lose her reputation, or she imagines that her achievements vanish into illusions. An ambitious woman may project her value onto the flawlessness of her professional, academic, or spiritual achievements. It is difficult, but eventually a woman may realize that pleasing, performing, and looking innocent all come with a need for power—power to be seen and valued according to perceived standards. A woman who needs this kind of validation is unconsciously submitting herself to hidden patriarchal values, including the power that keeps eros suppressed.

Turning inward for reflection and value, concentrating libido toward the inner world, becomes the priority in later life when a woman feels the inner imperative from her core to become more of herself, regardless of what others think. She may need to sacrifice the satisfaction involved in seeking worldly approval or avoiding the appearance of being the least bit unlikable. Lucy, for example, had long felt the need to be seen as patient, compassionate, and accomplished until she realized these expectations were holding back her individual development. The following dream opened her eyes.

> My husband and I are standing on the edge of a cliff overlooking a great valley. Right below us is a tree with two limbs sticking out over the edge. On one limb is a little dog, and on the other limb is a bunny. They are each jumping up and down playfully. It is funny and cute, but I worry that the bunny is going to fall off the tree limb and down the steep cliff. And then the dog (innocently, it seems) grabs the bunny in its mouth and drops it.
>
> The bunny falls down the cliff, and I know it is going to either die or be seriously maimed. I am so upset that I run away and go sit on a bench next to an old shed. I am crying and in deep grief at the thought of the bunny down at the bottom of the canyon with a broken body. My husband, on the other hand, runs down a narrow trail that goes to the bottom of the canyon to go find the bunny. I think he is brave to do this, to witness the suffering, but

I also feel that he is trying to make up for something that can't be undone. It all feels very despairing.

Lucy identified the soft nature of the bunny as the instinct for innocence, the part of her that maintained peace in her relationships at all costs. In the dream, the bunny was most likely killed by the puppy, which we understood to represent an unconscious, innocent, and immature instinct to please. Both bunny and puppy—innocence and pleasing—were balancing precariously on the high limb. It was innocence that had to go first.

As a child, Lucy learned to use innocence as a way to smooth over her relationship with her father, and she never stopped. She was his favorite of three children and knew how to flatter him. As a teenager, she became aware that he made patronizing comments toward her and didn't really see her emotional or intellectual intelligence; she had already grown beyond him psychologically. She didn't know how to change the dynamics and continued to flatter him rather than talk about her own experience. She felt it was imperative to keep the peace, even though it meant squelching her own thoughts and feelings—her own reality—so her father could remain the authority in all ways. She could never confront him because she feared he would see her as disagreeable. This was not so much a problem in her relationship with her father per se; he wouldn't have been able to understand it. But in other relationships, Lucy was called to develop beyond those patterns. Hers was a positive father complex, which we can clearly see has its own inherent dangers.

Lucy's tendency to placate others for the sake of controlling their impression of her spilled over into personal and professional relationships. Even though quite accomplished and respected in her field, she was constantly afraid that others might see her as a poser or as someone who was falling behind professional standards. She worked very hard, often too hard, to quell this fear. In order to appease her fantasies of what others thought, she gave more energy to troubling relationships than she should have, a tendency that with men left her vulnerable to sexual violation.

When she had this dream, Lucy was somewhat aware of her need to be seen as innocent, but she was surprised to see what her strong grief for the bunny was indicating—that she was identified so strongly with innocence. She also realized that she had been making herself small for the sake of others or to maintain the status quo, and like many women caught in this problem, she had considered the trait virtuous. The dream was telling her it had come time for her innocence to die.[70]

In the dream, it is her husband, her own positive masculine side, that can witness and carry the suffering of this death and somehow know that it must be endured. This points to an important development on the positive side of the animus compared to the dream in which he couldn't accept the reality of the ugly man. Here he is strong enough to carry the necessary sacrifice of innocence as an aspect of individuation. Likewise, Lucy could feel how her innocence had lived itself out and needed to die.

As Lucy could let go of the need to be seen as innocuous, she could finally accept a long-term depression, which for years had been running in the background of her self-effacement. She could see that the depression was trying to bring her into contact with her own depths, insisting that she let go of a need to be seen a certain way. In the past, she had been ashamed of her depression because she thought it meant she was a failure. It is one thing to have a depression, another to feel ashamed of it, and yet another to pretend it doesn't exist in order to uphold appearances. Realizing how destructive this was to her soul, Lucy resigned from professional situations that exhausted her. She began to demand more time for herself so she could relate to the depression and contemplate its meaning. She was risking the possibility that she might appear selfish or that others would see her as less likable, but in the end her desire to connect with the self was stronger than her fear of others' perceptions. She delved into the sheer joy of being alone, less and less concerned about what others might think of her for doing so because her inner life had become her orienting priority. She began carrying herself in life more as a self-willed woman and less as a maid to others' perceptions.

---

[70] Von Franz, in *The Golden Ass of Apuleius,* discussed the "wrong kind of pity" as it appears in Psyche's journey. Crossing the river Charon, Psyche is instructed not to have pity on an old man she sees drowning. "Not to have any sentimental love for something that is doomed to die and has to go is very hard. This applies also in analysis: a neurotic attitude in the analysand naturally cries out for our pity, but to give in here would mean to keep alive something dying or already dead. To have pity and love, combined with the reckless 'cruelty' to allow the condemned thing to die, is very difficult in practical life," 126.

The Role of the Dark Feminine

All sister-rescue fairy tales include a supernatural antagonist—wizard, demon, or devil—who kidnaps and tortures women. In other tales of feminine redemption, the antagonist is not a supernatural being but an actively destructive father figure. In the Grimms' "Allerleirauh" and Charles Perrault's "Donkeyskin," the father wants to marry his daughter when he realizes she looks just like her dead mother. In "The Handless Maiden," the father unwittingly sells his daughter to the devil. In psychological terms, these tales depict how a father can force his daughter to remain undeveloped, even though he doesn't seem to be doing so. Being threatened by a feckless father may seem less dangerous than being threatened by a demon, but underneath the civilian clothing, the father is driven by the same devil who sabotages the feminine more purposely. Father-daughter tales tend to be a bit more sophisticated than tales of demons and wizards because they are a step removed from nature. But in both types, there is a marked absence of feminine figures; the mother dies, plays a minimal role, or is not mentioned, indicating that eros is missing and needed for renewal.

Psychologically, the father-daughter tales describe how a negative father experience can be the basis of a debilitating negative animus complex, as we have seen with Pearl and Sarah—and with Lucy, once she could see her father's spiritual lethargy. On the personal level, fathers with undeveloped eros likely cannot see *any* female as an individual, and their daughters are doomed to become just one of the herd. Their daughters are not real, not objective individuals to them but extensions of the unconscious anima. Such men do not have the capacity to relate to any woman as an individual. A typical experience for a woman around such an unrelated man is that he can't remember who she is, or he mixes her with other women because her individuality does not register with him. Some men tend to impose themselves on women, psychologically and sometimes sexually, actively devaluing a woman's individuality or her existence outside of his fantasy. If a woman falls for this kind of behavior from a man, it means that her eros development also belongs to the old generation. She can't discern how eros is trying to develop in her in a way that could change the insidious patterns.

In Cinderella-type tales, including the Russian "Vasilisa the Beautiful," it isn't the father but a feminine figure who is the main antagonist of the heroine. In most of these tales, both parents have died or departed, and the heroine is left at the mercy of a stepmother who relentlessly demeans her. In psychological terms, fatherly logos is missing and motherly eros has died. Again, there is a need for development in both realms. The jealous, debased stepmother working against development represents regressive feminine energy that remains frozen in collective, stoic patterns.

In her discussion of "Vasilisa the Beautiful," von Franz suggested that it takes almost superhuman power for a woman to extract herself from identification with her mother, especially if her mother's influence is repressive. She has to find her way out of an old, established way of valuing life that remains in unconscious collusion with one convention or another and stifles her development. Cinderella tales depict a woman's journey in facing such a femininity, the mother generation in her own psyche, in which individual differences are ignored or tacitly threatened through lack of relatedness.[71]

Interestingly it is the witch, Baba Yaga, who helps Vasilisa destroy her stepmother. Vasilisa survives and apparently gets on Baba Yaga's good side by asking her the right questions and refraining from asking the wrong ones. The tale makes it clear that asking her the wrong question would get Vasilisa killed rather than save her. The witch's seeming cold-bloodedness is really an uncompromising preference for the right attitude—psychologically for individuation, which is clearly her goal no matter how she promotes it. Likewise, a woman with a powerful negative mother complex has to differentiate between that aspect of the mother archetype that promotes individuation, even when it feels a bit cruel, and the aspect which actively tries to prevent it through ties to convention and rationality.

One of my analysands, Sylvia, throughout her childhood suffered physical and psychological abuse from both parents, though it was

---

[71] See Chodorow, *The Reproduction of Mothering*, for a well-researched discussion of how mothering qualities and practices are passed through the generations, and how difficult they can be to change.

instigated primarily by her mother, a woman who suffered from a demonic animus possession. She wrote of her mother:

> She invaded every aspect of my life, even my thoughts. She shamed me about my body and budding sexuality. She railed at my attempts to write. She short-circuited every possibility of my becoming a whole person with a sense of efficacy in the world. When I fought back verbally, she encouraged my dad to hit me with his belt—even when I was a senior in high school. Once she stood by as my dad sat on top of me on the bed and hit me. She said, "Now, don't hurt her—don't hit her where it shows."

Sylvia had two siblings, and all three children were convinced that they were living in a haunted house. They heard terrifying noises coming from the attic, saw ghosts, and witnessed blood seeping from a ceiling. All had serious childhood illnesses and suffered lifelong depression, stemming from the fact that in childhood they were saturated with the experience of being actively unwanted by their mother, and their father passively going along with the abuse. Sylvia had a special relationship with her aunt and uncle that helped her survive with more of her identity intact than her siblings and the strength to find analysis later in her life. Through some kind of grace and intuition for her own development, she was able to resist the regressive influence of her parents, though it was a lifelong struggle. Neither of her siblings grew into strong adults.

The Archetypal Trauma of Threatened Individuality

Pearl, Sarah, and Sylvia had childhood experiences that dealt traumatic blows to the formation of their individuality. Such an experience introduces a child to a dark fate, which she can sense, though she may not be able to verbalize it. She is exposed to the immense power of the archetypal realm since parents who commit such dark crimes are in the grip of something much larger than themselves. Pearl's dreams of being stalked by an immortal demon, for example, reflected the archetypal experience of her individual reality being targeted, as if a deific force were insisting that she should not exist. When both father and mother inflict that message, the trauma can become insurmountable for people with little support. Even after decades of therapy, Sylvia carried a sense of profound inferiority and existential loneliness into her 70s yet somehow knew in her bones that she was at the same time healing and growing.

A dream of a haunted house similar to her childhood home helped Sylvia turn an important corner. She wrote about her memories of that house: "I dreamed for years of a labyrinth on the third floor that was populated by evil beings, including my mother, who appeared as a witch. These dreams continued until my parents moved out of the house when I was in my 40s." Remembering these dreams helped Sylvia realize the fact of archetypal evil as it existed in her childhood home and haunted the psychic atmosphere. She could see that, for one thing, her mother was caught in an aspect of the unconscious that is oriented toward death, as we see in the wizard, unable to allow individuality to flourish. I repeatedly told Sylvia that there is nothing more evil than killing a child's individuality or making a child feel like he or she should not exist. When Sylvia could feel the truth of that fact and acknowledge the archetypal dimension of her mother's drivenness, she then could see that her parents themselves were not the demons but that they were possessed by demons—at the mercy of archetypal forces.

Psychic Rage

Rage is an inevitable result of being imprisoned in innocence. Pearl and Sylvia both experienced extreme bouts of rage that took them over at times, their sense of feeling unseen exacerbated by those primal areas of the unconscious that also remain unacknowledged. The spirit of the unconscious as well as the nature mother roil in the fact that they aren't being seen, and this lends considerable energy to a woman's anger when *she* feels unseen. I have known more than one woman who, in the grip of a rage attack, would punch herself violently. Cutting, purging, and other forms of self-harm are expressions of archetypal intensity acted out rather than contained in a creative process. But anger can be an important emotion if it is contained in creative work, where it helps a woman align with the side of the psyche that is yearning for recognition and development. Even as she becomes intimate with her shadow, she will realize that her rage is nothing less than the inner drive for individuation—confined, imprisoned, unrealized psychic energy, bursting to be seen and expressed for its psychic vitality.

From Unconscious to Conscious Dismemberment

As Jung recounted many times, a confrontation with the shadow normally ends as a defeat for egocentricity—for the ways we may be fooling ourselves with our certainty. Meeting the shadow means we are no longer naïve or innocent, and neither is our idea of the divine, as Eve discovered; we confront our one-sidedness, our righteousness, and in the process discover we have been rejecting a perspective that is trying to fuel individuation.

The self-knowledge that comes from a woman's encounter with the negative animus includes the shocking awareness that we discussed at the beginning of this chapter: She has been cooperating with—believing—the negative messages telegraphed to her throughout her lifetime. Her feeling for herself has not been strong enough to keep her from being abducted by conventional animus thoughts. At the same time, she has been trying to compensate for the negative messages by proving herself worthy. And yet even that behavior is another capitulation to the worldview that is tormenting her—painful for a woman to see and so difficult to bring to consciousness. But if she can find a relationship with the greater perspective offered by the self in individuation, she may find the strength to face these realities in the context of the greater goal. In that case, she is no longer the victim of unconscious dismemberment by the animus; rather, her shadow and the negative animus complex together become the objects of dismemberment.

For example, Sylvia at one point realized that to compensate for her feelings of inadequacy, she had been holding up the illusion that she had a perfectly happy family when really there were fierce difficulties in her relationships with her adult children. She was subjecting herself to the ideal of the happy family and performing *as if*, but she was secretly ashamed that her family wasn't living up to that ideal. Although she was a good mother, she was participating in the same charade imposed on her in childhood, hiding away dark secrets. She was obeying the ideal almost as if it were a religious conviction: Partly to uphold her position in her work community and her social circles, she felt that her family must be perfect.

Sarah had to admit that she loved the attention she received from being such a good hostess. Pearl wanted approval from her professor, even as she felt how dubious that need was. She even realized she was using her beauty to evoke approval from her professor and other men—meaning she was actively evoking an anima projection that was once completely unconscious. (Jung called women who charm men this way "anima women." I'm here to say that a woman can be possessed by the animus and also be an anima woman at the same time.)

We all recognize tendencies in ourselves to perform to an outer standard, women as well as men. The penchant may serve us well up to a certain age. But the self, waking us up to the destruction in the illusion that we "should" be perceived a certain way, throws the shadow of that need right in front of us. We might be performing in order to control our world, which amounts to a power problem. Or we might be constantly trying to hide an exaggerated inferiority, which amounts to a negative inflation and anyway is just as egocentric as a positive inflation. What is really missing is an eros connection to our wholeness, a femininity in our own consciousness, which can reflect without judgment what the psyche is telling us and accept darkness as meaningful rather than ignore it or condemn it.

As the shadow is seen and accepted, and as dreams help a woman accept herself the way she really is, eros may be brought into daily life as a natural function rather than a performance. This is a development that may not be evident for some time, but slowly, genuine eros builds up through contact with the wisdom that reaches us from the unconscious and forces us to be honest with ourselves. I am not speaking of eros that we expect in being blessed by a perfect life but eros for life as it is, including the shadow. It is an eros that is sometimes incredibly generous and accepting, as some experience in the Virgin Mary, and other times brutally honest, like Baba Yaga, for the sake of the truth.

For Sarah, the sacrifice of an old, pleasing dynamic meant in part giving up her typical relationships with mother-bound men, in which she retained most of the power. The thought of a relationship with what she called a "grown-up man" was actually frightening to her, but she could see it was necessary to give up infantile relationships if she were to experience real love. Synchronistically, a man appeared in her life, and she fell in love with him in a way that she had never experienced before. Although the relationship didn't work out, the new experience of love exposed her to the positive side of the animus—something she found quite surprising so late in life. She experienced a profound sense of redemption in her capacity to love an ordinary man for who he was, without subjecting him to power demands.

Sylvia could eventually love her children without having to pretend that their relationships were anything other than what they really were. Loving people for who they are and valuing one's own life as it is are developments of genuine eros that do not occur out of willpower alone. One can decide one day to be more loving, but if the shadow is driving our motivations unconsciously, we won't really understand what we are trying to love. The capacity for genuine love grows slowly out of our honest work with the darkest aspects of ourselves. It is slow because we are also redeeming the unfathomable comprehensiveness of eros.

Summary

A woman may find it almost impossible at certain points of life to discern whether suffering serves development or whether it does not. Yes, she has a shadow like everyone else, and that must be suffered and integrated as best she can. But no, she is not to blame for that shadow as the old animus opinions and the old god-image would have her believe. In fact, in her shadow she may discover what makes her uniqueness whole. Accepting life as it is, including the shadow, means she doesn't so strongly feel the need to split off darkness and pretend to be innocent. She may actively reject the animus torture that either punishes her for having a shadow or convinces her that suffering through a shadow realization is not worthwhile. Keeping that differentiation in mind is like balancing on a razor's edge at times. The difference between destructive self-criticism and meaningful suffering in the service of individuation does, over time, become easier to discern and feel, and a woman knows with more and more certainty when she is genuinely related to the unconscious.

6

Circulatio

As we've seen, it can be very difficult for a woman to catch the negative animus in action until she experiences his tricks over and over again. Each time she sees his effects on her, she builds up consciousness about him and resistance toward his destructive tendencies. Her focus on the overarching process of individuation depotentiates his power in any given moment to grip her emotionally or to destroy her connection to the eros of the self. In other words, a woman begins to contain the animus rather than the animus containing her; this is ultimately the meaning of the fire at the end of "Fitcher's Bird." It is possible to become familiar enough with the fiery dynamism of the animus to catch it in consciousness and to realize its aim in the context of individuation—to identify its archetypal reality. The repetitive nature of this work isn't wrong; it constitutes an overall pattern of development, a circulation around the center that over time stretches into a spiral.

Around and Around: Building an Eros Connection to the Center

Kat grew up in an evangelical family with Calvinistic ideals in which, simply put, a thick wallet was considered a sign of God's approval.[72] She struck off on her own as a teenager, long having realized that she couldn't participate in her family's worldview. She had a strong spiritual drive as a child but felt suffocated, and then alienated, by her family's insistent religious views. When I met her, Kat was in her mid-30s, divorced, building the career she wanted, and raising two children. She lived on a tight salary with inadequate child support from her ex-husband. Although the divorce was an important step toward independence, her financial poverty and the sheer exhaustion of being a single mother

---

[72] My thanks to Dr. David Senn for this phrase.

plagued her with a sense that somehow her life was wrong or that she was being punished for some vague sin. Feeling very much alone, she fell into depressive episodes during which she could hardly drag herself through her days. She simply believed that she was a hopeless failure. Even though she did not participate in the family religion, somehow the religion was participating in her, convincing her that she was innately a failure. Her thoughts along these lines so effectively degraded her feeling for herself that had she not had children, she thought she could commit suicide.

In analysis, she began the long process of examining the dynamic fantasy thinking that tortured her, especially when she had any contact with her family. I could see a clear discrepancy between the real merits of Kat's life and her perception of her life as worthless or punishing. It is typical for the negative animus to spin unconscious fantasies about how horrible life is, how lonely and how unfair, creating an emotional reality that is completely cut off from the courageous valor of a woman's ventures. On top of that, he implies to such a beleaguered woman that she is to blame for her life being so difficult. She becomes a double victim—a victim of circumstances and a victim of self-blame. She is too easily convinced of her victimhood, partly because the shadow secretly loves to wallow in self-pity.

It can help in such cases to suggest to a woman that she take a written inventory of the positive, blessed realities of her life as data that prove the negative animus thoughts objectively inaccurate—a sensory exercise that can help deactivate a dark intuition foreboding certain failure. Kat was working in her chosen career; she was moving up the occupational ladder; she and her children were healthy; she was intelligent, strong, resilient, and creative. She loved her work. She could hang on to these realities while she was with me but would lose touch with their value once she went back into the world and faced the laborious facts of her life. This was an indication that her eros connection to the self wasn't strong enough to sustain her on its own. In one sense, the sisters in the fairy tale who don't protect their eggs represent this state, in which eros for the self is not strong enough to fend off a debilitating, dismembering attack.

The goal for Kat was to stabilize over time the sense that yes, life is difficult but that doesn't mean she or her life is unworthy. Her process was slow and tedious, but gradually Kat could see that in blaming herself for life's difficulties, she was cooperating with the family complex, remaining too gullible to the idea that she wasn't getting what life was supposed to deliver to a deserving woman. In her awareness of this dynamic was the seed of a new possibility. According to images in her dreams and in sandplay, as she confronted the debilitating thoughts and began to objectify them, a potential renewal was set in motion at a deep level.

Many of her dreams compensated for her negative opinions, showing her how strong she really was, reassuring her that her life was on the right track. Over time, the dreams helped solidify her sense that she was doing the right thing above all in taking loving care of her inner development. She began to feel seen and supported by the unconscious rather than beleaguered by it. In several of her sand trays, this shift was indicated by the fact that she placed eggs in meaningful situations. In one tray (fig. 16), a white stone egg and a red marble sphere are placed on vases, directly across from each other, showing a relationship between the red and the white as opposites—red in alchemy representing the fiery drive of the unconscious and white the capacity of that fire to be contained.

Figure 16. Kat's Sand Tray with an Egg and Globe
One of Kat's sand trays had an egg and a globe elevated in twin vases and facing each other, suggesting a relationship between the egg of individuation, its need to be contained, and potential wholeness. These figures are surrounded by trees, also symbols of individuation. Author's photo.

The globe and egg are surrounded by four trees, symbols for individuation. The placement of the trees suggests that the potential for individuation was constellated in all four directions of psychic development. Outside the trees are four more figures, including three positive feminine figures and a minotaur brandishing a sword. The minotaur may represent a threatening primal energy that works against individuation, or he may be protective toward individuation; he could represent either or both sides of the animus. His overall influence is incorporated into the whole; he need not be excluded from the overall goal of wholeness.

In another of her sand trays (fig. 17), Kat placed in a bed an egg-shaped stone with a circular blue opal embedded in its center. Then she surrounded the bed with fire and protective animals, including Pegasus, who helped Bellerophon slay the Chimera. This arrangement appeared in the upper left side of the sand tray. It indicated in every way that something vital was trying to get born from the egg stone. The fire and instinctual life energy surrounding the egg could represent threats to the life in the egg, but for Kat they seemed to be expressing urgent support and protection, the fire another image for the burning drive of psychic life wanting to find containment and purpose in her relationship with the psyche.

On the right side of the tray, Kat placed several figures from Egyptian death and resurrection mythology. The tray as a whole presents a juxtaposition of birth and death, the two sides of individuation. One god-image (her family's) was dying as the other (her own myth) was trying to come to life. The great question for her in this moment, as for many women, was whether the egglike potential for individuation could be felt and understood—if her love for individuation and her understanding of its intentions could become strong enough to mitigate ingrained, threatening patterns.

"Good" Is What's Good for the Egg

The appearance of an egg or other symbol for individuation in a dream, active imagination, or sandplay image can reveal a person's

Figure 17. Kat's Sand Tray with an Egg-Shaped Stone

Kat placed a jeweled egg, protected by fire and animals on one side of the sand tray and by death and resurrection symbolism on the other side, including a sleeping Osiris guarded by two Bastet figures and Horus. The fierceness of a jaguar and a dragon seem to protect the psychological death process that needs to take place as something new is getting born. Author's photo.

relationship to the self and the dynamics that surround it, though the egg itself may not necessarily indicate a mandate for a fully engaged, conscious individuation process. For example, in a sand tray by a woman named Deira, an egg is confronted by a threatening, fire-breathing dragon,

Figure 18. Deira's Sand Tray

The egg, place in the center of the tray, is threatened by a fire-breathing dragon on the right. A dark feminine image and an apple tree indicate how the fruits of individuation grow side by side with the darker experience of the unconscious, which still carries a threatening quality for this woman. However, the dark queen, placed directly next to the tree, could mean that the archetypal feminine would fiercely protect individuation the way Baba Yaga does. Author's photo.

an image for primal energy in the psyche that may or may not want to become conscious (fig. 18). Such a standoff shows us how development constellated in the unconscious also may be challenged in the unconscious, quite naturally, by the side that doesn't want to develop. The tray may suggest that a relationship to the unconscious may be too threatening for Deira. On the other hand, the dragon in this case could be fiercely protective or offering heat that would enliven the egg, contributing to individuation. The baby dragon in the bottom right corner of the tray may indicate the possibility for the unconscious to become less threatening in the future; on the other hand, it could represent a new generation of threat.

Behind the egg and the dragon in this tray stands an apple tree, another symbol for individuation. The apple tree offers the fruit of knowledge, of transformed consciousness. It stands next to an evil queen, which symbolizes the dark side of the feminine that, like the dragon, can either be devouring or protective of individuation. The tree and the queen are not in confrontation but side by side. Is the queen protecting the tree, or is she blocking access to it?

Deira faced a horribly traumatic negative mother complex involving infantile sexual abuse, and so the unconscious naturally felt tremendously threatening to her basic existence. She was challenged to differentiate her personal mother complex from the archetypal devouring feminine if she were to engage with the unconscious at all. The tray presents the possibility for the dark queen and the dragon to become fierce protectors of individuation rather than devouring threats if Diera could engage with the unconscious in a sustained way.

The number 5 is important in this tray. There are five flat circular discs separating the two parts of the scene, and there are five figures participating in the scene, with the egg in the center. Five is the number of human reality: We have five limbs, including arms, legs, and head; five digits on each limb; and five senses. The emphasis on this number, with the egg in the center position, suggests the possibility for a union of opposites to be brought into reality or into Deira's living relationship with consciousness. Overall, the possibility for an engaged relationship with

Figure 19. Hartley's Sand Tray

An egg, centered on a mound and surrounded by animals and humans, marks an important centering process in a woman who was threatened by regression into drug addiction. The tray depicts a circulation around the center, although not in a spiral. Such a mandala image is a sign for an experience of being centered around an inner core of development, but does it necessarily point toward an engaged process of individuation? Author's photo.

the egg of individuation seems fully constellated as a possibility, yet it remains open whether the ego can approach the unconscious at this time, given the natural, underlying threats.

In another case, a woman named Hartley went through a very engaged sandplay process and created beautiful images, including one featuring an egg at the top of a carefully constructed, tiered mound (fig. 19). This tray was an important healing indicator for her as she worked through the danger of falling back into drug addiction. The egg in this case is at the center of a mandala formation and indicates the constellation of the self underneath consciousness, a natural development in nonverbal sandplay work that suggests the completion of a certain level of psychological healing through contact with the center, even if the center remains mainly unconscious. The egg and its potential seem very well protected by numerous animals and human figures lined up in concentric circles, as if they are parading around the egg.

The image could be emphasizing that the figures are moving forward, indicating progress. The psyche also may be emphasizing that the figures are going around in circles and not moving upward in a spiral toward the egg, which is the shape that symbolizes ongoing individuation. In other words, the image could indicate a completion in the psyche that does not necessarily need to develop further in conscious life.

Likewise, the snakes on the rim of the tray could indicate a further potential for development or they could be framing a healing achievement that needed to be preserved. As it turned out in Hartley's case, the snakes were indicating a need to keep the current inner constellation of stability safe from intrusion. Further contact with the unconscious may have been disruptive at that time. The self was constellated mainly beneath consciousness, and this was enough for Hartley; she simply did not have a need or an interest to engage the symbolic dimension of her work in a conscious process of individuation.

The egg images in all these trays, a symbol for potential individuation, have something in common that may easily be missed. In each image, good and evil appear, but they are redefined in terms of what is good or evil for the egg. What is good psychically is that which supports individuation, at whatever level is appropriate for the individual. What is evil in these images is that which destroys individuation or the individual's connection to psychic healing via the self. These images show us again how the psyche's need to transform through us forces us to reconsider collective notions about what is good and evil in our lives.

Forgetting and Remembering to Protect the Egg

During her analysis, Kat developed an intense, creative process of spontaneous painting. In her images, powerful creative energy could take form and help her build a meaningful relationship to the transpersonal dimension of that energy. But even as this process was strengthening, she experienced a serious invasion. Desperately in need of more financial stability, Kat began to display her artwork for sale, hoping to develop another income stream. Dreams warned her against this, but she still wanted to try.

Unfortunately, the exposure of her intimate creative process to the evaluation of the outer world proved to be too hurtful; it reenacted the very family dynamic she was trying to move out of. She ended up feeling destroyed when her artwork wasn't understood or appreciated and when it didn't sell. She compared herself with other artists who seemed more successful. She reasoned in partial accuracy that her lack of success stemmed from the fact that her artwork did not belong in a world that was blind to its meaning, that the world is full of unconscious people who could never understand her profound connection to the transpersonal realm. It is typical for animus thoughts to be basically true on one level yet strike the same old chord that isolates a woman from life. Kat felt like a victim to the ignorance of the world, which sparked a new generation of grief.

In this situation, Kat did not protect her egg of development from the evil that can be inflicted by collective standards as she was imagining them. She once again fell into desperation about being recognized and valued from the outside. She gave up her artwork as a "waste of time" in the midst of a severe depression. She went through a tragic loss of connection to the self—a death that can occur in the deepest darkness before the dawn. We can feel in this setback how Kat tried to adopt a heroic mantle, as if she could change the world, or at least influence its perceptions, through her artwork. This extraverted approach betrayed her unique creative connection to the self; it had not yet formed enough strength to resist a temptation from the demon of success. This repetitive reexperiencing of dismemberment by the judgmental mindset is symbolized in the fairy tale by the repeated murders of maidens for God knows how long, an image for how that mindset can be so powerful and enduring, even as we are getting a handle on it. The experience can convince a woman that the self has betrayed her or that she just cannot make any psychological progress.

I do not understand why some women must suffer so much in the process of feeling the supportive reality of the self in a steady way. I have seen depressions lasting for years in which the unconscious is trying hard to connect with a woman, and just when she begins to feel the meaning of her suffering, she suddenly decides that her dreams are useless or that she isn't being given sufficient comfort against her bitter disappointment. She is again abducted by the judging mindset, which offers her no magical solutions to her suffering. An eros connection to the self again is at risk of being murdered, and it can be excruciating to witness.

Thankfully, as Kat worked through her depression, she courageously realized all over again how important it was to provide a secluded container for her creative inner life, whether through painting, journaling, or writing. She knew she needed to keep her creative work to herself and protect her love for it by remaining profoundly introverted, even anonymous, about its existence. The depression had dismembered another layer of naïve feeling that was still connected to the evaluations of a prestige-oriented worldview. This process of dismembering a judgmental mindset can be inexpressibly painful. But what it destroys in false hope is built up in genuine connection to the self—a felt sense of its desire for one's individuality above all else. I don't mean to suggest that Kat should never try to sell her artwork; the possibility depends on what the unconscious needs from her at any given time in her life.

As she experienced a renewed, strengthened contact with the unconscious, Kat did an active imagination in which an image for the self made an unmistakable appearance. In an exercise, she asked the unconscious, "What is the one word that I need to know?" The answer she received was, "You will find the word hidden in the egg." She created a painting in which she depicted what such an egg might look like (fig. 20).

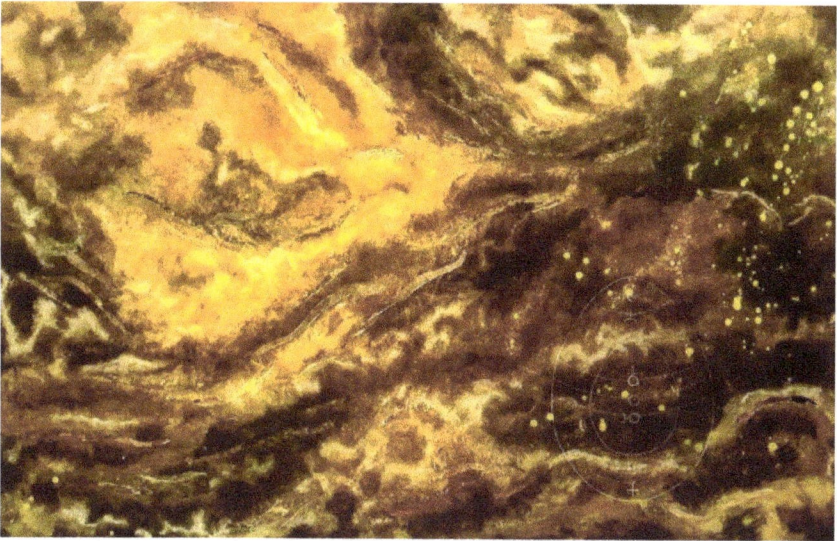

Figure 20. Kat's Painting of the Cosmic Egg

Kat's painting was the result of an active imagination in which she asked what was the one word she needed to know. She heard a voice say, "You will find the word hidden in the egg." This image hints at the cosmic dimension of the egg of individuation, but also the possibility or need for grounding the meaning of the egg in the "earth" of Kat's personality. Artist's photo.

Through active imagination and painting, Kat rediscovered the egg of individuation as an inner yet objective developmental phenomenon. In her painting, the egg has a cosmic dimension, revealing the archetypal layer of individuation and how it is related to one's astrological stars. Kat could see that in her relationship to the unconscious, she was being led into a mystery that was barely expressible, but her collective attitudes and values really had to die to make room for that mystery—to protect the divine secret hidden in her relationship to the self. The experience of being rejected by the prejudices of the outside world could be healed only by the penetrating recognition that persistently emerged from the self, reparenting her as a child of the cosmos. The word hidden in the egg refers to the logos quality of this strong feeling realization and reminded Kat that she needed to put effort into understanding the meaning of her deeply felt psychic images.

Circulatory Distillation

Kat's process, in which she gains, loses, and regains her connection to the self is typical. Like most of us, she felt she was going around in circles, reexperiencing the same problem repeatedly. In fact, individuation is a process in which we circulate around the center but in the shape of a spiral rather than a concentric circle. Each go-around with a complex creates a bit more consciousness so that when we find ourselves in a familiar situation, it is important to remember that we have come to a new level of development with that situation. This can be one of the most important reminders an analyst may offer an analysand in times of deep frustration. The struggle is familiar, but that doesn't mean she hasn't gotten anywhere. She is revisiting the complex with a new level of understanding and experience, and now she must take in this fact and understand how she has changed. If she once lost a connection to the self, she now more strongly feels its value. Eros for the self, once murdered, can be resurrected in a stronger, more conscious iteration.

As she develops a growing understanding of her complexes and realizes how she has grown through a long process, a woman may begin to feel a deepening appreciation for the very process that is demanding so much of her. She may in certain, unexpected moments realize how her particular suffering has brought her to an experience of the transpersonal realm that otherwise would not exist—in anyone. In other words, with each rotation through a stubborn complex, the self becomes more real to her, and therefore more real in the world. The self, through its own volition and velocity, draws into its orbit a bit more of her psychological substance, building up its reality as the living center of the personality.

This mysterious process, in which consciousness develops out of the unconscious and moves into the orbit of the self, was identified by alchemists who projected the psychological event onto their meditative laboratory work. Paracelsus called the gradual, circulatory development of the self a *"retorta distillatio ex medio centri,"* which Jung understood as a "circulatory distillation" meant "to extract the volatile substance, or spirit, from the impure body."[73] The distillation expresses exactly the psychological development we have been discussing, when with each

---

[73] Jung, "Paracelsus as a Spiritual Phenomenon," *CW*, vol. 13, par. 185.

rotation through a familiar complex, a bit more volatility is extracted out of that complex, the "impure body," and integrated into the relationship between ego and self. Consciousness is gradually distilled out of the unconscious through this circulatory distillation, and the self becomes more substantially realized. In other words, the self is built up out of unconscious material as it gradually becomes a conscious, living reality in a person's daily life.

Each dream image represents an unconscious content whose symbolic meaning can be extracted and taken into the personality, strengthening the relationship between ego and self through the ongoing circulatory process. Variations on the same image may appear many times, until we understand it well enough and integrate it into consciousness thoroughly enough that its volatility no longer motivates us without our knowledge. The self generates this ongoing production of images through its own circulatory movement, pulling toward itself the content and energy that is needed for its ongoing development.

Projection is the primary tool the self uses to draw more of the psyche into its orbit. When Pearl realized that her father complex was projecting itself onto her professor, she could begin to see how the complex motivated her when it was activated. She was naturally attracted to the professor she saw in her imagination, until she became suspicious of him; at that point, the dynamics and the content of the projection could enter the conscious orbit of her relationship with the self. The whole experience was orchestrated by the self, the central dynamism of which constantly pulls unconscious contents into view. Projection is a natural part of our psychological development, instigated by the self. But the ego is needed to complete the transformation—to bring what was unconscious into consciousness and thus part of a relationship with the self.

Paracelsus observed something crucial in the activating center of the *retorta distillatio* and called it a "volatile midpoint," "a fiery, radiant centre." He compared this center to the sun in the heavens, the heart in a human being, and the yolk of an egg, all of which emphasize the autonomous ability of the center to attract to itself what it needs to develop. Psychologically speaking, the midpoint, the center, the "volatile spirit" is the aspect of the self that can attract everything in the personality that belongs to it, through its heat and its centripetal volition.

Development of a Living Being

Paracelsus also saw that the radiant center of the self contains a balsam, a substance that not only drives the circulatory process of development but, like a yolk, gradually transforms into a living being as it draws more life substance to itself. Jung collected a series of quotes from Paracelsus and others describing this balsam:

> Like the sun in the heavens, the balsam in the heart is a fiery, radiant centre. We meet this solar point in the *Turba*, where it signifies the "germ of the egg, which is in the yolk, and that germ is set in motion by the hen's warmth." The "Consilium coniugii" says that in the egg are the four elements and the "red sun-point in the centre, and this is the young chick." Mylius interprets this chick as the bird of Hermes, which is another synonym for the mercurial serpent.[74]

The "germ of the egg," the "red sun-point in the centre," or the balsam is the kernel of a living being, a "young chick" or "bird of Hermes." In the alchemical imagination, the dynamic energy is a spirit, which means it has the propensity to become consciously understood and reoriented toward development, even realized as an aspect of the inner god-image, here symbolized by a fully fledged bird. It is the same volatile substance, the dynamism that motivates us at first unconsciously, like the animus that drives fantasy thinking but eventually may be realized as an aspect of the Anthropos.

The development of the chick, an image for a potential renewal of the self, is set in motion when the hen warms her egg, tending to it instinctively. In these egg images, we have another paradox: While the yolk of the egg is hot and volatile, at the same time its development into a living chick needs the external heat of the hen. Translated into psychological language, this means that while the self is a living dynamism and contains its own heat and its own aims, it needs the ego's warm attention if it is to renew itself, organizing into a living reality in life.

As Jung noted, the alchemist Mylius called the chick born from the balsam of the egg "the bird of Hermes," which is "another synonym for

---

[74] Ibid., par. 188.

the mercurial serpent," the dark spirit that provokes consciousness, as we have been understanding the wizard in "Fitcher's Bird." Some alchemical texts described the living center as the Anthropos or the original human, "the inner spiritual man" (or the inner Christ), the "spagyric foetus," the *filius philosophorum*, whose redemption from volatility makes him a panacea for humanity.[75] Jung verified that with these analogies, the alchemists were describing "the activation and development of a psychic centre, a concept that coincides psychologically with that of the self."[76] Clearly, these descriptions include the dark and dynamic aspects of the psyche, the unconsciousness that is yearning with its own fire to be united with consciousness. Redeeming the psychological aim of that unconscious energy can be a panacea for humanity because it stops projection, for example mitigating our tendency to blame our neighbors for our own unconsciousness.

All of these analogies are related to nature, to chemical activity and organic development that can be observed in plants and animals, reminding us that the principle of growth has its own aim, according to the individual life it nurtures. In a human being, that natural growth can become consciously realized—as a divine or autonomous phenomenon with its own compelling magnetism, pulling the ego into relationship with it anyway it can. In this sense, we can understand the wizard or the serpent as an agent or aspect of the self, breaking a path through which consciousness can begin to relate to the unconscious by forcing attention onto its autonomy. Likewise, the negative animus forces us to pay attention to his autonomy and leads us to a relationship with the whole unconscious.

Symbolically, the development into a living being means that as the self draws once-unconscious contents to itself and unites them with consciousness, the union of the two gradually becomes a living reality. Like a tree growing out of soil, the self with the help of the ego miraculously transforms the unconscious, the earth in which it grows, into consciousness. Slowly in this process, the self comes alive in consciousness, and the ego begins to realize the self as a new, living

---

[75] Ibid., pars. 185 and 187.

[76] Ibid., par. 189.

center. Eventually, the personality goes through a second birth in which the self rather than the ego becomes the primary guiding light.

We see the paradox: The balsam that moves the self—the drivenness that is at first unconscious, even tormenting us through projection—is the lifeblood of the self. What we first experience as incompatible and uncontrollable in the unconscious is the same energy that we eventually realize as the balsam of the self. In other words, every unconscious problem, even every illness, contains its own healing, when it can be seen in the context of individuation.[77]

The circulatory distillation, then, is a paradoxical operation. The energy in an unconscious complex belongs to the self and needs the ego to realize this. To the extent that the complex remains rejected, it remains volatile, motivating us in mysterious ways toward objects and people that seem fascinating. The volatility itself, the autonomy, provokes us to wonder what is driving our fascination, inexplicable yearning, and relentless judgment. In other words, the unconscious and its dynamism, even its torture, is the *prima materia* of our relationship to the self. A dynamic, unconscious complex may plague us, but it is our very own, fired by our own energy. Our complexes belong to us from the time we are born, or from early in our lives, and they contribute to the psychological matrix of our wholeness through the very dynamism that torments us into becoming conscious of them. The unconscious and its drivenness is not to be rejected, therefore, but related to and understood as well as possible, with as much eros as possible. The longer we reject what we don't like, the longer we suffer its autonomy. Such fire is the stuff that drives wars and other power dynamics with the ego assuming it is in control.

Accepting this fact may require a difficult, hard-won sacrifice of certain expectations for life to be as it is "supposed to be," based on our collective expectations for goodness, or rationality, or the illusion that we can win a heroic victory over the sometimes brutal dynamism of the unconscious. Individuation is an integration, not an exclusion, of the heat of the life energy that is constantly in movement, sometimes in a tortuous way, sometimes even in an evil way. Our worldview is turned

---

[77] My thanks to Brigitte Huber for this insight, which came out of her unpublished work with the mythological healing processes attributed to Asclepios.

upside down when we realize that individuation is a transformation of darkness through relationship with darkness. What frightens us wants to be understood and consciously connected to the center; the ego is essential for that mediation.

Since the alchemists were men, it makes sense that their images for the self were predominantly masculine and focused on logos images as the divine center of development. The following dream gives us an image for circulatory distillation in a woman's psyche.

Eros and the Self

This dream from Sandra presents an image of the gradual building up of the self through a circulatory distillation—in this case around the heart:

I see in my mind's eye how love develops in a woman, in what I can only describe as her spiritual or subtle body. There is a movement, a circulation around a light in her subtle-body heart. Eventually, I realize, a seed is circulating around the light. The movement of the seed creates an energy field, or a spiritual field of love, which she can feel growing as if it were physical. This field of love never goes away once it is developed. The growing love in her subtle-body heart connects her to her own "real" heart-center, and it also connects her to the reality of another person.

Here, a central light gradually increases its strength by attracting and integrating light particles that are hidden in the darkness of its surroundings. In this dream, the central light is the heart, drawing more and more of those sparks into its orbit—the sparks representing potential points of consciousness within the unconscious aspects of the personality. As those contents are made conscious, the heart is built up as the center of the personality. The image depicts individuation as a building up of eros consciousness, which becomes a woman's living experience of the self; in other words, the building up of the self is specifically a development of eros, the opposite of judgmental power.

The dream emphasizes that the completion of this process is the establishment of eros as a reality in life. As the light of the symbolic heart develops, it is translated into the reality of the dreamer's ability to love—something she can feel growing "as if it were physical." The light that develops in the heart "connects her to her own 'real' heart-center, and . . . to the reality of another person." Based on this image, we can see that the goal of development is for eros to become real in the world, helping guide a woman's life.

I cannot ask analysands enough times if they can *feel* the new development taking place in them as they understand the meaning of their dreams over time. Encouraging rational people to discover even a sensory experience somewhere in their body of how the self is transforming within them, or how it is interested in them personally, can help them connect to the reality of the self that is developing in them. If a woman can feel new eros developing as a result of her connection to the self, even as a momentary sensation that she can pinpoint or an image that comes to her spontaneously, she may be able to carry that reality with her into the world and relationships. Eros develops out of her own nature, from her own ecosystem, and is truly indigenous to her but also an objective reality, having been fed by an objective process. There is nothing foreign or synthetic about it.

Consciousness and eros, so innately linked in this image, indicate that individuation has as its goal the distillation and development of conscious eros out of the *prima materia* of Sandra's life, including the very dynamism of the animus that once could destroy her experience of love (as we saw in her dream of her husband and the spring flowers in chapter 5). The development of eros that is personal and yet objective may help us further understand why the devil in Barbara Hannah's dream implored women to deal with the darkness in their own lives: doing so has the potential to bring a new, more inclusive love into the world.

According to this dream, eros that is built up out of the unconscious through its volition—through its own energy—has an eternal quality and is indestructible. It cannot be contaminated by false aims or power, and antiquated attitudes are no longer capable of subjugating it. This is essentially because eros is created from darkness—from dark experiences, from the shadow that so long has been rejected and yet offers a new way of valuing life. The darkness becomes integrated into the central light of the heart, increasing the ego's capacity to consciously love through light and darkness alike. In the fairy tale, this is the meaning of the resurrected sisters being returned home with a basket of gold. Psychologically, they represent eros that has been redeemed from the unconscious and now can become consciously treasured and visible in the world—truly a miracle.

In the dream, the heart is composed of light, and a seed circulates around it. A light that attracts a seed would be identical to the light of nature, the *lumen naturae*. Likewise, in his work, *Astronomia Magna,* Paracelsus described the midpoint of the psyche as having the quality of the *lumen naturae*. Jung quotes him as saying, "Nothing can be in man unless it has been given to him by the Light of Nature, and what is in the Light of Nature has been brought by the stars."[78] Paracelsus also called this inner light "the *Quinta essentia,* extracted by God himself from the four elements, and dwelling 'in our hearts.'" He called it the *corpus astrale*, the "firmament" and the "star in us," or "the star in man." He added that meditation, through which we may reach the imaginal realm, "is the active power of the *astrum* (star) . . . of the higher man within."[79] Paracelsus is referring to the true imagination that connects with the divine inner phenomenon, the nous through which we experience the inner Anthropos.

Paracelsus's description of the imaginal realm as something that is derived from the light of nature helps us understand how, in the dream, eros is first built up in the subtle body, or in the realm of the true imagination, guided and organized by the light of nature. The imagination on this level is something divine and guided by the objective self so that we are not fooled by our egocentric preferences. If eros development is built up through the light of nature in the imaginal realm, through the very nous that connects us to the divine, we again see the identification

---

[78] Jung, "Paracelsus as a Spiritual Phenomenon," *CW*, vol. 13, par. 148. Jung noted that "the astrum theory had been foreshadowed in the *Occulta philosophia* of Agrippa, to whom Paracelsus was much indebted."

[79] Ibid., pars. 148 and 173. The term *corpus astrale* is also used by Ruland in *Lexicon alchemiae* (1612).

between the divine psyche and nature's wisdom. Eros that is built up this way is absolutely genuine.

The dream suggests that the life that develops at the core of a woman's psyche is not a logos phenomenon but primarily a living eros, an enduring feeling connection to the pulse of existence, which itself brings meaning into the fore as a potential alternative to judgment. We will explore the alchemical understanding of the self as an eros-oriented, world-healing phenomenon in the chapter about Mercurius. For now, we consider more fully how a woman's work with the animus may turn from a negative to a positive condition—and how her process shifts from what the alchemists identified as the first part of the work to the second part of the work—from the egg to the bird.

Part III

Protecting the Egg:
Turning from Negative to Positive

7
Tending to the Objective Reality

At the pivotal moment in "Fitcher's Bird" when our heroine protects her egg, she is described as "clever and crafty." Disobeying the wizard not only by entering his forbidden room but also by keeping her egg out of it, she changes the whole course of the fairy tale. Besides saving herself and her sisters from demise, the fairy tale says that the wizard "now had no longer any power over her and was forced to do whatsoever she desired." She hides her revived sisters in his basket with a dowry of gold and instructs him to carry the basket to her home without stopping to rest. He obeys her directions, showing us that power has been transferred from the masculine to the feminine realm. The heroine and her sisters now direct the wizard's movement, even as he remains convinced that he is going to marry her.

For a woman struggling with the animus, such a shift in power to the feminine side would represent a profound psychological change in which her nourishing relationship with the self has become more prominent than her identification with the animus. Tending to individuation, she can now more consistently direct her spiritual life toward creative work that is devoted to inner life as organized by the self. She is developing an understanding of her psychological situation from the objective point of view of the self, and this means her consciousness is becoming more reflective, more feminine, her relationship to the unconscious more positive. Von Franz wrote about the beginning of this critical shift in the ego's capacity:

> When real reflection comes up, you can always see it the minute you look into that person's eyes, for he or she is . . . suddenly quiet and objective about themselves and willing really to look at the thing. I would call that a numinous moment, which nobody can bring forth. It is a wonderful

thing when it happens to someone, this suddenly becoming quiet and truthful and really "bent back reflectively" upon oneself, looking really for the bottom of the psychological truth, to find out the difficulties. The moment of reflection, of the possibility of becoming conscious—because only thereby is a progress in consciousness possible—this is the moment of the birth of the sun out of the egg. When the egg appears in a dream, then you know that this moment is approaching, but now the birth of consciousness, as an active self reflection, is at least possible, it is constellated. The libido is concentrated in one point and now it can come out.[80]

"The moment of the birth of the sun out of the egg" is an image for consciousness getting itself out of containment in the unconscious (for a woman, out of the animus). As we shall see in our exploration of philosophical egg symbolism, this wonder—that the ego can find its way out of the unconscious and then tend to the unconscious as an objective, even divine phenomenon—was of great interest to the alchemists. For a woman who has been charmed by an old god-image her whole life, we can't underestimate what a miracle it is for her to emerge from her identification with antifeminine attitudes and genuinely tend to the egg of individuation as her own. In this shift, the animus too becomes more of a positive, guiding spirit, primarily because she can see him that way; his challenges are carried in her strengthening, reflective capacity, which allows his very real, persistent energy to contribute to the process of individuation.

The Pure White Egg

When the wizard returns home and sees that the heroine's egg has not been stained while he was away, he assumes that she has obeyed him and has *not* gone into the forbidden room—that she is pure to his way of thinking, and thus purely his. But the heroine is not the innocent maiden that the wizard supposes; she has seen his evil side and is secretly working her way out of marrying him. The situation in which sublime

---

[80] Von Franz, *Creation Myths,* 231.

purity still seems to be the standard corresponds to a psychological state in which the conventional aspect of the negative animus is still active enough to seduce a woman into the old ideals of innocence or the need for worldly recognition. She may feel heroically immune to negative animus effects or tempted to expose her discoveries to the world too soon, as Kat did with her artwork. Although the animus will always pose this danger, a woman who over time gets to know his tricks well enough can develop a certain amount of immunity to his influence, mainly by keeping track of her dreams and fantasies daily.

The heroine's work thoroughly cleaning the wizard's house can be seen as an image for such steadfast work with the unconscious. The value of humble, ongoing psychological housework mitigates the dangers of inflation, regressive identification with the animus, or spiritual materialism. The psychological house must be cleaned every day, that is, dreams understood on a daily basis, their meaning brought into life, to continue building a relationship with the self. Women who have endured lifelong criticism from the negative animus often discover bright shadow aspects in themselves—strengths they haven't yet seen or felt, giving them strength and confidence they hadn't imagined. Some important dreams must be pondered over a lifetime until their unique meaning is understood.

Any woman who has recognized the animus and the shadow and how they have been operating behind her back has worked very hard already, and it is important that she take in this sense of achievement. Deservedly, she wants to feel that she is free and clear of the animus, at least for a little while. Inevitably, however, she will find herself in the grip of animus dynamism, reminded again just how powerful he really is. Individuation is not about getting rid of the animus or even his unconscious nature. He will always be connected to the unconscious. He will always have the ability to carry a woman away in certain moments; but if she accepts the humbling reality of this fact, she also allows his inspirational side into her life as an aspect of her individuation.

As an example, I have more than once committed to presenting a lecture before I was ready to do so, my eager and intuitive animus convinced that I *could* be ready. In one case, I was to present three one-hour lectures on a topic that fascinated me—"Fitcher's Bird." The closer

I got to the first lecture, however, the more I realized I could not wrangle the material into the coherent form I had imagined. I found myself unable to bring my thoughts to a point, no matter how hard I tried. Even though many in the classroom enjoyed the lectures, I was not happy with them. I knew I had been carried away. It took me some time to stop punishing myself for this "mistake" and realize that I had been launched (to say the least) into a line of research that was much larger than I realized at first. My performance at the lectures was not the important thing. Knowing this, I could accept the fact that being carried away in inspiration is both torturous and meaningful. Punishing myself for getting carried away, however, would have meant that the critical animus was taking over. In my larger relationship with the self, certain dreams let me know that overall I was on the right track.

In truth, it's easy to forget just how wizardly the animus can be. A woman must constantly be aware of the conflict that exists between the animus that loves perfection and the animus that pushes for development no matter how messy or embarrassing it is. Once she accepts the wizardly quality that can lead her sometimes clumsily into new adventures, the negative side has much less power to cut her off from life, inflate her with pride or power, or deflate her with shame.[81] If a woman assumes she is done with the animus altogether, she inevitably falls into the danger of feeling herself to be a pure white egg—that she could or should do no wrong. I don't know how many times I have heard women ask, "Is it enough, already? How many times do I have to go through this?" Or, "After all these years, how can I still not see it?" The idea that one day the devil will be conquered puts us right back into the Christian idea that the devil shouldn't or doesn't exist, and we are again alienated from the psyche as a whole. The goal for a woman is not to rid herself of the animus but to come to terms with his idiosyncrasies as well as she can, realizing again he is a daimon from the transhuman realm with an animal level as well as a spiritual level and aims she cannot fathom. Sometimes the best she can do is keep the animus from ruining her feelings for herself.

---

[81] I heard a story from a friend of von Franz that each time she gave a successful lecture, she made sure to go home and do menial work, like cleaning and taking out the trash, to protect herself against inflation.

In the fairy tale, the heroine cleaning the wizard's house is an image for psychologically "cleaning" the animus complex, which means, again, not eliminating the complex, which is impossible, but getting intimately acquainted with the animus complex and the shadow that has been cooperating with it. If the animus is a system of thought, the shadow is a system of valuing that goes along with the thoughts and supports them, often throwing over a woman a mantle of inferiority. Reviewing our examples—Pearl's *feeling* for herself as a freak is a shadow phenomenon, a feeling that too easily cooperates with animus accusations of being a freak. Likewise, Kat's feeling for herself as a failure brought her to her knees too easily when the thought occurred to her that her poverty proved she was a failure. The cooperative shadow listens to accusations of failure from the conventional animus and then convinces a woman they are true, and further that she should be ashamed of herself.

The fact that the heroine cleans the house "from cellar to garret" tells us that the process of disengaging our values and our feeling life from old animus attitudes needs to be quite thorough. From my own experience and observing the experience of other women, I can say with all certainty that this is a difficult, lengthy process fraught with backsliding and repetition, though it is not without joy. A woman through this process sees and feels how strong she really is, gradually developing enough awareness to defend herself against old opinions in a way that feels genuine to her. Over time, her eros connection to the self, which has always been in the background nourishing her with dreams develops a living quality. She begins to feel her validity in relationship with the self as the main foundation of her life, and this protects her in perilous moments. Even though inflation or deflation may threaten her, neither will lead to an emotional massacre. Her goal, always at the forefront, is to continue to tend to the objective reality, the egg of individuation, so it may develop as fully as possible in her life not only as a personal reality but also as an expression of larger meaning. She is engaged with knowing the world soul through her own soul, and this becomes more and more present in her life.

The Universal Egg

In her book *Creation Myths,* von Franz pointed out that egg symbolism appears in many creation mythologies to symbolize the birth of the world. In Phoenician, Indian, and Egyptian mythology, the egg represents the cosmic potential out of which the world is born. The 18th-century Bhagavata Purana is a series of verses describing all of creation emerging continuously from a cosmic golden egg, the Hiraṇyagarbha (fig. 21). In the Chandogya Upanishad, the nonexistent potential of the world forms itself into an egg that rests for a year and then breaks open into a silver half, which becomes the earth, and a golden half, which becomes the sky. In Indian and Egyptian mythology as well as alchemy, the yolk of the egg is associated with the sun as the source of life energy.

Figure 21. *Hiraṇyagarbha* (Golden Cosmic Egg) by Manaku

The egg in this picture represents the eternal presence of creation floating in the waters of existence, like a seed that contains all that will come to pass. The swirls in the background could represent "concentric whirlpools and eddies, like giant rings of time on endless waters" (Goswamy, *Manaku from Guler*, 146). This painting is an illustration from a Bhagavata Purana series, dated 1760 CE. From Bharat Kala Bhavan Museum, BHU, Varanasi, India, accession no. 240.

Psychologically, creation myths in which an egg symbolizes the beginning of the world express the beginning of consciousness, especially consciousness of the cosmic dimension of existence. Von Franz describes the individual experience as a "sudden illumination" that marks a new awareness of the self:

> We know that every time a human being makes real progress in consciousness, makes this evolutionary jump toward a higher level of consciousness, the whole world for him has changed; relationships change and the outlook on the outer world and on his own situation changes. There is a complete rebirth of the world. The golden germ or egg motif shows the constellation of this possibility by an enormous concentration of energy in this one center.[82]

In the process of individuation, the self dawns to consciousness over time, evolving from a potential to a felt reality as more and more energy is devoted to individuation.

The Egg and the Bird: First and Second Parts of the Work

In the fairy tale, the heroine gains power over the wizard when the egg becomes the focus of her attention, a shift that eventually leads to a compelling ending in which she will make an appearance as a marvelous bird. In alchemical symbolism, the egg and the bird represent the first and second stages of the opus. The first stage represented by the egg corresponds psychologically to the birth of the sun out of the egg, as von Franz described it—when a person awakens to the fact that the objective psyche exists and has a perspective to offer.

In alchemy, the second stage of the opus, represented by the birth of a chick, corresponds psychologically to the slow development of the self as a reality in life, just as we saw in the previous chapter in the image of the heart that was growing through the integration of orbiting sparks of light. As we reflect upon dreams over a period of time, repeatedly extracting symbolic meaning from our unconscious situation, we bring our experience of the self as a source of knowledge and wisdom more

---

[82] Ibid., 232.

strongly into the world. Ongoing attention to the egg of individuation leads to the second part of the work in which a reorientation toward the self becomes a more constant, steady part of life, though this is a process whose goal seems always to be developing.[83] We will explore the alchemical stages of this development in chapter 12.

As an example, we can consider how a woman despairing of her loneliness may at some point take up the ethical challenge to ponder her despair in active imagination instead of falling into self-pity (first part). Already she anticipates that the unconscious may have something to say about her sadness; she has an expectation that her depression is meaningful. She takes her emotional state into the vessel of active imagination and finds an image, and *if she can absorb the symbolic meaning of that image*, she will experience a phenomenal change in herself psychologically; she may even feel it physically, as if the transformation were cellular and she is carrying the change materially into her life (second part). As this process is repeated, the arc of her life changes, and she may honestly know that she is no longer driven by the animus in a neurotic or destructive way— even though he may still sometimes overwhelm her with inspiration. His energy is consistently contained in her ability to reflect on its meaning, and she feels the real value of her own development.

Although there are two stages to the work, these stages are in constant circulation, one building on the other throughout life. We are constantly engaging with the unconscious to understand a new problem (first part) and bringing its meaning into life, changing our way of thinking and feeling, thereby connecting with more strength to the self (second part). In the latter part of life, the second part of the work may develop into a steady, consistent state that imparts profound meaning.

---

[83] See Abt, "The Great Vision of Muḥammad ibn Umail" and "From the First to the Second Part of the Work" in *Book of the Explanation of Symbols*, for additional symbolism about the shift from the first to the second part of the work. *Kitāb Ḥall Ar-Rumūz* (*Book of the Explanation of Symbols*) is a 10th-century Arabic text written by Muḥammad ibn Umail, also called Senior.

Incipience and Stability

As an analyst, I may be able to see an increase in the stability of an analysand's relationship to the self more clearly than she can, especially if she is in a depression or conflict. I want to emphasize that a felt relationship to the self, as healing as it may be, does not necessarily end a depression, not right away. But it can make the depression meaningful, if a negative animus thought system does not succeed in destroying that meaning by claiming that the process is hopeless. As we saw in Kat's and Lucy's struggles, a felt relationship to the self allows a woman to at least move out of the idea that her depression is wrong, which can give her the strength to stand in her predicament for all she is worth, giving in less and less to fear or despair or a temptation to condemn her own experience. Absorbing the meaning of her dreams, taking the time to bring the healing balsam of the self into her felt reality through active imagination or creative work, her depression may turn into an experience of feeling deeply seen by an objective entity.

As we have observed in the previous sandplay and art images (figs. 8, 11–12, and 16–19), the appearance of an egg or egg shape in dreams or active imagination often points toward individuation as a potential that is forming in the unconscious before a person realizes it is happening. Of course, other symbols besides the egg, such as a stone, heart, mandala, tree, pregnancy, etc. may represent this potential, depending on the individual. In some cases, the symbol anticipates a lifelong, steady relationship with the self. Jung reported such a case in his work with analysand Kristine Mann, who came to him for analysis with a strong, intellectual animus but a sense of being stymied in her life creatively. Early in her analysis, she portrayed herself in a seascape, "stuck fast in a block of rock" on a seashore "strewn with boulders" (fig. 22).[84] Jung understood this image of stuckness as indicating she was identified with the animus, that is, unable to move in her relationship with the unconscious. Noticing that she accidentally shaped the stones like eggs, Jung knew that

> the unconscious made use of the patient's inability to draw
> in order to insinuate its own suggestions. . . . The egg is
> the germ of life . . . the vessel from which, at the end of

---

[84] Jung, "A Study in the Process of Individuation," in *CW*, vol. 9i, par. 525.

the *opus alchymicum*, the homunculus emerges, that is, the Anthropos, the spiritual, inner and complete man. . . . From this hint I knew what the unconscious had in mind, namely individuation, for this is the transformation process that loosens the attachment to the unconscious. It is a definitive solution, for which all other ways serve as auxiliaries and temporary makeshifts.[85]

Mann went on to produce a beautiful series of mandala paintings that reflected ongoing individuation and a strengthening experience of the self, as an inner, centering and reordering phenomenon with a life of its own (fig. 23). Her images testify to a deeply introverted, evolving relationship to the self, one that began stuck in the unconscious and slowly made its way into life, beautifully expressed through her mandala images of its phenomenology.

Figure 22. Seascape
When Jung's patient drew the rocks in her dream as egg shapes, he knew that the unconscious was pointing toward individuation. Her sense of being stuck in life he saw as an animus possession. From Jung, "Study in the Process of Individuation," CW, vol. 9i, picture 1. Reprinted with permission from Princeton University Press.

[85] Ibid., pars. 529–30.

Figure 23. Selection of Mandala Paintings
From Jung, "Study in the Process of Individuation," CW, vol. 9i, pictures 2, 3, 22, and 24. Reprinted with permission from Princeton University Press.

I have heard various descriptions of the wonder a woman may experience when she begins to feel the nourishing reality of the self in her life, allowing her to endure as best she can her own human darkness. Lucy realized the miraculous freedom she might have in her life, knowing she didn't have to commit to exhausting projects anymore in order to prove herself. One analysand told me she had the experience of feeling as if she were gradually becoming more real, not only psychically but also physically. Another came to know immediately when she felt a certain sensation of anger when things weren't going her way that the animus was warning her about her own pride, and she was amazed that this did not send her into a spiral of shame but that she could accept the feedback, which made her relationships more meaningful. Another reported that on a certain day, she was able to look in the mirror and for the first time in her life not hate herself for her appearance. She could see herself more clearly, as a normal, ordinary human being with a soul shining through.

Another realized suddenly, after she had the following dream, how after decades of being alone, someone could fall in love with her:

A man I have met tells me he is so happy to be with me. We are apart now, but he still feels happy. He is not lonely or sad being away, but happy that he has this love for me. Then suddenly he has returned. I wasn't expecting him, but there he is, in the next room. I am just getting dressed and am bare-breasted, and we walk to each other across the room. I don't feel ugly because I know he sees me as beautiful. We embrace so warmly, and I am amazed. I am in the world in a new way; I don't hate my body. I know that I am loved.

Such moments are miraculous for women who have experienced a lifelong alienation from the eros of the self. They represent a real transformation in consciousness, when the feminine side of the self is contributing to a woman's perceptions, helping her stay out of identification with demanding perfectionism and its one-sidedness. It means that eros is being redeemed, along with the positive side of the animus.

8
Redeeming the Positive Animus

As the wizard carries the resurrected sisters back to their home, he is easily tricked into thinking that the heroine is watching him. He sweats and complains about the heavy load he is carrying, not realizing the sisters are goading him on from inside the basket on his back. The demon character in all the sister-rescue tales is tricked the same way and seems incapable of discerning how he is being driven. In some of the tales, the demon is told he must never look inside the box or the bag that he is carrying, and he dutifully obeys. Although the wizard in "Fitcher's Bird" is not instructed this way, he shows zero interest in the contents of his load. In all of the sister-rescue tales, whether the devilish character is a wizard, a troll, or an evil horse, what stands out in this moment is his sheer stupidity and lack of curiosity.

Psychologically speaking, the lack of curiosity reveals how uncreative and lazy the orthodox side of the animus really is. A slave to convention, he is devoid of ingenuity and simply cannot come up with anything new. Rather, his power has existed in his relentless momentum—the way he just keeps driving a woman's thinking in the same old way. But when a woman is related to the self and its larger picture, she can see that momentum and the stale, repetitive thought system in action, and gradually, they lose their power to compel her. Old opinions no longer hold her in sway because she is connected to the living meaning of the psyche. Importantly, this shift in direction is an aspect of the enantiodromia that she must take in hand: She has a chance to redirect the volition of the animus toward individuation. Now is the moment when she can and must steer animus energy in a creative activity that engages her intellect and is meaningful to her life, if she hasn't already. She must work to change the momentum of her own thinking—to consciously contain animus dynamism and channel it toward an expression of her life meaning.

Putting the Animus to Work

Forcing the wizard to carry his heavy basket without rest, the sisters in "Fitcher's Bird" follow the same pattern that is carried out by a witch in the fairy tale "Goose-Girl at the Well." In that tale, a count meets an old woman in the woods and offers to carry her huge bundle of kindling. Then he discovers how heavy the load really is, especially when the witch jumps onto it herself and subjects him to endless chatter and bad jokes, and he begs for a rest. But the witch, like the sisters in "Fitcher's Bird," will not allow even a brief sit-down. She insists the load is not nearly as heavy as he thinks it is.

When they finally reach her home, the witch rewards the count with a pearl, which leads to the redemption of the goose-girl, the heroine in the tale. In the end, the count and the goose-girl are married and inherit the witch's house, which magically transforms into a castle. We realize the witch is really the nature mother, and her forcing the count to carry her load was an initiation. The magical power that the "Fitcher's Bird" heroine and her sisters display in directing the wizard so mercilessly suggests that they too have archetypal powers and are putting nature's wisdom into practice.

In psychological terms, a woman in connection with the wisdom of the suprapersonal feminine knows the necessity of putting the lazy animus to work, specifically geared toward the long journey of individuation. It is up to a woman through her connection to the self to focus the animus on this path and make sure he sticks to the task, to remind him constantly that he now serves the feminine perspective. He is in service to the unconscious as a whole, not to worldly expectations. A woman must be constantly vigilant about his tendency to get lazy and fall back on old patterns. Otherwise, it may be impossible to bring the animus into humble service to the symbolic realm. He will always want perfection and accolades, and he will always be in a hurry to get things over with, so to him the road may seem unreasonably long, the load uncommonly heavy. His indolent conventionality will bar a woman from creative work by bombarding her with thoughts about its futility; he simply cannot imagine the possibility that life could have new meaning. Like the old god-image from which he stems, he cannot begin to fathom his own obsolescence.

Tragically, this dynamic can keep a woman from discovering the means or forming the commitment to yoke animus energy to creative labor, even when she knows she should. Such passivity perpetuates a low-level neglect of the unconscious—a paralysis, even, of her relationship to the self. She may not value strongly enough her own viewpoint, or she may not have the tenacity to articulate that viewpoint, which can be an enormously tedious task. A woman who doesn't face the sacrifice of time and energy required for a careful creative life in which genuine thinking is engaged in the pursuit of meaning actually feeds negative animus opinions that her life is meaningless. This is a typical animus trap that cheats a woman out of her own psychological gold. It tends to have the most power in women whose thinking function is their weakest and who are thus vulnerable to inertia in the process of discovering meaning.

Creative work brings a woman immeasurable value when she can accept her vulnerability in the process and learn through inevitable mistakes, which are suited to the task of humbling a proud animus. Via creative work, she develops a connection with her own real thinking function, differentiated from unconscious fantasy thinking. She discovers her inner partner, her true, indigenous animus, the drive to discover her own myth and its meaning—an inner brother who can be rediscovered when unfettered from the negative animus.

The Brother as Native Animus

At the very end of the tale, "the brothers and kinsmen of the bride" arrive at the wizard's house, revealing the fact that the heroine has brothers. They and their kinsmen save the heroine from a terrible marriage by locking the wizard in his house and setting it on fire. Similarly, the heroine in "Bluebeard" summons her brothers to her aid when she knows Bluebeard wants to murder her for looking into his forbidden room and discovering the wives he killed before she came along. While waiting for their slow arrival, she distracts Bluebeard with a series of clever delays.[86]

---

[86] Marina Warner, in *From the Beast to the Blonde,* points out that the heroine's delay tactics are similar to Scheherazade's in *One Thousand and One Nights,* who keeps her would-be killer waiting 1,001 nights while she tells him stories.

In both tales, the brothers make a late appearance, breaking a tension in which the heroine's fate has been uncertain.

In psychological terms, the brother represents a woman's closest opposite—masculine energy that is related to her and interested in her individuation, identical to the inner companion she remembers from childhood adventures. [87] A natural inner logos, typically he has to be freed from engulfment in familial or cultural complexes through her individuation. Anytime a brother or brotherly image appears in a woman's dream, we can suspect that the indigenous inner spirit is trying to be felt for what he is in the moment. Early in a woman's individuation, the brother animus may be inundated with familial ways of thinking. Later, he may be indicating a redemption out of those ways. The brotherly animus may appear as an actual brother or as another positive man who feels brotherly and supportive.

It is difficult to express how important the transformation is, or how much it contributes to a woman's renewal, when she can finally feel the presence of the positive animus—her very own logos capacity—and consciously accept the effort he demands of her. Such a transformation between the ego and the animus is so thoroughgoing and so deep that it is symbolized as a death and resurrection in this fairy tale, as well as in mythology and alchemy.

The Transformation of the Brother-Sister Pair

In "Psychology of the Transference," Jung interpreted the symbolic meaning of a series of alchemical pictures that appear in the *Rosarium Philosophorum*, which describe the dissolution and re-formation of a relationship between a king and queen, also referred to as brother and sister, or Apollo and Diana (fig. 24). These pictures portray the depth of transformation that takes place between masculine and feminine realms as a person deepens his or her relationship to the self, though to make this clear for women, we will have to translate the alchemical material and

---

[87] See Lara Newton, *Brothers and Sisters,* for personal stories about this psychological relationship.

Jung's explanations from the masculine to the feminine perspective. To start with, it is important to clarify that we are discussing the brother-sister pair as representing the masculine (logos) and feminine (eros) aspects of one individual as these principles transform through the individuation process. At the same time, the queen stands for a woman's consciousness and the king her unconscious (the personification of the animus); as this relationship transforms, so does the relationship between eros and logos.

Figure 24. King and Queen, Brother and Sister

The king and queen, or brother and sister, at the beginning of the transformation depicted in the *Rosarium Philosophorum*. The two represent an original union between consciousness and the unconscious, or at the same time between ruling logos and eros, masculine and feminine aspects of the personality that govern consciousness. Picture 2 of the *Rosarium Philosophorum: Secunda pars alchimiae de lapide philosophico* (Frankfurt, 1550).

Jung explained that when a person is meant for individuation, "whenever this drive for wholeness appears, it begins by disguising itself under the symbolism of incest, for, unless he seeks it in himself, a man's nearest feminine counterpart is to be found in his mother, sister, or daughter."[88] As long as his feminine, unconscious side is projected, he

---

[88] Jung, "The Psychology of the Transference," *CW*, vol. 16, par. 471.

never sees the unconscious—his own anima or psychic "sister." It may take a man a long time to finally turn inward to develop a relationship with the unconscious if he is reluctant to face the anima standing at the threshold.

As we have observed, the same courage is needed for a woman to face the animus standing at that threshold. Using Jung's phrase, unless she seeks it in herself, a woman's nearest masculine counterpart is to be found in her father, brother, or son. Projection by nature replicates the original, unconscious, psychologically incestuous relationships with which we begin our lives. These familiar relationships felt godlike in childhood in that they surrounded our consciousness; as children, we experienced our parents as archetypal beings. In this sense, Pearl's yearning for recognition from her father and later her professor, like anyone experiencing insecurity, was at its deepest level an appeal to that archetypal, godlike realm to reassure her that she was wanted in the world.

When Pearl could see that she was seeking from her professor what she originally sought from her father, she could understand the original, incestuous quality of her projection. She was seeking the positive animus in her father first and in her professor later on. The projection could dissolve as she developed a direct, conscious relationship with the animus by working with the dreams he sent her and doing her best to understand their symbolic meaning. Paradoxically, a conscious relationship between ego and animus is also depicted as incestuous, but in a positive way; it means a woman is no longer dissolved in or identified with the unconscious animus but has a conscious relationship with him. She has separated enough from the projection onto her father, brother or son that she can absorb new meaning from the symbolic aspect of her projection. [89]

The transformation of the king and queen in the *Rosarium* picture series represents how in one person the original, incestuous relationship with the unconscious dissolves and dies through the individuation process, and how it is reborn according to the self. In the end, the king and queen are depicted as a crowned and winged hermaphrodite (fig. 25), indicating

---

[89] Similarly, the uroboros (the snake eating its tail) can depict either an unconscious relationship to the unconscious or a conscious relationship with the unconscious. When the snake wears a crown, this indicates that the circular relationship has become conscious.

Figure 25. New Hermaphrodite

The new hermaphrodite, or the original king and queen renewed and reunited, is a symbol of wholeness that is unimaginable prior to connection with the unconscious. The couple represent a conscious union between consciousness and the unconscious, as well as a new union of archetypal logos and eros manifesting a realized experience of the self. Picture 10 of the *Rosarium Philosophorum: Secunda pars alchimiae de lapide philosophico* (Frankfurt, 1550).

that the union between consciousness and the unconscious has moved out of the old mainstay and become oriented toward the manifestation of the self as a living phenomenon. In this transition, a woman may feel connected to the animas in a new way as he is slowly disentangled from her inherited state of mind.

For example, Pearl's animus projection onto her professor lost its power over her as she began to uncover the fact that it was pointing toward a deeper relationship with the unconscious as a whole. Separating from the old father mindset, she could become closer, more consciously related to the innovative side of the animus and his way of understanding her life. Reflecting this development, her dreams began to present her with positive and brotherly masculine figures who were supporting her. Like any woman experiencing this transition, she had to make her preference known—she had to differentiate between the old and the new animus.

Tension between the Positive and Negative Animus

As a relationship with the unconscious deepens and the old animus inertia is challenged, women's dreams tend to reveal a struggle between negative and positive sides of the animus, one stuck in isolating precepts, the other striving to bring her a new connection to meaning. Pearl had several dreams revealing the two sides of the animus that will help us understand what that looks like symbolically. We see how the death of an old worldview is trying to take place, and at the same time a resurrection is trying to occur; the ego's influence is needed to tip the balance. Pearl's dreams challenged her to be clear about the difference between the negative and positive, to build up her preference consciously, and to make that preference known to the animus.

The positive animus corresponds to the winged youth in an alchemical allegory called *Introitus apertus ad occlusum regis palatium* by Eirenaeus Philalethes (George Starkey, 1628–65). The winged youth is a positive and inspiring masculine spirit who "flies away" when the waters of life are approached by a devilish, thieving spirit.[90] The negative side of the animus often takes the role of an aggressive thief or a beggar, as we have discussed, never revealing his proximity to the sacred waters of life. The positive animus tends to be more shy. He often needs a woman to confirm her interest in him and purposely connect with him.

In the following dream, the positive and negative sides of the animus are vying for Pearl's attention and energy:

I am in a strange land. It's postapocalyptic and so there are not too many survivors. There is a man who is abusing me, and because there are not a whole lot of people around, I just sort of take the abuse—like this is the only relationship I can have. There is one other man—he's got long blond hair, kind of a hippie and looking a bit like Jesus. He shows interest in me, and I am attracted to him. I want him to save me from this other horrible man, but for whatever reason, our love isn't strong enough. I lose him in the dream.

---

[90] Barbara Hannah discusses this allegory in *The Animus,* 1:59. Also see Jung, *Mysterium Coniunctionis, CW*, vol. 14, pars. 27, 84ff.

The dream-ego is being tortured by an abusive relationship. She is aware that she is taking it passively, as if an abusive relationship is all that is possible for her. She can't feel a strong enough love for the positive man to make that relationship possible. She finds herself facing a psychological, "postapocalyptic" state that feels hopeless.

An apocalypse symbolizes a far-reaching transformation in which an old worldview has come to an end and a new way of life is trying to manifest itself. Edward Edinger points out that it symbolizes the earth-shattering realization of the objective psyche, or the onset of a new god-image.[91] In Pearl's dream the apocalypse is over, but now she is left with a choice that will impact the rest of her life. My sense at the time was that her realization of the self had begun to take shape but that a loving connection with the animus had become imperative to her deepening relationship to the self as something she could understand and feel as truly her own. She may even have been in danger of the negative animus destroying any eros connection to the self that was possible for her to feel at the time. There are moments when an analyst feels the need to pray as she watches an analysand struggle with this difficult transition, wondering which side of the animus will carry the day.

The new possibility presented in the dream is a loving man whose hippie appearance reminded Pearl of Jesus. He represents the potential for a new, loving connection to the inner spirit of the unconscious. In the dream, Pearl could see the potential for that relationship, but her love for the positive side wasn't yet strong enough to save her from the abusive side. The psychological inertia was difficult to overcome. Yet the unconscious is showing her a real potential—how she could help turn around the momentum of hopelessness by loving the animus who loved her. When we discussed the dream, I encouraged her to make a clear gesture toward the positive animus by devoting herself with more energy to the images he brought from the self, through journaling and active imagination.

The event precipitating this dream was a regressive, out-of-control temper tantrum that was partly a reaction to stressful life events— ordinary life with young children and a career, which could sometimes

---

[91] See Edward Edinger, *Archetype of the Apocalypse*, for a full exploration of the psychological meaning of the apocalypse.

feel impossible. Her experience of rage echoed childhood tantrums that flared when she felt invisible and "freakish," inadequate and unseen. The tantrum simply picked her up and carried her into that old way of thinking and feeling about herself, convincing her that she would never be understood, that she was a terrible mother. In the blink of an eye, Pearl was overtaken by the dynamism of the old animus thoughts, and she exploded. *But this time, she could see it happening.* She consciously felt the autonomous dynamics, even as they took hold of her. Her ability to observe the animus in action also meant that, even as it was activated, the old, destructive union was beginning to die.

Now, it was necessary for Pearl to take a stand against the negative relationship and commit to the positive one, and this could only be done through conversations in active imagination and by tending to her dreams on a daily basis. A world-changing event was at hand. Believe it or not, a new, loving, and positive animus was taking shape, and if Pearl could relate to him as a psychic reality, the transformation would bring nothing less than a new worldview in which she and the animus were related to each other via the self. Sensing how important this was, she could commit herself in a new way to her dreams and her journals, and she began to read about depth psychology with more devotion.

On several occasions, Pearl dreamt of an old boyfriend who was trying ardently to make a connection with her. In one dream, he ran around her house several times to get her attention, wanting her to know he was available for relationship. In the dream, she debated with herself about whether or not she could love this man, whom she described as a "basic, imperfect but loving man." Can she love a man who isn't ideal, according to her old way of thinking? She would have to lower her standards. In other words, she would have to make it clear to the judgmental animus that she aims for a more loving kind of understanding in the masculine realm—a spirituality that is actually related to her individuality.

In another of Pearl's dreams, the positive side of the animus appears as an unknown man trying to connect with her. In the following dream, she begins to accept and even long for this new connection:

> *I am at home alone, in the bedroom. My husband and children are gone. A man appears. He is tall and strong with a proportionate build . . . perfect, really. He broke into*

the house using his tools, but he was completely silent. He was silent coming in and now he is silent as he enters the bedroom and approaches me. The whole dream is silent. I know he is an intruder and wants to violate me, but I want him, too. In fact, we have the most passionate sexual encounter. I actually still tingle when I think about it. He leaves afterward, but we make a silent agreement that I will break into his house next. He lives three houses down and has his own family. I woke up yearning for the secret pact.

Here the positive animus is just as intrusive as the negative, but by the same token, he is having some success in piercing the conventional veil of right and wrong. He wants to connect rather than to intimidate. He wants so much to be felt and pursued, just as Pearl does. The sexual energy in the dream, intense and lingering, expresses an acute yearning for something new to develop between consciousness and the unconscious. This dream reminds us that sex contains its own numen. The animus is interested in a direct relationship, not in being projected, and this requires a full-blooded connection. The fact that the connection is secret and silent makes it all the more intimate and conveys the sense of destiny and adventure that individuation offers.

Another of Pearl's positive animus dreams involves an old lover: *I am in my high school boyfriend's house. We are in a large room with many windows. Natural light is flowing in. There are many plants and chairs. We are older now. He has changed. He has become a wise man or he is becoming a wise man. We fall in love again, and he says that he has never forgotten me. I feel so happy to be in love. I wake up feeling really good.*

Pearl remembered the boy in her dream as someone who encouraged her creative life. In outer life, the boy was too fond of recreational drugs, but in the dream, he is portrayed as wise and loving. When women dream of revisiting an old lover who has matured or healed somehow in the beyond (even if it's not true in real life), such dreams can indicate that the animus has been transforming as she has been tending to her egg of individuation. His transformation represents a resurrection in the unconscious that is trying to make its way to consciousness.

In another dream of the struggle between positive and negative animus, Pearl was driving in a car with a man she didn't trust. Even so, she felt an attraction to him, which later reminded her of the abusive atmosphere of her postapocalypse animus. This man forced her out of the car and into a river, where he tried to kill her. Suddenly, an unknown man came to her rescue. He was dressed in a red, hooded garment, and he somehow pulled her out of the river and saved her life. She painted a picture of this man, who seemed related to the Jesuslike figure in the earlier dream (fig. 26). In this picture we can see how the positive side of the animus was coming more actively to life, appearing spontaneously in a moment of peril. In saving Pearl's life, he couldn't have made his intentions any clearer. Psychologically, he really does want to rescue her from a dead existence with the abusive, judgmental animus. The redness of his cloak symbolizes drive energy, suggesting that the driven energy of the animus is entering a redemption, becoming connected with new meaning in Pearl's life.

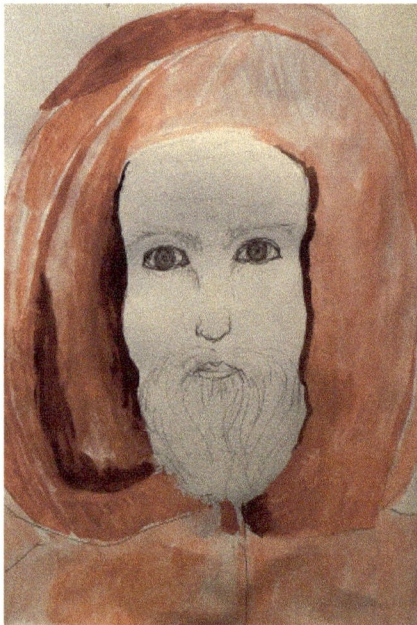

Figure 26. Pearl's Picture of the Unknown Dream Figure

In Pearl's picture of the unknown dream figure who saved her life, we can see that the positive side of the animus is coming to life for her, and in this sense he is both rescuer and rescued. The red of his garment emphasizes his dynamism and his connection to creative life energy. Adding color to the face would indicate a stronger feeling connection to him, but even without color he conveys a certain spiritual beauty. Artist's photo.

Another woman, a creative writer named Chance, had struggled most of her life with a brutal animus that tortured her endlessly with thoughts that something was wrong with her, her life, or her reputation, criticizing and blocking her from realizing her tremendous talent for writing. As this dynamic began slowly to turn to its opposite, she dreamt that a beloved, charismatic, and intimidating writing coach ("X") greeted and acknowledged her lovingly during a writing workshop, even as she panicked about her performance. The encounter was numinous:

I am at a beautiful place at the edge of an ocean with a stony beach. We are gathered in anticipation of a writing conference. We've all been given one assignment in advance. I am working on it, using an old typewriter that is pale green in color and very flat. Tapping away on the keys, time is running out, and I need to get a paragraph done, but oh lord, there's no paper in the typewriter. I'd forgotten to put it in, so used am I to working on a computer.

I find paper and put in a sheet and roll it up, ready to type, but someone else's words appear. I read and reread them—something I wouldn't say or write. I don't recall the words. Don't know why I hesitate so long. Am feeling panicked and in despair. I can't get the writing done in time, just as I missed one assignment in the last writing course I did with X.

Then I see X as though in a perfectly composed photograph. Framed against a radiant blue sky with bright curly white clouds, he appears, his piercing blue, all-seeing eyes gaze out to sea to the left. He's wearing clothes he'd never wear: an expensive tweed jacket not unlike the shabbier versions my father used to wear, or not even that, more like an eccentric disconnected Englishman. [X in real life wears very fashionable elegant clothes.]

It seems to be X, but maybe it's not exactly him. Either way, he's smiling warmly and acknowledges me as well as all the other adoring students who are in awe of him as I am. But he occupies a completely unreal kind of space quite separate from my reality.

The feeling of the dream is: Something wonderful is about to happen.

The feeling of X's warmth was life-affirming for Chance and calmed her anxieties about finding her own words. Working with this dream, when Chance could see that the outer man, the writing instructor, was carrying the projection of the positive, highly creative animus, she could allow herself to experience the attention in the dream as coming from the psychic realm, the inner creative force, and this tempered her need for attention from the outer man. She could feel, at least for a time, that she truly was meant to write and that the psyche wanted her to write: The words that appear on the typewriter come from out of nowhere, that is, from the other side of consciousness. The numinous moment of recognition and the sense that something wonderful was about to happen were related to the development of more strength and confidence in her writing as something that was meant to be.

Chance later had the following dream, which brought into the picture her lifelong connection with African culture (she is White). The dream needs no comment, other than to remind us that the man represents the depths of masculine energy that wants to be integrated as a true partner in creative work, and not projected.

I'm in an old dreary house, a sort of communal space like an art center. I hear African drumming coming through the walls, and it thrills me. There's music in the streets, reggae music, a feeling of joy and life pulsating. I go up to the floor, and a woman is dancing to the music of a couple of drummers, absorbed in moving to the rhythm.

I see an African man I love. He's tall, kingly, assured of his power and appeal, Nigerian, dressed in regalia. I go to him, looking up at his regal head against the sky. He bends down and kisses my open mouth deeply. I'm ecstatic. He tells me he is enjoying this relationship for as long as it lasts. I smile. I know I am the age I am in this dream—old, too old for intimate relationship or to be found attractive by men. I know it isn't going to last long, but it's a memory of joy, my sensuality and delight in life itself.

This is one the most rewarding motifs in women's dreams—that of an originally negative masculine figure has transformed as a result of her psychological opus. After many years of analytic work, Sandra, in her 60s, had a remarkably healing dream about a lover who had haunted her since she was 18. He was 20 years her senior and had abandoned the relationship without a word, leaving Sandra plagued for most of her adult life with the ideation that her great love had found her inadequate and abandoned her. She had worked with many dreams about this man over the years and had this one during an intensive creative project, a musical chronical of her life. She dreamt:

> *I seem to live near my old lover, Henry. One day I find myself going into his house. I didn't mean to but somehow I ended up there. I look around a little bit and call hello, but I really don't want to find him. It is Christmas time, and he has a tree, but it's not decorated. It's a tree with leaves that are dark green on one side and almost glittery light green on the other side, as if the tree had its own way of lighting itself up.*
>
> *In another scene I find myself in Henry's house with a boy. We are playing with honey. The boy is spreading honey on my lower legs and hands. Henry joins us and watches us for a while. Then he brings up an old saying— it is about women and the smell of honey. He is making a sexual comment. I hope he doesn't want to have sex with me because I'm not interested.*
>
> *Another time I'm with Henry, just talking. I look into his eyes, which are very blue, and remember his left eye is lazy. It always seems to be turned a little bit to the left. I had forgotten about this.* [Though in real life he has brown eyes and no lazy eye.] *In this conversation he really seems to want to connect with me. We look into each other's eyes for long periods of time, recognizing each other. His eyes are so deep blue and friendly and curious. At some point we end up just balancing our bodies next to each other or on top of each other, as if we are levitating together.*
>
> *In another part of the dream, I am living across the street from him. One of his friends has given me a birthday card from him that says, "Happy Birthday Forever."*

Sandra said that this version of Henry was different—more relatable, approachable, and less arrogant than he was in outer life. His unusual blue eyes are very different from the brown eyes that he had in outer life. They were more spiritual and yet more feeling, and the left eye always turns left—toward the psychic realm. The appearance of blue in dreams can signal the need or the achievement of a spiritual transformation; in this case, the blue seems to indicate that a transformation had occurred in this animus figure. What was negative in the spiritual realm had become positive, the result of many years of work and a reorientation toward inner development.

The Christmas tree symbolizes new light and new life emerging out of the darkness. This particular tree has leaves that are dark green on one side and glittering or reflective green on the other, unifying light and dark. The honey is an eros substance that comes from nature. Sandra's legs and hands are being covered in this substance by a younger male figure in a way that is sensuous and renewing. The honey is applied as if to define her standing in the world (legs) and her work in the world (hands) as saturated in natural eros. The dream-Henry links the odor of the honey to the *coniunctio*. In the dream, Sandra isn't interested in a union with him on the sexual level, but in the next part of the dream, they seem to be engaged in a union on the spiritual level, gazing into each other's eyes and balancing together in levitation. Sandra felt the experience as a spiritualization of erotic love with no loss of intensity. The levitation can also be seen as indicating the achievement of the *coniunctio* (the goal of the *Rosarium* pictures) on the symbolic level.

The dream overall signals a miraculous transformation of Henry energy from negative and demeaning to positive and supportive. Henry sees Sandra for who she really is and loves her spiritually. We sense the eros development that goes along with this transformation, bringing Sandra and the inner, spiritual Henry together through a genuine alliance that had developed over the years of her intense work with individuation. The birthday message, "Happy Birthday Forever," speaks to the eternal aspect of her birth and her life, living "across the street" from the inner Henry, who had been in the background of her development for more than 40 years.

The New Son

Dreams of sons may signal a development in which a woman, through her relationship to the self, has helped bring about new development in the masculine realm that only she could birth. An example:

> *My son is about 8 years old. I am making a big effort to get*
> *him to feel how much I love him. I hold him in my lap as I sit*
> *on the ground and tell him over and over that I love him. I*
> *am kind of curled around him. I hope he isn't embarrassed,*
> *that he can take it in, really feel it and take it into the world.*
> *I notice that his hair, always blond, is especially shiny and*
> *has orange sparks, blinking off and on like a sparkler.*

This dream tells us that a new spiritual reality has developed in the dreamer, indigenous to her, born of her own psychological flesh. The age of the son in this dream (8 years old) represents the possibility or the presence of a development of wholeness that is highly differentiated (divided into eight parts rather than four). The orange sparks in his blond hair hint at the sparks of light, or divine scintilla, in Mercurius, the spirit of transformation and enlightenment. This is a powerful dream of how a woman may feel intense love for the spirit of the unconscious as it has developed in her—as it only could develop in her, through a relationship with the psychic realm he introduced her to.

While going through a difficult time with her outer son, Sylvia had a dream that depicted him as a handsome young man who had been taking voice lessons and was about to perform in a recital that she was eagerly anticipating. The dream makes a clear distinction between the outer and inner son, helping Sylvia realize that, on the inner level, a new son—a new spirit developing out of the unconscious—had a voice that was ready to be heard.

One of Sandra's dreams gives us another image for a newly formed, newly felt masculine entity that is very closely related to her, even if not by blood.

> *I am in a very large bed, kind of a community bed. I am on*
> *the right side. Across the bed a baby is waking up with his*
> *father. The baby looks at me, and we smile at each other. We*
> *have a clear, strong connection. The father says, "He wants*
> *to hug you." The baby gets out of bed and runs around to*

my side. I pick him up, and we hug. He says to me, "I am Indian." He means, from India.

A baby boy from India symbolically is an Indian spirit, meaning he comes from a spiritual tradition that for at least 5,000 years has recognized the divine reality of the self. There is a strong emotional connection between the woman and the toddler. They are related not by family but via the self, making him the son of her psychic life, a *filius sapientiae*. The birth of a mother's son symbolizes on the deepest level a new spirit, a new image of the divine born out of the feminine realm, the unconscious psyche, redeeming both the feminine principle and the spirit of the unconscious.

9
Eros Resurrection and Redemption

To bring her sisters back to life, the heroine exercises a magical power normally reserved for the gods, reminding us that she is connected to the archetypal realm. The tale makes it clear that she has appropriated the wizard's power and can get him to do whatever she asks, even tricking him into carrying her sisters, hidden a basket stuffed with gold, back to her parents' house. The heroine doesn't return with them but stays at the wizard's house, cleaning and preparing a wedding feast, and then she appears in her wondrous bird costume of honey and feathers.

Psychologically speaking, we've seen that the sisters' resurrection and return to upper life and the appearance of Fitcher's bird in the forest symbolize two levels of redemption. The sisters reappearing at home represent eros that is redeemed in life, when a woman naturally feels a new kind of eros in the way she lives. The appearance of a wondrous bird in the forest represents a concurrent, numinous event in the collective unconscious in which a new feminine reality makes its presence known in territory that was once exclusively masculine. Together, these events fulfill the death and resurrection archetype in the feminine realm, bringing profound religious meaning to the tale.

Redemption through a Confrontation with Darkness

The redemption and resurrection of the feminine principle in "Fitcher's Bird" evolves out of a dark, murderous situation, reminding us how difficult it has been and how long it is taking for eros to make itself known again as a transhuman factor that can renew spiritual life. As the devil in Barbara Hannah's dream suggested, since women are the ones who can deal with the dark side and with evil where eros has been mired, we know how important it is that women participate in this redemption.

But we can also see that darkness itself has a part to play; evil is included in the picture. In the alchemical view that has compensated for the purely masculine pattern of death and resurrection since the early part of the first millennium C.E., the transformation of psychological life by coming to grips with darkness is as much a transcendent event, as legitimate a spiritual experience as any encounter with the light side of the psyche. According to the alchemical view, it is even necessary for human beings to confront their own little corners of evil, because as Jung put it, "Christ's work of redemption was regarded as incomplete":

> Whereas the Christian belief is that man is freed from sin by the redemptory act of Christ, the alchemist was evidently of the opinion that the "restitution to the likeness of original and incorrupt nature" had still to be accomplished by the art, and this can only mean that Christ's work of redemption was regarded as incomplete. In view of the wickednesses which the "Prince of this world," undeterred, goes on perpetrating as liberally as before, one cannot withhold all sympathy from such an opinion. For an alchemist who professed allegiance to the *Ecclesia spiritualis* it was naturally of supreme importance to make himself an "unspotted vessel" of the Paraclete and thus to realize the idea "Christ" on a plane far transcending a mere imitation of him. It is tragic to see how this tremendous thought got bogged down again and again in the welter of human folly.[92]

The restitution of human beings to their original and incorrupt nature in this passage refers to the restoration of individuals to their naturally divine state, in which they can realize what Christ is not by imitating Him, but by going through what He went through. An "unspotted vessel" is not a person who imitates Christ in form but rather a person who suffers through the reality of God's opposites as they appear as a matter of fact in his or her own life and reconciles them to whatever extent is possible.

A woman who, through the analytic art of self-examination, confronts the reality of her shadowy participation with a destructive, judgmental attitude goes through a mortifying experience, as we have

---

[92] Jung, *Mysterium Coniunctionis, CW*, vol. 14, par. 27.

seen. Suffering through the transformation such a discovery induces, she is gradually decontaminated of unconscious opinions, criticism, pleasing, and performances that are not true to her. She is forced to confront the illusions and pretensions that make her in any way false. Imitating Christ or those she admires will not make her more of herself, but bearing her own shadow will. If she were imitating Christ according to the church, she would be attempting the impossible task of eliminating the shadow rather than facing it as a valid, inner reality that helps define who and what she is. Her personal life is the only place where a real redemption can take place because there, she has a chance to reckon with, and indeed to carry, her own burden of archetypal conflict.

The heroine's knowledge of the wizard's two-sidedness—her understanding of the fact that he is a murderer who only seems to promote innocence, increases her power over him. She has seen the side of the wizard that insisted she remain innocent, and she has seen the side that tempted her into the pangs of new knowledge. She doesn't use that power to condemn him, to become one-sided herself, but to redirect him in returning her sisters home. Then, remaining at his house to clean and prepare, she continues working with the tension of the opposites that she has discovered.

The fairy tale presents these two events as occurring in parallel—returning the sisters home and cleaning the wizard's house, enduring the tension. In psychological terms, these are images for the parallel processes of working with the animus shadow and returning eros to life. I find it amazing that the fairy tale links them so clearly. It would mean that as a woman becomes more conscious of her own darkness, eros is being redeemed in a way that changes life. The animus facilitates that redemption when his volition is directed toward individuation.

In a woman, this would mean that she can finally accept the role of the negative animus and the shadow in her individuation. She is constantly facing the darkness of not knowing and the possibility that she may fall into another dark situation herself. But the fact that she knows about this tension and is willing to hold it changes everything. The change in attitude, in which she no longer needs to be constantly identified as innocent or right is by itself a miraculous redemption—an acceptance of the paradoxes of the unconscious in her own life. A woman may finally realize, for example, *Aha! This very suffering that I have been going through all this time, this is exactly the thing that I was born to transform!* In that case, she can protect herself from thoughts that her individuation isn't going fast enough or her suffering isn't being relieved well enough and so on, as her work continues. What seemed irredeemable is redeemed in the very fact that darkness is acceptable, and the lower god—what we always considered a demon—is included rather than excluded.

Such a realization may seem to drop out of the sky as if by magic, but it is actually the result of the ego's persistence over time, honestly confronting the inner struggle with the animus as it has appeared in life. The dismemberment a woman endures in the inexplicable drivenness of her thinking about herself now transforms into a willing endurance of tension between the old god-image that has entrapped the animus and her own individuating inner spirit. Her main goal is not to fall into one side or the other but to understand unconscious drivenness as an innate, transpersonal imperative for transformation. In this way, she transcends an imitation of Christ, bringing into life the capacity to bear the opposites in herself, and making it possible to bring genuine love into life.

A woman's capacity to see the archetypal two-sidedness of the animus depotentiates him of his possessive power—especially his power to make her one-sided, toward herself or anyone else. Her moral compass shifts away from collective ideals about what life is "supposed" to be. She can finally see that what she has been going through is individuation— because she has been tending the very dynamism that life has given her to tend. She is incorrupt not because she has achieved perfection in the eyes of the world but because she is more genuinely herself. Every aspect of this awakening contributes to the eros redemption that the world needs.

The Feminine Needs the Feminine

The resurrected sisters find themselves carried home in the same basket on the same back that carried them away from home. They make sure the journey as instigated by their younger sister is complete and that their parents receive the gold meant for them. In psychological terms, this means that eros development and redemption symbolized by the sisters is now under the auspices of the feminine realm, where the womblike basket belongs symbolically. This is the essential transformation that defines the tale's enantiodromia: Eros is protected by the feminine, and animus energy is redirected accordingly. This is the most vital psychological transformation expressed in the sister-rescue tales, and it is especially emphasized in "Fitcher's Bird."

In a woman, this transformation in which eros is returned home under the auspices of the feminine would mean that eros is protected in a felt relationship with the self and that it can be felt in life. Feeling and relatedness, renewed through a long opus with darkness, are allowed to exist and become visible in personal life. The negative animus has less power to wreak emotional havoc when natural eros is protected this way, when it has regained its spiritual relevance. His destructive tenor is depotentiated. Genuine new feeling has a chance to be felt. A woman's consciousness, in other words, has become more feminine— more reflective and inclusive, more related to the unconscious, and more consciously loving.

At the same time, it would mean that the feminine principle itself has recovered creative and protective powers in the psychic realm. We can observe the thread of this transformation taking place in the work of Sandra. In her dream about daffodils and lilies (p. 123), Sandra saw how her animus thoughts were capable of destroying her relationship with her husband as well as her own feeling for the spiritual growth symbolized by miraculous spring flowers. For years, Sandra continued to hold the tension of her critical thoughts about her husband, some of which could be quite convincing, at times even telling her that she should leave him. But she did not act on those thoughts; she held the tension between a genuine urge to leave and knowing in her heart that her relationship with her husband was meaningful. She did not fall into the destruction of eros. This dream and others helped her see that the real separation being called for was between the negative animus and his projection onto her husband. Still, along the way, the temptation to act out a concrete separation or to blame her husband for her misery at times became almost overpowering. She continued working with her dreams, holding the tension, pouring animus energy and love into her creative work. Eventually, she had the following dream:

Twice this happens: a newborn baby with dark hair is given to her brother and then falls to the floor. The second time it happens, I see that the brother is incapable or unwilling to hold the baby, and so she just slips from his unresponsive body onto the floor. The mother is very concerned and tries as much as she can to comfort the baby. The third time, she gives the newborn to the baby's sister, who wraps her in her large, protective arms. I wonder if it is possible to comfort the baby enough, or if these falls and the experience of being dropped will always haunt her. I am glad to see that in her mother's and then her sister's arms, she is calming down and seems to feel safe.

The dream suggests that new feminine development in the psyche, symbolized by the newborn girl, needs to be held by the feminine if it is to survive. In the dream, even the baby's brother cannot or will not hold on to her. The image indicates that new feeling development must actually be felt, as simple as this may seem. The baby represents a feeling connection to the self or a new development in emotional life. It needs to be held, protected, and carried as a precious new entity, as a mother would protect her daughter.

We had to surmise that Sandra's dream-baby represented eros per se, manifested in the vulnerable form of a newborn, a mystery asking to be held. Sandra took the baby into active imagination, where she continued to hold and care for her. Another dream of a slightly older infant girl appeared several weeks later, and this time the precocious baby could talk, indicating the potential for logos to develop in tandem with this new eros reality, once it was allowed to exist without question, valued as an unknown psychic entity.

Working with these images for a period of time, Sandra was surprised by a new realization. After fantasizing about leaving her husband for years, holding that tension for so long, she suddenly became aware of the fact that her love for him had become as real as it had ever been in their 40-plus years of marriage. Besides this, she also felt another dimension of love that went beyond their personal relationship. She described the experience as washing over her like a wave. Her husband was not the perfect partner for her, according to her worldly, intellectual judgment, but their love was rooted in something so deep in the psyche that it could not be destroyed. Eros for her husband had developed enough strength and scope to encompass the imperfections that her critical thinking would cause her to reject. Her love had developed an eternal dimension, a fact that was presaged by her dream of a man with whom she experienced a "cosmic constellation of love" (p. 118). This dream of being embraced in the eternal dimension brings an image for the penetrating experience of transpersonal eros as a *kosmogonos*; Sandra's experience of her deep psychic connection with her husband meant that such eros was being realized in her lifetime. Sandra's work with the negative animus and the shadow brought about the realization of a comprehensive eros, freed from fossilized ideas of what love is supposed to be. This is another way we can understand how consciousness becomes more feminine, able to accept the love that life offers.

Here we can see the ego's astounding responsibility to recognize and honor eros as an objective phenomenon that needs restitution in consciousness, especially crucial when cast in the balance of collective human development. According to this dream and Sandra's experience, a woman can help, and even *must* help, the Great Mother in the gestation of eros for its own sake, carrying it in the fiber of her being as a mystery that needs help making its way into the world.

In the fairy tale, once the sisters are taken home and the wizard's house is cleaned, the heroine prepares her epiphany as Fitcher's bird. Again, these parallel events help us see that as newly alive eros appears in everyday life, the feminine side of the self builds itself up in the deeper layers of the psyche. Eros becomes more real at both levels. This mutual transformation in personal and objective realms helps us understand how profoundly life may be impacted by one person's individuation process.

The Lost, Scattered, and Re-collected Inner Divinity

Death and resurrection represent the archetype of continuous transformation and renewal, which we clearly observe in nature and which is modeled by gods and goddesses from all ages who die and resurrect, disappear and reappear, or are dismembered and reassembled in a new form. Jung reported that Dionysus "was actually called ὁ ἀμέριςτος καὶ μεμεριομένος νοῦς (the undivided and divided spirit)."[93] The death of Christ on the cross and his resurrection create a later example of the divided and undivided spirit—a spirit that remains whole even as it is dismembered, dies, and renews itself. As psychological images, the dying and resurrecting gods portray the ability of the archetypal realm to transform continuously, dissolving and reforming itself, refreshing itself in itself.[94] Then it wants to bring its newness into reality through consciousness. We are not necessarily aware that the inner transhuman being—the regulating self—is going through a transformation unless we are in relationship with it. In that case, we share and facilitate its transformation.

Jung described the renewal of the god-image as a mutual endeavor between ego and self. He explained how individuation, "the integration or humanization of the self," is "an act of the ego's will," and yet, also a sacrifice of the ego as it comes to terms with its limitations and realizes it is not the captain of its ship after all. The self, too, "demands sacrifice by sacrificing itself," in other words, by giving up its mysteries to consciousness, including the fact that it needs to be made whole.[95] Individuation is initiated by the archetypal realm, yet it requires a partnership with the ego to recollect and manifest aspects of the self that have been lost, unconscious and want to come together in a new way in conscious life.[96]

Aside from the myths of Inanna and of Demeter and Persephone, the motif of recollecting a dismembered or mortified deity survives in the mythology of masculine gods. We find the symbolism in fertility cults, Gnostic creation mythology, Christianity, and alchemy. For example, in Basilides's version of a Gnostic creation myth recounted by Hippolytus, an original, "nonexistent god" is scattered throughout the world in the form of light-seeds.[97] In the human realm, each light-seed is an inner

---

[93] Jung, *Psychology and Alchemy, CW*, vol. 12, par. 91 and note.
[94] "Refreshing itself in itself" is from Eleazar's text, reprinted in sections in Jung, *Mysterium Coniunctionis, CW*, vol. 14, pars. 591, 622, and 624.
[95] Jung, "Transformation Symbolism in the Mass," *CW*, vol. 11, pars. 399–400.
[96] Ibid.
[97] Hippolytus, "Refutation of All Heresies," in Roberts, Donaldson, and Coxe, *The Ante-Nicene Fathers*, 5:100ff.

Christ, born into an individual psyche with the potential to awaken that person to the fact that he or she carries a divine entity in their soul that needs to be united with other aspects of itself.

If people become aware of the inner Christ or Anthropos, they know they carry in themselves an aspect of the godhead (similar to knowing Brahman through *ātman*). The godhead is recollected through human knowledge, or gnosis, of him as an objective spiritual being in the reality of individual human life. Psychologically speaking, these mythologies reflect the fact that we each carry a spark of the self in our being, and all individuals are needed to bring the sparks together in themselves, so that their individuation contributes to a collective realization of the evolving image of the divine that the self is mediating day by day. The new god-image seems to want to bring itself wholly into reality but can only do so individual by individual.

All Things Woven Together

The divided and undivided god became more obviously psychic in early alchemy. In some of the earliest alchemical texts, the Gnostic alchemist Zosimos of Panopolis (ca. 300 C.E.) described his vision of a process through which the immortal inner man is created, at the moment of death or in the process of individuation.[98] In his vision, he witnessed the torture of "men burning and yet alive," their bodies boiled in a crater.[99] He saw them suffering, undergoing the process of mortification, casting off the body as they became spirit, remaining awake for the whole excruciating process. In comparing Zosimos's visions of "unendurable torment" to Christ's sacrifice on the cross, Jung explained that such suffering was not only a projection of the alchemist's personal experience as he worked on the philosophical stone but also the suffering of the stone

---

[98] Zosimos would have been familiar with Egyptian mummification practices, through which the dead body was made immortal. In Egypt, the creation of the inner immortal man was projected into the afterlife. See von Franz, *On Dreams and Death*, and Abt and Hornung, *Knowledge of the Afterlife.*

[99] Jung, "The Visions of Zosimos," *CW*, vol. 13, par. 86, vision 3.6.1, p. 63.

itself, an image for the inner god-man moving from the unconscious into consciousness:[100]

> Zosimos sees himself as a homunculus, or rather the unconscious represents him as such, as an incomplete, stunted, dwarfish creature who is made of some heavy material (lead or bronze) and thus signifies the "hylical man." Such a one is dark, and sunk in materiality. He is essentially unconscious and therefore in need of transformation and enlightenment. For this purpose, his body must be taken apart and dissolved into its constituents, a process known in alchemy as the *divisio, separatio* and *solutio*, and in later treatises as discrimination and self-knowledge. This psychological process is admittedly painful and for many people a positive torture. But, as always every step forward along the path of individuation is achieved only at the cost of suffering.[101]

The homunculus is another image for the Anthropos or inner Christ of the Gnostics. At first, suffering in the unconscious, he is not a heavenly god but a leaden one, that is, unconscious and unredeemed within the human psyche—invisible to those who don't yet have the eyes to see. He represents the lower, dark half of the divine, the "hylical man" who is "sunk in materiality," rejected by a worldview that cannot accept a god that is innate to the reality of a human being, a lower divinity whose connection to matter makes him suspicious. Such a god therefore remains dark from the perspective of a one-sided, spiritual worldview, as we saw in Birkhäuser's *The Outcast* (fig. 15). He suffers in the unconscious of humanity, but his constant goading of our certainty seems to indicate that he wants to be reconnected with the upper, spiritual domain that we consciously identify as God. We have no idea how the inner divinity suffers from its split condition except when this suffering enters our personal lives.

Through *divisio, separatio,* and *solutio,* the inner god-man may become known, but the unconscious human being suffers too in this

---

[100] Ibid., vision 3.1.2, p. 60.
[101] Jung, "Transformation Symbolism in the Mass," *CW*, vol. 11, par. 411.

transformation, most likely unaware that his or her suffering is linked to the inner divinity. The torture intensifies so long as a person is ignorant of or continues to reject the existence of the inner god-image or its dark aspect, as we have been exploring in terms of the negative animus. The ego's certainty about the world is broken down as it realizes it is suffering because its own divinity is suffering in unconsciousness; the conscious and unconscious worlds really are intermingled. In a poignant, well-known passage, Zosimos described the mutual transformation between the human and divine realms as one that is mirrored in nature down to the minutiae:

> And all things are woven together and all things are undone again; all things are mingled together and all things combine; and all things unite and all things separate; all things are moistened and all things are dried; and all things flourish and all things fade in the bowl of the altar. . . . The weaving together of all things and the undoing of all things and the whole fabric of things cannot come to pass without method. . . . For nature applied to nature transforms nature. Such is the order of natural law throughout the whole cosmos, and thus all things hang together.[102]

The way that "all things are woven together and all things are undone again" analogizes the woven reality of spirit and matter—consciousness and the unconscious—and how they need each other in the process of renewal. The details of the process seem to be impossible to fully describe, except that they follow nature's principles of transformation—which, Zosimos sees, are themselves divine.

As the ego comes to terms with this struggle, accepting that the development of consciousness is not entirely an experience of bliss, its own role as handmaiden to the divine realm becomes more fully apparent. Human consciousness is needed as the medium through which the god-image dissolves and is recollected, as we saw with Jesus Christ and Mary Magdalene. Without becoming integrated into the conscious realm—into the way we live our lives—the transformation of the divine cannot be

---

[102] Jung, "The Visions of Zosimos," *CW*, vol. 13, par. 87, vision 3.1.4, pp. 64–65.

completed. Felt consciousness, or conscious eros, is needed to make the new god-image real, to bring it into the matter of life.

Organic, Collective Eros

In *Projection and Recollection in Jungian Psychology,* von Franz discussed the psychological significance of Stoic, Gnostic, and alchemical mythologies in which a god descends into human life in the form of dissipated sparks, seeds, or light or in the image of a human being and wants to be recollected and made whole again through the individual-by-individual realization of its presence. A natural result of this realization, a kind of byproduct of individuals consciously participating in such a recollection, is that they develop a deeper feeling connection with each other. Von Franz said,

> The mythologems . . . depict a process of re-collecting that proceeds from the god-man or the light-man or some similar Anthropos-Redeemer figure and that unites the many single human souls into a unity, that is, into a genuine community. Therefore not only does the individual becomes a whole in himself but a community comes into being that also represents a whole. In antiquity this whole was called the Anthropos. Psychologically it means that an organically united community becomes visible. A group of human beings of this kind is not organized by laws or by the instruments of power; to the extent that each individual relates to the self in himself he will quite naturally assume his rightful place in a social order of a psychological kind.[103]

An "organically united community" is one based on a unifying relationship to the shared soul—in other words, a community oriented around the realization of the self, in which each individual has a sacred role that is all his or her own, and yet is part of a collective effort. We saw an example of such a reality in Elise's dream of the religious center built

---

[103] Von Franz, *Projection and Recollection in Jungian Psychology,* 172. Von Franz provides an excellent summary of Gnostic and alchemical ideas of how the original god-man is distributed throughout humanity and seeks to be recollected in consciousness.

like a mandala into the backside of a mountain. The center was oriented around her own personal myth, and it united feminine and masculine, nature and spirit, in a new symbol of God to which everyone in the community contributed.

The Redemptive Power of the "Lower" Divinity

In the *Visions* seminars, Jung discussed another aspect of the rejected lower god as it appears in the symbolism of the frog in the fairy tale "The Golden Ball."[104] Here he helps us see that in rejecting the hylical man, we reject the wholeness of the divine, and in rejecting the wholeness of the divine, we reject ourselves as we are, a mix of dark and light. We remain identified with a god that we think is only light.

> But the frog, symbolizing man as he is, can only obtain to the dignity of a healing symbol when it is compensatory; that is, when it meets an audience, an individual or a public, that identifies with the superior man within. For if we, in the form of frogs, identify with that beautiful Prince Charming, we necessarily suffer from inflation, and then we are one-sided and unnatural, because we cannot possibly be that superior man. We know how Nietzsche tried to be, and he overdid it altogether and was threatened with the ugliest man; that is the reason why he broke down, and the reason why we break down when we assume a quality which is not ours. Therefore, it is redeeming or healing for us to accept ourselves as we are, instead of always wanting things to be different. We say: he would be very nice if only he were not so in so, or: I could really except myself if I were not what I am. . . . But wisdom begins only when one takes things as they are; otherwise we get nowhere, we simply become inflated balloons with no feet on the earth. So it is a healing attitude when we can agree with the facts as they are; only

---

[104] Jung, *Visions*, 532ff. Also see Jung's discussion of the two Adams (the primitive man and the original man) in Eleazar's text, in Jung, *Mysterium Coniunctionis, CW*, vol. 14, par. 596ff.

then can we live in our body on this earth, only then can we thrive. . . . Just the thing that is ugly and repulsive is the thing that leads to redemption, just as the princess got her Prince Charming out of the skin of the frog.[105]

Human history, including certain horrors of the current day, shows us the evil that is done when we are "inflated balloons with no feet on the earth," unable to see our unconsciousness, or the shadow of our god-image. According to "The Golden Ball," as well as "Fitcher's Bird," what we originally consider repulsive can lead to redemption when we own it as our other half. What repulses us the most in others likely is a projection of our own unconsciousness. We saw this in Lucy's dream of the repulsive man who suddenly appeared in her bed and shocked her into realizing that he was the spirit behind her creative work. Pearl's gorilla is another example of how a less desirable figure may seem repellent but have a redeeming function when we can relate to him. The frog, the drug addict, the outcast, the gorilla, and the wizard are all images for the "lower" aspect of wholeness. Von Franz pointed out that the frog also represents the "vital impulse" of the unconscious itself, including its desire to be realized as the source of consciousness.[106]

I had a dream many years ago that offers another view of the frog as a redeeming symbol from the lower world. In this case, the frog represented a genuine condition of humility in the face of nature. I was camping in a Wyoming wilderness area when I dreamt of a tree frog:

> I see a glowing, bright green tree frog sitting on a narrow willow twig near my campsite. The frog is pregnant with a human baby, which is gestating in the tip of its right thumb. I can see the fetus growing inside the frog's translucent thumb-womb, and I know that when this child is born, it will become the savior of humanity.

The frog in my dream was not ugly and repulsive but quite beautiful, and vulnerable because it was so delicate. For me, the tree frog had a special meaning as a species whose decline in population should

---

[105] Jung, *Visions*, 545, emphasis mine.
[106] Von Franz, *The Feminine in Fairy Tales*, 22. It is said that von Franz, who loved frogs, died with a jade frog figurine in her hand.

awaken us to the effect of our arrogance toward nature and our willful ignorance of how, as Zosimos said, "all things are mingled together and all things combine"[107] in nature and in the psyche. The dream implies that the child of the frog could be an Anthropos—an original human being imbued with such awareness, born from the lowly perspective of the frog, so that our lost interconnectedness with nature would be infused into the consciousness of humanity once again, integrated as a holy imperative. Inborn consciousness of our humble place, our froglike dependence on nature, would contribute to a new god-image that could save us from the demise resulting from our own hubris. In this case, the inner god-image is miraculously half frog, half human, carrying in its essence the wisdom of nature, as the alchemists saw in Mercurius.[108]

I felt, too, that the world-saving child born from this frog was somehow related to my love for the man I was camping with—the man who later became my husband. The dream supported my intuition that my love for him was important, not just on a personal level. Our experience of personal love helps us know that what saves the world is our *feeling* for how all things are woven together. Our mere knowledge of this fact so far has not saved us. Through feeling, valuing our connection with nature and the unconscious, we may also realize how the objective psyche is the weaving.

Recollecting the Divine Feminine

The maidens in the beginning of "Fitcher's Bird" are abducted and dismembered before they can enter life in any effective, mature way. Their demise takes place at the wizard's house in the forest, which of course symbolizes the collective unconscious. This means that the dismembered sisters, like the Gnostic Christ or the men burning yet alive in Zosimos's vision, represent psychic figures suffering through a transformation, their suffering exacerbated by the fact that they are unseen, lost in the unconscious. The fact that they are feminine makes them even less visible to collective consciousness than the masculine devil.

---

[107] Jung, "The Visions of Zosimos," *CW*, vol. 13, par. 87, vision 3.1.4, pp. 64–65.

[108] My thanks to Gotthilf Isler for his insights regarding this dream.

The suffering of the feminine principle on such a deep level is expressed in the words of a Shulamite in an alchemical text by Abraham Eleazar:

> For Noah must wash me in the deepest sea, with pain and toil, that my blackness may depart; I must lie here in the deserts among many serpents, and there is none to pity me; I must be fixed to this black cross, and must be cleansed therefrom with wretchedness and vinegar and made white, that the inwards of my head may be like the sun or Marez, and my heart may shine like a carbuncle, and the old Adam come forth again from me.[109]

This text seems to be a first-person expression of the anima in a man as she suffers to become known to him as an inner divinity—describing what it would be like to be rescued from nonexistence. She suffers in deep, dark unconsciousness—until, she says, "the inwards of my head may be like the sun or Marez, and my heart may shine like a carbuncle." When her head and heart shine with light, this is an indication that finally she has been realized as a divine factor. The "old" or original Adam (not the Adam of the Fall) that may come forth from her is another image for the Anthropos; this is a clue that the Shulamite is an image for the unconscious condition of the feminine side of the psyche, which has existed since creation but has been denied for the last two millennia. This passage gives us a profound expression of how the inner divine feminine, for which the collective unconscious is one image, suffers to be known as the source of consciousness, She Who Gives Birth to God.

We can see how important it could be for a woman to realize that she is participating in the resurrection of the scattered, divine feminine that for so long has endured being invisible. But a woman identified with a conventional animus, a worn-out way of thinking about the divine, will find it as shocking and difficult to grasp as any man that the psyche

---

[109] Quoted in Jung, *Mysterium Coniunctionis, CW*, vol. 14, par. 591. Edward Edinger discusses this text in *The Mysterium Lectures,* chapter 21.

itself is a divine phenomenon, and even a feminine one, and further, that it is seeking realization in the intimate details of her own personal life.[110]

Mother-Daughter Renewal

The myth of Demeter and Persephone expresses a feminine version of the death and resurrection archetype, told as disappearance and return. Persephone's abduction by Hades into the underworld symbolically is identical to a death, especially as her mother experiences it. Perhaps the myth's most enduring motif is Demeter's intense mourning for her daughter after she vanishes. She is motivated by fierce love for Persephone as she endures multiple misfortunes roaming across the world, searching for her daughter and imploring the other gods for help. Her agony and her love for her daughter are so ferocious, she neglects her role as fertility mother. Nature cannot renew herself on earth, and human beings cannot not be fed. Finally, Zeus intercedes, tasking Hermes with bringing Persephone back to the upper world. Because Persephone has eaten even as much as a pomegranate seed while in Hades's realm, she will have to return to him for half of every year. But while she is with her mother, Demeter's joy brings light and fertility back to the human realm.

Persephone returns to the upper world a changed woman. She has become a queen with intimate knowledge of the underworld, of darkness. She is no longer naïve but has been initiated into the mysteries of life, death, renewal, and sexuality—apparently the fundamental elements of the Eleusinian mysteries that induced profound experiences of renewal in those who attended the secret rites.[111] The myth conveys the powerful yearning of the feminine to know and renew herself from one generation to the next through dissolution and recollection; the Kore, too, is a divided and undivided spirit.

---

[110] In *Aurora consurgens,* sometimes attributed to Thomas Aquinas, the author describes his earth-shattering encounter with the anima, the inner divine feminine. In this seminal text we see how the feminine side of the psyche, in which we would include the fact of its intrusive reality, is nearly impossible for a Christian man to acknowledge without an alchemical perspective.

[111] See Kerényi, *Eleusis,* and Foley, *The Homeric Hymn to Demeter.*

In the Greek world, people participated in the goddesses' renewal through rite and ritual and reflected on the presence of divine feminine renewal as a matter of course. The interrelatedness between the archetypal feminine and the life of human beings was sanctioned and celebrated—something we can hardly imagine these days. In "Psychological Aspects of the Kore," Jung imagined a woman's experience of the renewal of the transpersonal feminine in an especially beautiful passage:

> Demeter and Kore, mother and daughter, extend the feminine consciousness both upwards and downwards. . . . We could therefore say that every mother contains her daughter in herself and every daughter her mother, and that every woman extends backwards into her mother and forwards into her daughter. This participation and intermingling give rise to that peculiar uncertainty as regards time: a woman lives earlier as a mother, later as a daughter. The conscious experience of these ties produces the feeling that her life is spread out over generations—the first step towards the immediate experience and conviction of being outside time, which brings with it a feeling of immortality. The individual's life is elevated into a type, indeed it becomes the archetype of woman's fate in general. This leads to a restoration or apocatastasis of the lives of her ancestors, who now, through the bridge of the momentary individual, pass down into the generations of the future. An experience of this kind gives the individual a place and a meaning in the life of the generations, so that all unnecessary obstacles are cleared out of the way of the life-stream that is to flow through her. At the same time the individual is rescued from her isolation and restored to wholeness.[112]

Through the mother-daughter archetype, a woman may find a sense of her own immediate meaning, participating in the sacred unfolding of life. A mother through her daughter feels that she has joined a long line

---

[112] Jung, "The Psychological Aspects of the Kore," *CW*, vol. 9i, par. 316. In this essay Jung provides several examples of the mother and the Kore symbols as they appear in the dreams of women and men.

of mothers and daughters, going back to the beginning of time, each generation born with the potential (even the literal ovaries) that she will pass on to her daughter. Less obvious is how a daughter may renew her mother, but this also happens when we honor the mother-daughter archetype in our psychological work.

We see in the myth that there is an intense closeness between mother and daughter that endures through a difficult separation. The emotional and psychological closeness remains constant, even though development requires that mother and daughter be differentiated. Symbolically, mother and daughter renew each other, but they do so by separating from each other and then reuniting; they divide and yet remain undivided. The paradox is key to a woman's individuation. It may seem impossible for a woman to break a psychological identification with her mother (or her mother complex), but the myth depicts the painful separation as a necessary evil, even requiring an abduction by the masculine that forces the daughter to go her own way. The masculine function of discernment is needed for a woman to differentiate herself from her mother psychologically, and to understand what is being asked of her in helping release the psyche from old patterns.

When a woman dreams of her mother or her daughter, she dreams of herself, as she has experienced herself in her mother or in her daughter. In her mother, she sees her own, old way of relating, and in her daughter, she sees a potential new kind of relatedness. Her dreams help her differentiate eros from what it has been in her life, identified with old mother patterns, and to imagine eros as it could be born in a new way. On an objective level, such dreams inform her how the feminine side of the self is dying to the old way and coming to life in its own new way—how the future of the feminine principle is trying to develop in her life.

Eros Renewal in Women's Dreams

The myth of Demeter and Persephone is a mother-daughter story that expresses eros development from one generation to the next, just as the Christian myth is a father-son story that expresses logos development from one generation to the next. Both myths describe renewal through a disappearance and return, even though, as von Franz pointed out, the feminine version has "nowhere been carried through and made a religious event."[113] However, women's dreams continue to document and carry forward the myth's phenomenal aims.

The following dream from Sandra depicts mother-daughter separation and reconnection on a highly emotional level, ranging from sorrow to joy. She had this dream while in a depression that had gone on too long:

> My daughter has died, and I am devastated. Her body is laid out in a dark tomb. I am in the tomb with her, saying a final goodbye and feeling impossibly sad. She lies on a bier of sorts, covered with a cloth, and some of her belongings are with her, some of them up high on a shelf above her. I take a final look around and then leave the tomb. But when I shut the door, I hear things in the tomb falling down, as if there has been a little earthquake. It will be fine, I tell myself; everything is going to be blended together in the end. But at the last minute, I decide to go back and make sure that her body is undisturbed. I feel in the dark for her and then sense that I must hug her one last time. As I do this, she begins to move. Then, we are hugging each other, and I am amazed. Is she really coming back to life? I say her name and ask her if she is there. She says, "Mama, I can't hear you." I know that she means she is still so far away in another dimension that she can't quite hear my voice in this world. But I feel her face so close to mine, and her voice though far away wrenches my heart. I hope I can help her feel my presence so she will be able to come all the way back to life.

Sandra awoke from this dream in a state of awe. It had taken her through the acute sorrow she would feel if her daughter in outer life were to die, and then the wonder of bringing her miraculously back to life. She had worked long enough with her dreams to realize that her dream-daughter represented future feminine development and that this was a dream from the archetypal realm. The dream moved her to feel as

---

[113] Von Franz, *The Feminine in Fairy Tales*, 21.

much unconditional love for that development as she felt for her real-life daughter.

We realized that the "little earthquake" that shook the tomb and piqued Sandra's concern was a gesture from Earth herself—we could even say from Demeter. The rumble brought Sandra back to her dream-daughter to check on her, and then embrace her, and hopefully bring her "all the way back to life." It seems that the Earth Mother and Sandra both participated in this miracle, sharing an interest in the daughter's reawakening. The daughter, too, had to work hard to hear her mother and will herself back to life. Symbolically, the dream brought Sandra a numinous encounter with the world-renewing Kore and helped her feel how she might help in that renewal by realizing the suffering taking place deep in the unconscious as her own.

This dream reminds us how the archetypal world needs the individual to participate in its renewal. Sandra's dream-ego can enter the darkness, the tomb where developing psychic eros lies as if dead, perhaps in a suffering like that of the Shulamite in Eleazar's text that is so deep it can hardly be felt, either in the world or in Sandra's own depression. Apparently, the psyche needs Sandra to feel the tragedy of the potential loss of eros in a deeply personal way. At the same time, the dream had a collective aim, expressing the emergency in the transpersonal realm, desperately longing for archetypal eros to be felt and thus redeemed. This dream shocked Sandra out of the self-indulgence of her depression and helped her realize that she and the self—the developing feminine—were suffering through a renewal together. She saw, too, that the meaning of her life had something to do with helping in this renewal.

In another mother-daughter dream, a woman described the following scene:

I dream that I am dreaming. In the inner dream, my daughter (about age 4) and I are praying together. We begin one of our prayers with, "O, God the Father who art in heaven," and my daughter adds without hesitation, "and God the Mother who art in heaven," to make sure we address both.

This woman reported that when her daughter was very young, they would pray together. Her daughter had a natural curiosity about religion even though they didn't attend any religious services, and at age 4, during one of these prayer sessions, she asked out of the blue, "Who is God's mother?" In the dream, she is naturally referring to "God the Mother" as a simple and obvious matter of fact. The dream-daughter says this in a dream within a dream, in other words, from a deep consciousness that lies within the unconscious. There, the inner daughter—age 4 representing a constellation of wholeness—naturally knows that God not only *has* a mother but also *is* a mother.

A woman named Sue had a lifelong difficult relationship with her mother, who may have been forced to marry her father when she became pregnant in England in the 1940s. Her parents moved to the United States, and her mother endured what seemed to be a loveless, authoritarian marriage to a man who never really acknowledged her or Sue. From childhood, Sue wanted to become a medical doctor, but her father refused to take her interests seriously, and her mother did not have the strength to advocate for her. Sue lived with a bitter, resentful animus much of her life; he was masterful at keeping an eros experience of the self just out of reach, in life and in the most profound dreams. But finally, Sue had the following dream of her mother and a man she suspected might be her biological father:

> My mother and a young British soldier are sitting at a round
> table. He is handsome and has fair hair. He is looking intently
> at my mother across the table with love and admiration. A
> glowing gold light, as if in a tube, encircles them, at heart
> level. I am standing behind my mother, outside the ring of light,
> looking at the young soldier. I am moved by this tender scene.

The ring of gold light provides a protective circle around the couple and suggests that finally a healing connection between the opposites may become manifested in Sue. She stands outside the circle looking in, which would mean that she has an objective view of the opposites inside the mandala, united through love. In an active imagination, Sue as a young girl popped herself under the light so she could be with the couple and feel the warmth of love between them. It is an impulse through which she might have an experience of eros as it exists between the psychic opposites now, after they had existed so long in bitter acrimony. Sue could even feel the uniting love subjectively, finally, as something that was developing in her. On the objective level as well, the dream might indicate a healing experience resonating toward the soul of Sue's mother in the afterlife. Another way to understand this kind of redemption is to think of it as karmic healing, that is, healing of ancestral wounds through the timelessness of the objective psyche.

Pearl had a touching dream that revealed how she experienced the mother-daughter model in analysis, through a self transference—a projection of the self onto me. She dreamt that she came to my home, where in outer life we held our analytic sessions. The house in her dream was not quite the same as the actual one, which means it represented the place where her inner analytic life was taking shape.

It's Thanksgiving Day. I'm in Laurel's home, about to have a session. She agreed to schedule a session with me on Thanksgiving (ha!?). In the dream, she was a woman who escaped a domestic violence relationship—long time past. So she was living in a safe and beautiful home that her perpetrator/ex-husband did not know about. It was springtime in the dream, and there was a lot of warmth and natural light coming in through the windows. I felt happy to be there.

I arrived 15 minutes before my session, and she had just finished cooking the Thanksgiving meal. All of her friends were at the table, a bunch of earthy men and women. She invited me to sit down with everyone and eat. When the meal was over, we went to have my session. I also met her daughter afterward. She had curly blond hair. She was so grateful that Laurel got out of the violent relationship with her husband—the daughter's father—when she was young; she felt like it was for her. She was taking a shower when I left.

In this dream, "Laurel," Pearl's inner analyst, had escaped the negative animus, culminating in a celebratory, springtime expression of thanksgiving, a sharing of gratitude at the time of year when new life is emerging in nature. New eros development is symbolized by the daughter of her inner analyst; she is grateful for her relative freedom from animus torture, thanks to the work of her mother. In other words, Pearl in the dream has a vicarious experience of the freedom and gratitude that result from a mother-daughter development (eros development) achieved through an encounter with the negative side of the animus.

In this layering of mother-daughter/analyst-analysand trans-formation, we have an image for what Jung described as extending feminine consciousness both upward and downward, or between the generations. The daughter (an image for the Kore archetype) is healed through her mother's healing. The daughter is showering, that is, being cleansed and renewed in the waters of the psyche—indicating an ongoing renewal on her own terms. The Kore is renewed by the mother and vice versa, or as Jung said, "Every woman extends backwards into her mother and forwards into her daughter."[114]

Figure 27. Pearl's Wise Woman

Pearl's wise woman appeared to her in an active imagination, in a bright green room she discovered inside a tree years ago. She regularly advises Pearl to this day. Artist's photo.

---

[114] Jung, "The Psychological Aspects of the Kore," *CW*, vol. 9i, par. 316.

In a way, the dream maps out Pearl's current and future development, perhaps hinting at the possibility that she may one day become an analyst. The dream-ego has an experience of what it might be like to live without an animus threat and how that freedom would make way for further generations of development in her own life. This dream helps us see how archetypal eros development may take shape when both analyst and analysand are women and when the self is constellated between them rather than the animus—how psychic renewal may pass from analyst to analysand via the mother-daughter archetype. We also sense how the feminine archetype itself is healed through a woman's understanding that she is participating in an archetypal renewal.

About two years after this dream, Pearl did an active imagination in which she found a staircase inside a tree, descended the stairs, and discovered a wonderful, underground green room filled with light and plants. The room was occupied by a wise woman, who has since advised Pearl on numerous occasions (fig. 27). Her green room has become her own container, a kind of egglike space, where she engages the unconscious on a regular basis.

The Stone and the Widow

After I gave a talk about animus and anima for a small public class, I received a call from one of the participants, Marta, a woman in her 80s, asking if she could enter analysis with me. She said that during the class, she felt a realization wash over her that she had been dealing with the negative animus her whole life and that probably she had inherited it from her mother. Now, she said, she absolutely must understand this influence in her life! She was also a devoted student of Jungian psychology and had been in Jungian-oriented therapy years ago. Right away, her dreams seemed to indicate that her work with the negative side of the animus could help redeem something in herself but also in her deceased mother in one direction and her daughter in the other.

After working diligently in analysis for about two years, Marta had the following dream:

A necklace has been found at a Denver high school where there is a high tower. It had been lost for many years and has been authenticated as belonging to Mary Lincoln (widow of President Abraham Lincoln). It is still in the tower where it was found, but persons are coming in the morning to remove it for further authentication and donation to a museum. A colleague and I volunteer to stand guard that night before the transfer occurs.

After everyone leaves, I become the instigator of a plan. I suggest that maybe we should go upstairs to the tower and see the necklace. We do, although we know this could bring a heavy penalty if we were discovered. We open the package and take out the necklace. It consists of small pearls strung together in several ball-shaped clusters; the balls of pearls are distributed on a gold chain. We put it away and think nothing more will happen and go downstairs.

Our boss comes in early in the morning before the transfer to the museum. Somehow she has guessed what we have done and asks us if we looked at the necklace. I say, cleverly, "We've got time. Do you want to see it?" She says she does, and then I know it will be all right because she will be in on the crime. We are getting up the third flight of stairs when I wake up.

Marta's association with Mary Lincoln began with the fact that she, like Marta, was a widow. Mary Lincoln was not just any widow, but the widow of a president, which in the United States is as close to royalty as we get, so Mrs. Lincoln is an image for the feminine side of a royal or dominant collective attitude, which Marta identified as supporting individual liberty. Mrs. Lincoln symbolized the feeling side of that attitude, the ability to value liberty. On a psychological level, Mrs. Lincoln represented Marta's inner capacity to liberate herself, her own value out of the unconscious, and to recognize the collective level of that experience.

The pearls in the dream-necklace reminded Marta of the parable of the merchant who sold all he had in order to buy "one pearl of great price" (Matthew 13:45–46), comparing such a pearl to a soul that is pure enough to enter the kingdom of heaven. In alchemy, the pearl of great price corresponds to the *lapis philosophorum,* which is sometimes called an orphan or a widow to emphasize its incomparable value. Whereas the pearl represents purity in the biblical parable, in alchemy it represents the high value of a realized, individual relationship with the self. Jung explained:

> The aim of the great religions is expressed in the injunction "not of this world," and this implies the inward movement of libido into the unconscious. Its withdrawal and introversion create in the unconscious a concentration of libido which is symbolized as the "treasure," as in the parables of the "pearl of great price" and the "treasure in the field." Eckhart interprets the latter as follows: "Christ says, 'The kingdom of heaven is like a treasure hid in a field.' This field is the soul, wherein lies hidden the treasure of the divine kingdom. In the soul, therefore, are God and all creatures blessed."
>
> This interpretation agrees with our psychological argument: the soul is a personification of the unconscious, where lies the treasure, the libido which is immersed in introversion and is allegorized as God's kingdom. This amounts to a permanent union with God, a living in his kingdom, in that state where a preponderance of libido lies in the unconscious and determines conscious life. The libido concentrated in the unconscious was formerly invested in objects, and this made the world seem all-powerful. God was then "outside," but now he works from within, "as the hidden treasure conceived as God's kingdom." If, then, Eckhart reaches the conclusion that the soul is itself God's kingdom, it is conceived as a function of relation to God, and God would be the power working within the soul and perceived by it. Eckhart even calls the soul the *image of God.*[115]

That Jung referred to the soul as "a personification of the unconscious" helps us see the depth of his religious attitude toward the unconscious. The pearl, jewel, or *lapis* may be discovered in the

---

[115] Jung, *Psychological Types, CW,* vol. 6, par. 423.

unconscious as a "concentration of libido"—life energy that no longer remains projected onto the outside world, not even onto an outer god. In other words, the pearl represents the inner realization of the self, and conveys the high value of our individuality in that realization, in a felt connection to the eternal. The incomparable beauty of the pearl helps us imagine the precious eros quality of each unique, transpersonal relationship with the self.

For Marta, as for many women, actually feeling the value of the inner pearl is the single most fundamental challenge in the process of individuation. Her willingness in her dream to break the rules in order to closely examine the expensive necklace is an indication that her heart was unapologetically in the right place; wanting to see the pearl necklace firsthand was easily more important than the dream-boss' rules. To Marta's surprise, her role as the instigator of a crime did not cause her the slightest bit of guilt, in the dream or while talking about the dream; this was a sign that the self had moved further into the center of her personality, prioritizing individuality over innocence. Marta had embraced the crime of individuation.

Marta's dreams at this time were boosting her awareness for how she and the self could treasure each other, but as we discussed this possibility, Marta realized that the idea of her own soul being treasured was new for her. As a child, she did not feel overtly valued by her rather stoic parents, and she had really never allowed herself to consider that she could or should feel treasured. Synchronistically, just before she had this dream, she was recognized in public by two people she didn't know but who knew her reputation as a medical professional who had worked in Colorado her whole life and broke ground as a female leader in her field. After these encounters, Marta realized that her work was valued and respected beyond her expectations or her knowledge. This experience, combined with the notion and the feeling that the self also saw and treasured her, brought rare tears to her eyes.

The pearls strung together in the dream-necklace may represent many moments of experiencing the preciousness of the self—moments strung together to constellate a whole, enduring realization of its high value, a testament to Marta's long study over her lifetime trying to understand the phenomenology of the divine.

I suspected, too, that Marta's dreams were preparing her for death—not necessarily an imminent death, but the fact of death, including its potential to link her soul with eternity. In that case, her ability to take in the meaning and transpersonal value of her individuality, symbolized by widowhood in her dream, is paramount. Marta was not a sentimental woman and didn't have any illusions about her mortality. But this dream gave her an experience of the psyche that helped her accept and feel in her bones the archetypal dimension of her life—to realize something eternal in herself in a way that felt organic to her. Marta expressed to me how tragic it is when someone like Mrs. Lincoln, who lived such a difficult life (losing both a son and a husband), never felt the inner value of her struggles but forever complained about how unfair life was for her. Marta and I knew that as the guardian of a highly prized soul-image, she herself had overcome the danger of that kind of bitterness lingering in her life.

Eros and the Stone

I had the following dream while working on the symbolism of the egg, suggesting how the egg is also an image for the alchemical stone, or *lapis*:

> *I see a large egg held in a suspended nest of fabric, slowly coming into reality. Large hands polish it with a cloth, as if it were a gem. As it is polished, slowly turned and rubbed, cared for in the air, or in the sky, the egg becomes fully formed and revealed. It becomes more and more real and solid as the care continues.*

The goal of the work in this dream is to bring the egg into reality, through devoted care and loving contact. It is important in this dream that the egg is, on the one hand, suspended in air and, on the other hand, becoming more and more real through care and contact with human hands.[116] The egg-stone is being realized "up" in the symbolic realm, that is, as a living psychic reality. Ultimately, this is the goal of individuation— the gradual manifestation of the objective, eternal stone of the personality as a tangible reality, cared for as a symbolic treasure.

---

[116] See Abt's discussion of Ibn Umail's egg that "travels around the whole world" in *Book of the Explanation of Symbols*, 227.

Discerning the Genuine Stone

An important turning point in Sylvia's work was marked by a dream about precious stones. (Sylvia is the woman abused by both parents). However, in this case, the dream emphasized a need for discernment regarding a stone's genuine value:

My mother and father have given me a beautiful diamond ring. The setting is elaborate, with many small diamonds arranged around a central larger diamond. I am wearing the ring when all the stones fall out of the setting. I scramble to try to pick them up and know I have lost some. Even as I'm picking them up, I keep dropping them. I tell Mother and Dad about this and explain that I plan to have the stones reset. Dad says, "Oh, don't worry about that—the stones are not worth that much." It slowly dawns on me that the stones are not real diamonds. I am stunned by this news and feel betrayed by my parents.

With this dream, Sylvia understood in a new way that the eternal stone of the soul, the stone of highest value, was not and could not be bestowed by her personal parents. Rather, the stone of the soul is brought slowly into reality through living the symbolic dimension of life, as she was really living it. In contrast, her parents had taught her to value the elusive, ideal life that she had been clinging to in fantasy. It was important for Sylvia in this moment to feel the fact that her personal parents and their values were not the source of her individuality. She was being reparented according to a different value system in which the real diamond of her individuality was bestowed via the psyche.

From Death to Life

Sylvia recorded a dream and an extended piece of writing as she went through a profound development in her eros connection with the self. The dream came toward the end of an intense depression, which Sylvia bravely faced but which nearly brought her to a breaking point in her relationship with her longtime partner. We can see in this dream and in Sylvia's devoted work with it over time how the inner divine feminine itself is dying and coming to life, connecting Sylvia to their mutual experience in a meaningful way. The dream begins:

I am dancing and singing and cavorting with a woman. We are being overly silly. We embrace in the dance. I realize suddenly that she has become a decomposing corpse. I am holding her increasingly weightless form as it becomes skeletal. The silliness and joy have gone out of the moment, and I am left with a bundle of bones and cloth.

Sylvia took the dream into active imagination, and the imagery continued:

In my imagination, I solemnly carry this bundle away from the dance floor. I don't want anyone else to touch her. She is mine—mine to mourn and to honor and to bury. I want to sing over the bones. If I could sing them into rebirth, what form would that new life take? Then I see her dancing again, this time in ceremony. There is still joy, but the silliness has been replaced with a sense of the sacred.

We can sense the courage and emotion in this active imagination, as well as how much Sylvia is related to the imagery and the tenor of the dream. She wonders about "singing [the bones] into rebirth," and immediately the dead woman is alive again and dancing, the initial "silliness . . . replaced with a sense of the sacred." Sylvia and the dream-woman have entered the sacred atmosphere of the true imagination, the container in which new psychic life can become manifest, even out of a deathlike experience. Symbolic life came alive through Sylvia's encounter with the imaginal world and her honest grappling with her life as it was.

The resurrection in this active imagination, after burying the body and singing over the bones, is reminiscent of the fairy tale "The Juniper Tree." In this tale, a boy is killed by his jealous stepmother, who cooks him in a stew and feeds him to his unwitting father. His half sister—whose name, Marlinchen, connects her to Mary Magdalene—gathers his bones together and buries them under a magical juniper tree, eventually bringing the brother back to life through a series of actions and help from a special bird. The deep, symbolic meaning of gathering the bones or the body parts and bringing them back to life step by step, as we have been discussing, refers to the reassembling of the inner immortal being.[117] We can see in Sylvia's work how important it is that consciousness is involved in this gathering of an inner entity that hasn't before been brought together in consciousness, in anyone. Sylvia's own work, her ability to dream the images forward and contemplate their meaning, makes the recollection—the inner resurrection—possible.

Continuing to do active imagination and to write, Sylvia experienced the self through the imaginal world becoming even more present as a reality.

I see before me a portal to my own imagination.

That portal has always been there, and I have danced in front of it, daring myself to cross the threshold. Something is holding me back—not a person, though the image of my mother comes to mind. I have believed that I could not be creative because I lacked the positive animus energy that would have been ignited by my father's encouragement. My years of longing for death, identifying with death, come to mind—better dead than self-actualized! Better to die than to violate my mother's most powerful imperative: "Don't tell the truth!" Deaden the truth in me by being depressed, by overeating, by drinking too much alcohol, by treating my most deeply held values as if they are silly. This brings the tears. I have devalued my own needs, my own natural tendency to create!

Now I remember the dream of a temple located in a tropical forest. A candle burns at the entrance of the temple—a flame that can never be extinguished.

The entrance of that temple is exactly like the portal that appears now. It is the portal to my imagination, my creative potential. The portal is personal to me, and yet it existed before I was born, and it will continue to exist after I am gone. Dare I enter? How can I not? Entering means engaging in what is mine to do in the world. The act of engaging in my own creativity is the process and

---

[117] My thanks to Irene Gerber-Münch for her insights on this tale.

the goal. I have long ago begun to engage, but I have not been able to cross the threshold to full immersion. Getting here has taken the time it took. Finding the portal has been the work up to now. I have never NOT been on the path, engaged in the work. Everything I have seen and heard and said and allowed in my life has been the work. Locating the sacred portal is the natural outcome of doing the work.

Bringing consciousness and the unconscious together, Sylvia discovered a portal into the vessel of the imaginal realm, similar to the tree portal through which Pearl could enter her sacred room. As she contemplates entering that portal, she has the miraculous, life-changing realization that she has "never NOT been on the path." This is a resurrection experience and a moment of grace, in which Sylvia could see that her eros connection to her own divine center only seemed to be dead; now she was helping to gather the elements of that eros connection together.

Continuing to contemplate the dream, Sylvia found words that she felt from childhood had wanted to be expressed. We can sense the redemption taking place as she writes—as if she were living now as a daughter of the self. Her poignant writing leads her to the deeply held experience of the opposites belonging together:

I love words. I love these words. I love the insight and understanding that only writing can bring for me. I love the numinous images that arise from the words that I write. It is magical, this ability to bring images to life by describing them in words. It's like the heat and smoke arising from a fire, like the play of light on clouds and earth when the sun rises, like the smell and taste of skillfully cooked food, like a beautiful flower blooming on a plant that has adequate water and soil. But it's also like the nauseating smell of a decomposing animal, like the sorrow on the face of a child who is neglected or abandoned, like the devastation visible after a terrible storm, like the heartbreak felt when realizing a lover's betrayal. I don't know if these comparisons will hold up when I read them tomorrow, but for now, that makes this most numinous moment "real."

In this beautiful passage (which I find reminiscent of Zosimos's observation that "all things are woven together and all things are undone again"), the opposites come alive in a way that is unique to Sylvia. Eros is reborn in relationship to logos: Her deep love for the images is strengthened by her symbolic understanding of them. We can see how important it was to bring the emotional content of her experience into reality and brood over it devotedly. The meaning and the goal of death and resurrection in one woman is how it constellates the wholeness of her experience—dark and light together—with the eternal nature of the symbolic realm.

If a woman has been severely wounded by life as Sylvia was, she may for a long time find it challenging to feel the self in the background of her experience; she may not feel deserving enough. But if she can continue in her opus, her feeling for her life and her moral sense of herself have a chance to recover their original value. She may feel independence and agency, liberated from the ideals of good and bad that she has embodied. Creative energy may be directed toward individuation as the main endeavor of her life, with love its primary engine. We should not underestimate how miraculous this recovery can be—how much life energy may be redeemed when the inherent, transpersonal value of a life is resurrected out of what once seemed to be meaningless suffering at the hands of a judgmental mindset.

Birth of the New Feminine

As Elise went through a long, difficult illness, she had several dreams that helped her see that her attitude—trying to find meaning in her affliction rather than complain (too much)—was redemptive and even lifesaving, strengthening her relationship to the self through thick and thin. The miracle of such a development was expressed in a numinous dream of a newborn girl:

I am in a big house with friends. It is dusk, and the world is awash in glowing sepia tones. We are preparing to celebrate Christmas, and everyone is in one big room sharing presents. At the same time, we pass from one person to the next a newborn baby girl, amazed at her. She seems lit from within. The baby is center stage for me. I am riveted by her and the fact that she is alive in the world.

The infant girl is the center of attention because she holds so much promise. The atmosphere of wonder surrounding this baby suggests that she represents the feminine side of the divine, brought into life at the same time that we celebrate the arrival of the baby Jesus. In other words, the birth of new eros in this dream complements the traditional Christmas celebration of the birth of new logos. Everyone in the dream is joined in a shared experience of the miracle, making the dream one for the ages.

Part IV

The Wizard, the Egg, and the Bird in Alchemy

10
Mercurius and the Divinity of the Psyche

Jung's thoroughgoing encounter with the collective unconscious gave him the experience he needed to understand the alchemists' quest for the elusive nature god Mercurius. As they searched for evidence of Mercurius and his secrets in their laboratory retorts, the alchemists experienced the religious dimension of the psyche through projection, often in the form of visions. Some saw Mercurius as an outer god, others an inner one—the hermaphroditic Anthropos, the inner divine human. As a nature god with a feminine side, a wily, two-sided character, and a capacity to change without warning, Mercurius compensated for the purely spiritual, outer masculine god of the times, a god-image frozen in creed. The alchemists saw in Mercurius the feminine side of the divine, the dark side of the divine, and nature as an aspect of the divine, all of which had been deprecated in Western religious dogma.

In "Fitcher's Bird," the wizard's dual and ambivalent nature, his home deep in the forest, his connection to eggs, his elusive effects on life, and his final identification with fire all bear similarities to Mercurius, especially as a god who is identified neither with good nor with evil. More than one alchemist said Mercurius is "good with the good and evil with the evil."[118] Psychologically speaking, he is evil with those who are unconscious of him, and good with those who acknowledge him and try their best to grapple with him. For example, in "Fitcher's Bird," the wizard is evil with the naïve older sisters but better, if not good, with the heroine, who confronts his dubious nature. She is "clever and crafty" and actually outwits him—not something she could do without his help—leading to the tale's ending in which both she and he are at least partially redeemed.

---

[118] Jung, quoting H. C. Khunrath from *Von hylealischen... Chaos*; "The Spirit Mercurius," *CW*, vol. 13, par. 267. In *Mysterium Coniunctionis,* Jung attributes the same quote to Gerhard Dorn; *CW*, vol. 14, par. 699.

A trickster spirit named Mercurius appears in the Grimms' tale "The Spirit in the Bottle," in which a poor young woodcutter finds a bottle under a tree and opens it, accidentally releasing Mercurius. Eventually, he realizes the danger he is dealing with, but he, too, is clever and crafty. He tricks Mercurius back into the bottle, first securing from him a magical healing cloth that makes him rich. Jung discusses this tale, referring to it as an "alchemical folk legend" in his essay "The Spirit Mercurius":

> The mention of Mercurius stamps the fairytale as an alchemical folk legend, closely related on the one hand to the allegorical tales used in teaching alchemy, and on the other to the well-known group of folktales that cluster round the motif of the "spellbound spirit." Our fairytale thus interprets the evil spirit as a pagan god, forced under the influence of Christianity to descend into the dark underworld and be morally disqualified.[119]

Our wizard, much like Mercurius in "The Spirit in the Bottle," seems to be "morally disqualified" insofar as he is seen and experienced as evil even though he has redemptive aims. This is also true for the serpent in the garden of Eden who awakens Adam and Eve to the knowledge of good and evil and yet to this day is commonly regarded as strictly evil.

Mercurius, sometimes imagined as a serpent, manifests the inscrutable laws of nature and in doing so may defy conventional moral norms in a completely ingenuous way. His behavior and ethics are those of the natural world. He is fiery, identical with drive energy, which can support either life or death depending on circumstances. But he is also watery, symbolizing the life-giving substance of the psyche that can either refresh or drown the ego. Because he bridges, divides, and yet defies the opposites, Jung said, Mercurius "evades every grasp—a real trickster who

---

[119] Jung, "The Spirit Mercurius," *CW*, vol. 13, par. 246. A folk legend is the story of an actual person that gets told and retold over time, eventually becoming well known. The individual identities and events in the tale may, however, become lost and assimilated into archetypal patterns and motifs, in which case the legend has become a fairy tale. In this case, the tale remains something of a legend, insofar as Mercurius remains identified with the German god Wotan. But for the most part, Jung refers to the story as a fairy tale.

drove the alchemists to despair."[120] He personifies the objective psyche itself, always mystifying us with its paradoxical nature.

The Spiritual Forms of Mercurius

The symbolic roots of Mercurius go back to the Egyptian god Thoth, the self-begotten scribe of the gods and inventor of language, astronomy, mathematics, medicine, botany, and theology, to name a few. In Hellenic alchemy, Thoth was combined with the Greek god Hermes and became Hermes Trismegistus, the "thrice great" father of the Hermetic mysteries. Hermes' characteristics as the messenger spirit of the winds were incorporated into some images of Mercurius to emphasize his elusiveness. Hermes is also reminiscent of the Germanic Wotan, who has a windy, wandering, numinous presence associated with the sweeping powers of war and death. With these roots, Mercurius is ever embedded in the pagan world, even though in many alchemical images he is also analogous with Christ as a dying and resurrecting god. As a renewing, eternal spirit he is the *filius philosphorum,* son of the philosophers. Yet he is also the son of a mother (matter; *mater*) with the uncanny wisdom of the suprapersonal nature mother that is the source of all life.

Jung described the symbolic difference between the son of the father we are so familiar with and the son of the mother, who remains dubious to our worldview:

> We know that the mask of the unconscious is not rigid— it reflects the face we turn towards it. Hostility lends it a threatening aspect, friendliness softens its features. It is not a question of mere optical reflection but of an autonomous answer which reveals the self-sufficing nature of that which answers. Thus the *filius philosophorum* is not just the reflected image, in unsuitable material, of the son of God; on the contrary, this son of Tiamat reflects the features of the primordial maternal figure. Although he is decidedly hermaphroditic he has a masculine name—a sign that the chthonic underworld, having been rejected by the spirit and identified with evil, has a tendency to

---

[120] Ibid., par. 251.

compromise. There is no mistaking the fact that he is a concession to the spiritual and masculine principle, even though he carries in himself the weight of the earth and the whole fabulous nature of primordial animality.[121]

In fact, if we look closely at the alchemical picture of Hermes-Mercurius (fig. 28), we see that he has a fetus in his abdomen. He functions as the feminine principle but with a masculine name that concedes to the spiritual and masculine paradigm that our culture can accept as divine.

Figure 28. Mercurius in the Form of Hermes

The fetus in his belly indicates a feminine, gestational aspect in addition to his windy, unearthly aspect. As an image of a masculine spirit, Hermes retains the qualities of Wotan, a spirit of the winds. From Michael Maier (German, 1568–1622), *Atalanta Fugiens,* 1617, emblem 1; engraver Matthaus Merian (Swiss, 1593–1650).

---

[121] Jung, *Psychology and Alchemy, CW,* vol. 12, par. 29.

His existence spans rather than splits spirit and matter as Christ does. To say that he "is nothing other than the spirit of the world become body within the earth" suggests that he represents the whole psychic aspect of life, including its mysterious connection to matter and its heavy, unavoidable reality.[122] As a spirit, Mercurius is not separate from matter but intrinsic to it; he is the mystery of growth that only becomes apparent in matter or in a subtle dream image. In terms of individual psychology, it is helpful to think of matter not only as the material aspect of the body but as the whole, psychosomatic reality of a singular personality—the *reality* of one's personhood, including the psychic essence, the mercurial energy that is as unique as one's individual appearance.[123]

Mystery of the Opposites, Mystery of Life

Mercurius is identical to the life principle and yet he also represents death. He appears in living matter as well as metal. He is a motivating, separating, uniting, dying, and resurrecting force in nature and in the psyche. As an androgyne, he is identified with masculine, feminine, and bisexual divine figures, including the Anthropos, the *unus mundus,* virgin of the world, *sapientia Dei,* the *lapis philosophorum,* and the *filius sapientiae.*

Mercurius is the eternal stone of individuality in every person, as if that individuality always existed and always will exist, preserved by him. He is energy and solidity, permanence and possibility, masculine and feminine, good and evil, divided and undivided, spanning every pair of opposites. Mercurius makes matter grow and change, including the mysterious transformation of earth into living plants, which symbolically is identical to the transformation of unconsciousness into consciousness.

---

[122] The summary of attributes of Mercurius comes from Jung, "The Spirit Mercurius," *CW,* vol. 13, par. 261ff. Readers are encouraged to refer to Jung's full descriptions, including his thorough citation of alchemical sources, for a comprehensive and detailed understanding of this curious figure. See also Jung, "Synchronicity: An Acausal Connecting Principle," *CW,* vol. 8, for a discussion of the relationship between psyche and matter in synchronistic phenomena.

[123] Von Franz describes how individuality is projected onto physical appearance in *On Dreams and Death,* 6.

The alchemists tried wholeheartedly to locate Mercurius, contain him, and extract his essence in endless variations of operations and procedures. They were compelled to uncover the mystery of life as if it were a divine substance or a living being; then they would have the secret of creation, the essence of God. Mercurius in this sense is the "true gold" that they sought. In psychological terms, Mercurius is intrinsic to our individual reality and thus, as Jung explained, he is identical to the principle of individuation. As such, he is a separator, just as Christ brings a sword to separate one generation from another (Matthew 10:34– 35; also see Luke 12:49–53): Both Christ and Mercurius suggest that people become like an orphan, disidentified from the old generation in the process of realizing what they were meant to be, which is also to realize the inner god as he exists in them uniquely. But the alchemists saw Mercurius paradoxically as a uniter, potentially bringing together all who recognize him as a shared god, a shared substance. Whereas the alchemists saw Christ's suffering as saving the microcosmic human by redeeming his personal sins, the dying and resurrection of Mercurius as Anthropos saves the macrocosm, because he can unite humanity in the knowledge of him as its underlying unity, completing the work that, as Jung explained, Christ left incomplete.[124] For this reason, he appears in some alchemical texts as the second Christ and *servator cosmi*, the preserver of the world (fig. 29).

Ultimately, Mercurius is the source and yet the goal of the alchemical opus: He is the arcane substance, the *lapis philosophorum*, representing the ever-renewing self, always out of reach and thus ever needing to be rediscovered. He is the unity, duality, trinity, and quaternity of individuation, as well as its quintessence. As the drive of nature and the presence of nature's drive in humanity, Mercurius is, in other words, the psyche itself in all of its paradoxical manifestations—its images, its urges, its mysterious relationship to soma, and its eternal re-creation. He is soul substance, identical to Sophia and nous and, like them, longs to be known in the consciousness of humanity as its underlying oneness.

As a figure for Mercurius, the wizard in "Fitcher's Bird" drives life in old ways and new, spanning the opposites. He seems to have

---

[124] Jung, *Mysterium Coniunctionis, CW*, vol. 14, par. 27.

Figure 29. Christ as *Servator Cosmi*

The resurrected Christ as *servator cosmi*, or savior of the world, in the form of Mercurius, the *filius philosophorum*. He carries a staff with a cross attached to a flag with a cross, indicating the opposites endured and united at the archetypal and temporal levels. Final picture of the second Rosarium cycle that may be reflective of female psychology, *Rosarium Philosophorum: Secunda pars alchimiae de lapide philosophico* (Frankfurt, 1550).

paradoxically dark intentions to awaken the heroine to him as a reality that wants to be reconciled to itself.[125] In a woman, such a wizardly energy, functioning in and through the animus, brings her the entire world of the psyche, tearing open any tidy ideals she may have held about its intention to coddle her or to take away the burden of her sins. To make himself seen, Mercurius wants and needs her individuality and her honesty, and will do whatever it takes to bring her around. He seeks himself in her, depending on her to become conscious of him, to feel his presence, masculine or feminine, as an other who is nevertheless innate to her.

---

[125] See Jung, "The Phenomenology of the Spirit in Fairytales," *CW*, vol. 9i, pars. 384–455.

Aerial Spirit

Alchemists considered one aspect of Mercurius to be an aerial spirit, in other words having the texture of air. As such, he was personified by such gods as Hermes or Thoth, who "makes the souls to breathe."[126] In this aspect he was considered a nonmaterial, metaphysical spirit, a *mundus intelligibilis*, such as Aristotle's *intellectus agens* (active intelligence), which imbued the material world with divine or archetypal intelligence. In this sense, Mercurius is an active, causal force in the universe that activates and forms the essence of living beings, imbuing them in conception with the knowledge they are born eventually to realize. Similar to St. Augustine's *rationes aeternae,* Mercurius is the absolute, cosmically imbued truth of a person, perceivable to the human soul, if not to the physical eye.

In psychological terms, Mercurius as spirit represents the invisible source of our inimitable, inner truth, which Jung named the self, and which may lie in wait for a lifetime and never be seen or appreciated consciously. Yet even though he may remain mostly unconscious, such a phenomenon exerts a pressure, an energy that we sense belongs to us. We may feel lost in expressing that irrepressible dynamism, an essence that is absolutely original to our individuality, and yet we may also be relentlessly driven to do so.

One of the most common dream motifs expressing this problem, mainly for women but sometimes also for men, is usually a bit embarrassing. It involves finding ourselves in a public or otherwise awkward situation, needing to urinate. Urine symbolizes our unique psychic substance, a concentrated essence of the life energy that has passed through us and nourished us, tinctured us individually. The urgency in such dreams is the point, pressing us to feel how vital the impulse is—how much the psyche wants us to bring our individual essence into a container in our own, intimate way, no matter how inconvenient. The point is to find the right creative container in which our individual relationship to Mercurius may be brought into life, even if we are embarrassed at first by any lack of aesthetic sophistication. Expression is the point, no matter its perceived

---

[126] Jung, *Alchemical Studies,* par. 261, referring to passages in *Aurora consurgens.*

beauty. If we can articulate the inner animating spirit to any extent of our ability, we help redeem that spirit and uncover its contribution to our individuality, as Pearl did with her devil-man; we see another example of such a redemption from Sylvia in chapter 13.

Soul

Mercurius was also described as soul, which on balance has a more feminine quality than spirit. Jung explained:

"Soul" represents a higher concept than "spirit" in the sense of air or gas. As the "subtle body" or "breath-soul" it means something non-material and finer than mere air. Its essential characteristic is to animate and be animated; it therefore represents the life principle. Mercurius is often designated as *anima* (hence, as a feminine being he is also called *foemina* or *virgo*), or as *nostra anima* ... as ... the arcane substance.[127]

This passage expresses soul as something even more subtle, numinous, and perplexing than spirit. A finer substance, it lives more invisibly between the worlds of psyche and matter as the animating bond between them, penetrating but imperceptible. In other words, as obvious as an individual is in her uniqueness, the soul that makes her unique is easy to miss, lying behind the veil of material reality and less perceptible than her spirit. Likewise, dream images are invisible except to the dreamer, immaterial and yet with the power to move us, real in their capacity to transform. When we see the meaning and intention of a dream, we are penetrated by its subtle, insistent essence, its soul, and its elusive ability to motivate us, even though no one else can see it.

Helping us understand how difficult it can be to differentiate spirit and soul, Jung said that "*anima* often appears to be connected with *spiritus*, or is equated with it. For the spirit shares the living quality of the soul, and for this reason Mercurius is often called the *spiritus vegetativus* (spirit of life) or *spiritus seminalis*."[128] Explaining the religious weight

---

[127] Jung, "The Spirit Mercurius," *CW*, vol. 13, par. 262.
[128] Ibid., par. 263.

of Mercurius as the life principle for the alchemists, Jung said, "If consciousness participates [in individuation] with some measure of understanding, then the process is accompanied by all the emotions of a religious experience or revelation. As a god of individuation, or a divine inspiration towards increased wisdom, Mercurius was identified with *Sapientia* and the Holy Ghost."[129] As *Sapientia,* he is wisdom, and as the Holy Ghost, he is the spirit of Christ on earth, incarnated in the individual; again, he is both genders. In our devotion to the individuation process, we feel these realities weaving themselves together in our developing relationship with the self.

The soul quality of Mercurius was seen as "glue, holding the world together and standing in the middle between body and spirit."[130] Mylius saw Mercurius as the *anima media natura,* which also identifies him with the *anima mundi,* the invisible animating essence of the world. Avicenna called him "the spirit of the Lord which fills the whole world and in the beginning swam upon the waters. They call him also the spirit of Truth, which is hidden from the world."[131] Jung added:

> Another text says that Mercurius is the "supracelestial spirit which is conjoined with the light, and rightly could be called the *anima mundi.*" It is clear from a number of texts that the alchemists related their concept of the *anima mundi* on the one hand to the world soul in Plato's *Timaeus* and on the other to the Holy Spirit, who was present at the Creation and played the role of the procreator . . . impregnating the waters with the seed of life just as, later, he played a similar role in the *ombumbratio* (overshadowing) of Mary.[132]

Mercurius as *anima mundi,* the glue of the world, represents not only the interrelatedness of natural processes but also the mysterious joining of spirit and matter, in nature and in the individual. The alchemists went so far as to compare him to the god who stirred the waters of creation and impregnated the Virgin Mary. In these comparisons, they viewed

---

[129] Ibid., par. 277.

[130] Ibid., par. 263, citing Happelius.

[131] Ibid.

[132] Ibid.

Mercurius not as identical to any outer god but as the impetus within the god. Similarly, the Gnostics saw a higher, "nonexistent god" to have created Yahweh, whom they identified as an Archon, a god begotten by the nonexistent god though ignorant of that fact and needing to be brought to consciousness about it.[133] For the alchemists, Mercurius was identical to that nonexistent god whose mere presence forces humility onto even the most powerful of kings and gods.

From Jung's descriptions and references above, we can see how Mercurius permeates alchemical thinking as a bisexual divine entity with an unfathomable existence that drives individual life, the activity of the gods, and creation itself. He is the unseen wisdom in creation, having been with God (identical to *Sapientia,* Proverbs 8) from the very beginning, whether God knows that or not. He stands for the fine, still nature of the soul and yet the driving force of the spirit. As Jung understood it in psychological terms, everything that Mercurius portrays for the alchemists—spirit, soul, wisdom, matter, the life principle, the opposites, and transformation—carried their projection of the numinous psyche and its dynamism.

Begin with Evil and End with Good

The alchemists saw the destroying and renewing effects of Mercurius in chemicals and chemical activity, such as quicksilver, sulfur, or magnesium, which react without conscience but always in accordance with their unique "spiritual" nature. Jung elaborated:

> If Mercurius is not exactly the Evil One himself, he at least contains him—that is, he is morally neutral, good and evil, or as Khunrath says: "Good with the good, evil with the evil." His nature is more exactly defined, however, if one conceives him as a process that begins with evil and ends with good.[134]

---

[133] See Hippolytus's description of this myth in "Refutation of All Heresies," in Roberts, Donaldson, and Coxe, *The Ante-Nicene Fathers,* 5:100ff.

[134] Jung, "The Spirit Mercurius," *CW*, vol. 13, par. 276.

To begin with evil and end with good means, psychologically, to begin with unconsciousness of Mercurius, acting out his drivenness, and end with consciousness of him as a source of wisdom, containing his energy in some level of communion with it. Mercurius remains "morally neutral," but by the same token awakens us to our unconscious attachment to our moral views, which we so easily take for granted as sound. According to Jung in his discussion of the fairy tale "The Spirit in the Bottle," Mercurius becomes most devilish when consciousness is stubbornly intractable toward him, when he is bottled up in an artificial spiritual container, such as a puritanical worldview, and removed from nature.[135]

In the fairy tale, the heroine at first is enchanted just as all the other maidens have been, and she could just as easily die as they did, a too-innocent victim of an ambivalent spirit that devilishly demands obedience. The wizard at this point represents a nature spirit removed from nature, his mandate imprisoned in an idea of obedience. Really, he is trying to offer another way of life in which individuation radically transforms any maiden's idea of obedience. He wants relationship and needs someone to see him as such. After the heroine attends to her egg, indicating just such a recognition, the wizard's activity turns toward a more positive end. What we regard as the wizard's evil behavior, his incessant murdering of maidens, is the agent of this awakening. Like Mercurius, the wizard seems evil as long as we are not in conscious relationship with his aims. He is evil with those who are unconscious of him and follow the old spiritual rules, but relatively good with those who dare to be related to him (though we should never assume that he is predictable).

In some alchemical texts, Mercurius himself is the subject of torture, burning, mortification, or dismemberment. He is the dismembered god, as we discussed in Zosimos's vision (chapter 7), hidden in the unconscious, morally disqualified by our conscious attitudes yet aiming for his suffering to be redeemed through our realization of him. In terms of the psychological journey we have been discussing, a woman may finally become conscious of how her soul is suffering if she experiences what Barbara Hannah calls "insights that pierce the opinionating veil of

---

[135] Ibid., par. 247.

the animus."[136] When an insight is strong enough to pierce the veil of preciously held ideals and reveal their unconscious prejudices, she may realize that her experience of the self has been bottled up in those ideals, suffocating her development. In even the briefest realization, good and evil come closer together. According to the alchemists, what saves the world is not the elimination of evil but the act of reuniting evil with good, so these opposites may once again become relative and compensatory toward each other rather than split apart and destructive toward each other. If Mercurius is suffering through the angst of his wholeness not being seen and an individual becomes conscious of what he is going through, she helps unite good and evil in herself and in him.

Mercurius and the Positive Animus

In his role as shadow to the Christian god-image, Mercurius may come across as a demonic spirit when he tears us out of our inertia and goads us into self-knowledge that is beyond our expectations and our predilections. But unlike our idea of Christ, Mercurius is not one-sided. He is both destructive and creative, both loving and violent. He is, as I also suggest about the wizard in our tale, a light-bringer who acts like a devil when he has to open up and even destroy a closed system of thinking and feeling about what is godlike. He is good with the good until the good becomes false—and he knows what has become false long before we do.

Jung described the development of Mercurius in the alchemical world as reflecting a comprehensive archetypal reality that Christ's official image fails to encompass:

> Hesitantly, as in a dream, the introspective brooding of the centuries gradually put together the figure of Mercurius and created a symbol which, according to all the psychological rules, stands in a compensatory relation to Christ. It is not meant to take his place, nor is it identical with him, for then indeed it could replace him. It owes its existence to the law of compensation, and its object is to throw a bridge across the abyss separating the two psychological worlds by presenting a subtle compensatory counterpoint to the Christ

---

[136] Hannah, *The Animus,* 1:141.

image. . . . To the Christian mentality, the dark antagonist is always the devil. As I have shown, Mercurius escapes this prejudice by only a hair's breadth. But he escapes it, thanks to the fact that *he scorns to carry on opposition at all costs.* The magic of his name enables him, in spite of his ambiguity and duplicity, to keep outside the split, for as an ancient pagan god he possesses a natural undividedness which is impervious to logical and moral contradictions. This gives him invulnerability and incorruptibility, the very qualities we so urgently need to heal the split in ourselves.[137]

Like Mercurius, the wizard in the tale is undivided, invulnerable, and incorruptible, because he doesn't identify with good or evil. He defies moral contradiction in that he abducts and murders girls, insisting they obey him, but through that dynamic eventually connects the heroine to his larger, redemptive aims, which include the recovery of the feminine principle itself.

The wizard is the bridge between two psychological worlds that we may identify as conscious and unconscious but that have become unnaturally split, fixed to good and evil, respectively. To the extent that a woman experiences the wizardly, nature animus as the devil, she may also face in herself a stubborn Christian character that still sees nature, including her own instinctual nature, as something to be overcome.[138] Her expectation for a loving and cradling god will hold her back in her process of individuation, or even be destructive, if she is fated to move beyond that god-image and realize that the psyche is offering her a darker experience, but one that expresses wholeness. As Jung said, Mercurius is "bound to nature . . . [and] represents all those things which have been eliminated from the Christian model."[139] Because of his connection to nature and his half-evil, half-good essence, the alchemists observed what

---

[137] Jung, "The Spirit Mercurius," *CW*, vol. 13, par. 295; emphasis added.

[138] Ibid. For example the heroine, Lucy Honeychurch, in E. M. Forster's *A Room with a View* tries but fails to overcome her own nature and marry the man she thinks she should marry. She finally allows herself to love the man to which her own true nature is drawn. In this case, the positive animus prevails over the negative.

[139] Ibid., par. 289.

may be most difficult for us to realize—that Mercurius represents a higher light than Christ:

> Mercurius, that two-faced god, comes as the *lumen naturae*, the *Servator* and *Salvator*, only to those whose reason strives towards the highest light ever received by man, and who do not trust exclusively to the *cognitio vespertina* [evening knowledge]. For those who are unmindful of this light, the *lumen naturae* turns into a perilous *ignis fatuus*, and the psychopomp into a diabolical seducer. Lucifer, who could have brought light, becomes the father of lies whose voice in our time, supported by press and radio, revels in orgies of propaganda and leads untold millions to ruin.[140]

The *lumen naturae*, the light of nature and of the psyche, guides us to something like Christ as a spiritual reality, and then past Christ to the inner, hermaphroditic, undivided Anthropos. To the extent that a woman experiences the animus as undivided, she helps redeem him from a worldview that cannot see and would destroy his wholeness for the sake of religious or philosophical assumptions that claim to know what is good.

Dreams of Mercurial Animus Figures

Several dreams help us see how a Mercurius-like animus may appear and develop over time when consciousness can finally begin to take in his two-sidedness. Sandra had a dream of an animus figure that brings chthonic and spiritual aspects together:

> *I am an assistant in a hospital. I hear that an Arab family has been brought in, perhaps refugees. When I see the doctor approach a certain door, I follow him to see if I can help. I am curious about this family, especially the man who was with them. As the doctor opens the door, I see that man on the bed, naked, lying slightly elevated on his side, leaning on an elbow. He is as manly as one can*

---

[140] Ibid., par. 303.

possibly imagine, with strong legs and arms, and a phallus
that is incredibly virile, though not erect, and slightly
darker brown than the rest of him. His head and his hands
are large and strong. He has long, dark hair and a round
face with dark, penetrating eyes. He seems at once alert
and at peace, enlightened. We gaze at each other for what
seems like several minutes and take each other in. My heart
is pounding with a strange sense of recognition. Suddenly
I am aware of myself, and I'm not sure I should be here.

This dream figure is a refugee, which indicates psychologically that he is rescued from the unconscious, where otherwise he may have perished without being known in this world (Mercurius is sometimes called a fugitive spirit, difficult to catch). He comes from a long way away, an Arab, probably Muslim, which at its root is the religion of eros and connected to the origins of alchemy. His virility indicates that he is not only a spiritual man but also imbued with chthonic, creative energy. The sexual overtones tell us that he is ready to unite with the dreamer, that is, to become an active part of her psychological life. He brings her a singular experience of seeing and being seen in a private moment.

For Sandra this was a numinous encounter. The dream figure represents an inner spirit who is completely natural, of whom Sandra could say, "That is exactly the man for me." It is typical that as a woman goes through individuation and the animus becomes more integrated, he becomes more and more specifically related to her as an individual. He becomes less collective and less divided. As in this dream, a mutual seeing and realizing between the dream-ego and the animus manifests the strength of their unique connection. Her wondering at the end of the dream, "I'm not sure I should be here," reflects the fact that a deep psychological secret is being revealed to her. This animus figure is a godlike entity—phallic, erotic, and spiritual—without any sense of being torn. The self has presented him as a completely individual spirit who can recognize Sandra for who she is and knows that she can recognize him.

The following dream gives us an image of two very different animus figures: one represents conventional attitudes toward the psyche and the other a deep relationship to the psychic realm:

A gardener is working in my garden. He is a tall, dark-haired man, charismatic, slender, and focused on his work in the soil. He works very hard, at times examining the soil closely. George, the handyman, asks about the gardener. George seems to be questioning his intelligence or his motivation in some way, as if he is suspicious of the gardener.

But the gardener knows a lot about gardening. He also has another vocation, which I try to remember. I have to think hard, but finally I remember, and I tell George: the gardener is also a physicist! It takes me a few seconds to remember the word, physicist, *and when I do, I feel vindicated for the gardener's sake.*

In some ways the gardener is a simple man, and obviously he is very connected to the land and the garden. But he also loves physics and is related to the mystery of matter. It seems that he is not working as a physicist professionally at the moment because he can't find a job that is consistent with his line of research. So he is working as a gardener and maintains a practice in physics in his own private workshop.

The dreamer saw George the handyman as a collective man who adheres to convention and is suspicious of what he doesn't understand. The gardener/physicist is a different kind of man altogether. He is investigating the mysterious relationship between energy and matter in two different worlds, in visible and invisible nature. As a gardener he investigates visible matter and as a physicist he investigates invisible matter, in both cases trying to understand the energic mysteries that actually define them and make them tick. He wants to find out what makes matter grow and transform—the very mysteries the alchemists ostensibly were trying to uncover as they investigated how Mercurius makes things grow from soil and ultimately how he holds the psychic and physical world together.[141]

In symbolic terms, gardening and physics represent the cultivation of spiritual life—the mystery of how consciousness develops out of the unconscious, how unconscious energy affects consciousness

---

[141] I can only briefly touch on the topic of relationship between psyche and matter; I recommend von Franz, *Psyche and Matter*, for a psychological orientation.

life, and how their interaction is sometimes visible in the personality and sometimes invisible. The unconscious exists in the part of life that we can see growing and changing, and it exists in the part of life we can't see, in the deepest, smallest building blocks of psychological life. Physics seems to be observing that the more deeply we investigate matter, we find its solidity to be more elusive. Matter may be in fact a form of energy in its own right. Soil and its microorganisms are material, but only partly so. They are also are energic, harboring a mercurial, volatile energy that grows its own inscrutable way in each plant; the dream reminds us that the psyche is everywhere, veiled and unveiled. Likewise in psychology we are realizing the more deeply we investigate the psyche, we find its connection to some form of matter. The psyche indeed may become manifest in a subtle body form, an aspect of matter that has been postulated since antiquity as the substance of a unifying world soul.

The gardener/physicist cannot join the collective world of physics; at that deepest level of life he must maintain the integrity of his individual research in an introverted way, in his own laboratory, his own container, the place consciousness and the unconscious come together in him. He must be true to his own line of inquiry, involved in a psychic investigation of great meaning to him. In this sense he is a modern-day alchemist like any of us, exploring the mysteries of relationship between psyche and matter at the tiniest, granular level, asking, "*where* is the psyche and how does it affect my reality visibly and invisibly?" As this is a woman's dream, it indicates an integration of the animus as a unique and independent spiritual drive. He carries a line of inquiry into individuation that is both spiritual and scientific.

An analysand who was relatively new to me reported the following dream with an image that blends physical and spiritual love in a way that helps us understand how psyche and matter may be related to each other, in this case through eros:

An old literature professor is quoting words of love to me from ancient books, saying the words as if he wrote them for me, trying to express his love for me. I have a hard time at first understanding or believing his expression. But then he embraces me, as if forcing me to feel what he is saying. He wants me to realize the power of love to bring body and spirit together. And finally, as we embrace, I feel that power. I feel the love and the sex coming together in the most intense way I have ever felt. I can hardly contain myself. We become naked. It isn't so much that we want to have sex but that we want to be together in the physical vibration that is struck with the intensity of love.

This woman's connection to the reality of an inner spirit is completely attuned to her and yet has an ancient, universal presence. We sense here how eros as a cosmogonic force is the motivating power driving her connection to the animus.

In 2001, during my first two-week, residential course of analytic training, which took place in a Catholic cloister in the Alps of Switzerland, I had a dream that introduced me to a nature spirit with the deep historical reach of Mercurius. I had fallen asleep in my little room overlooking a beautiful Alpine valley and lake with my balcony door open to the spring breeze. House rules forbade the balcony door be left open at night, but I couldn't resist, and I felt just a bit criminal about it. I dreamt:

A creature has entered my room from the balcony. He is a monkey, but he also seems human. He jumps onto my bed and stands on me, gazing at me while I am sleeping. I am asleep, but I am awake. I can't move. He continues to examine me all over. Finally he sits on my chest. Then he licks my face, from the chin to the cheek on the left side, and then from chin to cheek on the right. My face feels wet, sensitive to the breeze coming through my door.

I awoke with a start, staring into the eyes of the monkey-man, who was still on my bed, gazing at me intently, and sat up straight. He jumped off the bed, but I could see him lingering in the darkness keeping an eye on me, hesitant to leave. My heart pounding, finally I found the wherewithal to turn on my bedside lamp. Although the creature was gone, my cheeks felt wet from his tongue. Gathering my wits, I wrote down the dream and the vision, still in the grip of its reality. I didn't know at the time that this monkey-man was probably a version of the Egyptian Thoth, predecessor to Mercurius. In my dream he performed what felt like an initiatory rite, even a fertilization, licking both sides of my face and leaving behind the wet sensation of his saliva—his essence. The dream and the lingering vision were powerful enough to help break through my ideas about the unconscious, to show me its crisp reality and its ability to penetrate everyday life. In making his existence felt, the Mercurius-like monkey-man undertakes a remarkably feminine task. He issued an unholy, unremitting demand to heed attention to his mother world of the psyche—to its phenomenal, substantial *reality*.

At the core of the animus is a daimon that wants love and attention as much as any woman does. In his yearning, he is also a she, always connecting. In each dream, the animus is unlike any other, as we see in the unique animus figures in all the dreams we have explored. The nature spirit clearly yearns to be felt in the human realm but will never appear as a quantity or a quality that is already known.

11
The Philosophical Egg and the Feminizing of Consciousness

The egg symbol has appeared several times in the psychological material we have been exploring, showing us an image for potential wholeness that begins forming in the unconscious as soon as a person pays attention to the unconscious. We have discussed how an ongoing devotion to the images that arise from a relationship with the unconscious may eventually bring about with the alchemists call the second part of the work, in which a living realization of the self develops. In the fairy tale, the heroine's attention to her egg symbolizes an awakening to the unconscious that brings about a profound change. Her cleaning and preparing at the wizard's house, leading to her appearance as a "wondrous bird" can be understood psychologically as a continuing, devoted opus with the unconscious that leads to a realization of the self. This development necessarily requires a consciousness that is more feminine, that is, more reflective and related to the unconscious rather than judgmental of it.

In this chapter, we explore how the egg and bird motifs appear in alchemical allegories of the philosophical egg, in which an egg may give birth to a chick in the alchemical laboratory—the "philosophical coop"—if it is tended according to nature's ways. The material helps us understand in more depth how the wizard, egg, and bird motifs in "Fitcher's Bird" may be derived from alchemy. We won't go into the tremendous details found in alchemical texts regarding these images, but hopefully our exploration will help us see, as if through the eyes of the alchemists, the fascinating symbolic process in which a bird slowly forms within the dark container of a well-tended, fertilized egg and projects itself into the world (fig. 30).

The philosophical egg is one of many names for the awe-inspiring, womblike alchemical vessel that brings new life into the world according

Figure 30. *Proiectio, Ceratio*

This is the final emblem of the series *De summa et universalis medicinae sapientiae*. The alchemical vessel is broken open like an egg shell, the *filius* having come alive and projected itself out of its container. Inside the egg is a waxy sphere resembling honeycomb. The honeycomb is an image for the *ceratio*, which is the softening of a substance that makes it capable of new syntheses, or new conjunctions. Psychologically the softened wax represents a personality that can be flexible and unify the opposites, rather than rigidly take sides. From *De summa et universalis medicinae sapientiae*, fol. 4, fig. 40, Bibliothèque de L'Arsenal, Paris, ms. 974 (18th century).

to nature's world-creating secrets. Other names for the vessel include the round oven or furnace, the Hermetic vase, the philosophical vase, the alembic, or the retort.[142] All are symbolic images for the imaginal container, the inner vision, or the subtle body that is formed when consciousness and the unconscious join for the purpose of creating new psychological life. The imaginal world that forms in the egg or the

---

[142] See Read, *Prelude to Chemistry,* 148ff, and Jung, *Psychology and Alchemy, CW,* vol. 12, par. 338ff, for more symbolism regarding the alchemical vessel and its mysterious influence on the alchemist.

alembic is not a function of personal consciousness alone; it is informed by the same divinity that creates life and transformation in nature, the same one that is good with the good and evil with the evil. In alchemical lexicon, Mercurius is the egg, he is the bird that emerges from the egg, he is the transformation from egg to bird and then again to egg, and he is the unsolvable riddle in which one or the other comes first. All of the images for the vessel, therefore, emphasize the need for a closed container, a round or oval shape that reflects the cosmic, life-creating nature of the work, and is strong enough to contain the volatile energy of Mercurius.

In some images, the philosophical egg is depicted as a microcosm of the world (fig. 31). It contains all the elements needed to produce life—

Figure 31. Cosmic Egg, "Subiectum Chimicum"
The egg, which is one form of the alchemical vessel in which transformation takes place, contains everything it needs for the production of the bird. Psychologically this means that the self contains everything it needs to become incarnated as a conscious reality. All four elements plus the gods Sol and Luna are available, as is the potential for them to affect each other, since they are in a container. From *De summa et universalis medicinae sapientiae*, fol. 4, fig. 2, Bibliothèque de L'Arsenal, Paris, ms. 974 (18th century).

earth, water, air, and fire, plus the divine influences of Sol and Luna. In psychological terms, the philosophical egg is the whole inner world of an individual, the psychic "shell" in which the bird of the self may be conceived and develop according to its archetypal origins and aims, eventually liberated from matter (the unconscious), and released into the world, finally known as the inner psychic divinity. The realization of this objective reality and its appearance in the alchemical vessel were considered to be world-creating; bringing the self into the world contributes to ongoing creation. The only thing the egg needs from the outside for the bird of Mercurius to be born is the alchemist's henlike attention.

Likewise, the self, the psychological equivalent of the inner divinity, lies in slumber in the personality until it is seen, nurtured in the imaginal realm, and finally liberated into the world, into a psychological reality, as a new spiritual entity. All it needs to fulfill this development is the ego's warm devotion.

Another Chicken-and-Egg Question

A mutual partnership between the ego and the self is not possible in every individual for the seemingly simple reason that the ego must first emerge sufficiently from its containment in the unconscious to have a relationship with the unconscious. This initial step is analogized in alchemy to the great mystery of fertilization, in which the opposites begin to relate to each other, fertilizing each other as discrete phenomena, and depicted in various allegories of the royal hermaphrodite, or Sol and Luna. Differentiation from the unconscious in service of a relationship with it is the preeminent miracle in the development of consciousness.

Psychologically, this first step of differentiation begs a chicken-and-egg question that is a bit more subtle than asking which came first: How can the ego give birth to the self when it is born contained in the self? The alchemists made it abundantly clear that this enigma, and the fact that the ego must become relative in the bargain, makes the opus uncertain, slow, and fraught with potential contamination. The "fertilization" for a woman requires that she disidentify from the animus in order to have a relationship with him. We have seen how difficult it can be for a woman to pull her attitudes and fantasy thinking out of the brine in which they were born, but this is the necessary first step.

To explore the mysteries of the philosophical egg, we look mainly at material from *Atalanta Fugiens* by Michael Maier (1568–1622), plus two passages from Ibn Umail's *Kitāb Ḥall ar-Rumūz*. Maier's work comprises a series of 50 "emblems" or illustrations printed from copper engravings, each accompanied by a motto, an epigram, a discourse of a few paragraphs describing the topic at hand, and even a musical fugue to fill out the sensory impressions of the allegorical material. We will explore discourses 8 and 30 along with their emblems, which expound on the mysteries of the philosophical egg, its fertilization, and how it develops into a bird.[143]

Woman's Point of View

As we explore the symbolism in these alchemical texts, we will keep in mind the fact that all alchemists describing the process were men. Although they were working toward the redemption of the inner divinity and his feminine side (the soul, the unconscious, psyche, Luna, and nature), we only have images for the male experience of that undertaking. As Jung noted, other than the material attributed to the legendary figure Maria Prophetissa, we don't know how female alchemists would have contributed to alchemical imagery.[144] Keeping this in mind, we will attempt to understand the egg and bird imagery in terms of a woman's experience in individuation.

Typically, a man differentiates himself from the unconscious through the anima, and a woman through the animus. I've observed this

---

[143] *Atalanta Fugiens* was written by Maier and published in 1617. For more about Maier's publication, see de Jong, *Michael Maier's Atalanta Fugiens*, and Maier, *Atalanta Fugiens: An Edition of the Emblems, Fugues, and Epigrams*, edited and translated by Joscelyn Godwin. I am using a translation from the British Library, Ms. Sloane 3645.

[144] See, for example, Jung, "The Psychology of the Transference," *CW*, vol. 16, par. 518. Also see Abt's descriptions of the experiences of Theosebeia, Zosimos's *sorror mystica*, in *The Book of Pictures*.

to be true regardless of sexual orientation or identification; the situation seems to be completely individual and needs to be observed without prejudice, that is, by suspending inner or outer gender assumptions and expectations. The symbolic process may surprise both analysand and analyst. This is a vital research topic that would be enlightening to pursue but is unfortunately beyond the scope of the present work. In a woman, man, or nonbinary individual, the feminine principle may be redeemed just by virtue of the fact that in analysis, the unconscious (feminine) psyche is recognized as the primary source of wisdom and the place where the gestational development of consciousness takes place.

We have already seen women's contributions to the symbolism of this process in such images as the devil-man in an egg, the egg being revealed as an image for the *lapis,* the dream of the circulatory distillation taking place in a woman's subtle-body heart, the cosmic egg containing the one word, and several sandplay images featuring the egg as an image for incipient inner development. We will come back to these and other images from dreams and active imaginations, especially Pearl's devil-man, to help amplify the symbolism of the philosophical egg and the transformations it expresses.

The Hen as a Model of Devotion

In discourse 30 of *Atalanta Fugiens,* Maier warned that if a new bird is to be born from an egg in the alchemical laboratory, the egg must be cared for in the same manner that a hen cares for her egg. He recommended that the philosopher or adept pay close attention to the hen's humble devotion:

> So likewise the Philosophers have their Eggs, which will passe into birds of the same kind if they are nourished with a temperate heat such as the heat of a Hen that setts, remaining upon them continually.... Wherein her Diligence and Industry is very remarkable; with what haste she eats and drinks and performs all the necessaryes of Nature, that she may run back to her Eggs least they should grow cold. Then with Force and Eagernesse she defends her Chickens; with how loud a voice like that of a Bell she calls and clucks them together; with what Endeavour she Bruises and Cutts with her Bill as with

a Knife the harder crumbs or grains which she administers to them. All of which is the work of Nature, and worthy of our admiration. And all this is done least Eggs should be wanting for the food of mankind or the production of Chickens.

This passage describes the profound, instinctual connection between the hen and her egg, emphasizing her faithfulness to protecting the egg. She is a model for the feminine side of the drive for life, the side that wants to bring new life into reality, a feminine spirit. She is diligent, protective, even ruthless in her attention, always devoted to her instinctual calling to nurture that life. She is never distracted from the goal of hatching her egg, and she would never reject anything in that egg. After it hatches, she protects her chick with "Force and Eagernesse" to ensure its survival and growth for the sake of an ongoing supply of chickens and eggs, the food of mankind.

The alchemist has to become familiar with these natural, feminine ways of protecting life, knowing when to be temperate and when to be fierce, so the life inside the laboratory egg in the philosophical coop may grow and develop in the same way as it would in a chicken coop. The instincts to care and protect are in the blood of the hen. In psychological terms, however, a rational man or woman might for a long time be separated from those instincts when it comes to caring for his or her own psychic development. As we've seen, if a woman is stuck in the incessant hurry of the worldly animus, she is probably detached from the instinct to take her inner life seriously, let alone to care for it with patience and stillness, or to protect it from the intrusions of outer-world demands and the seductions of recognition. Her feminine instincts may need to be recovered to tend to the egg of individuation according to the egg's needs.

The hen's activity illustrates what naturally happens when we realize the unconscious exists and has life in it. The potential psychological life that can be born through a relationship with the unconscious is precious, and we care for that relationship the way a hen cares for her egg, as if life depends on it. We keep the developing relationship to the self warm with daily attention and nourish it with all diligence. We document our dreams, but further, we amplify them and brood over them, allowing their unique meaning to give birth to itself and work its way into our lives. Even as we strive for understanding, we learn to sit and wait when the path seems unclear. Sooner or later and in the fulness of time, something new will get born.

Slowly, the meaning of the work clarifies, and so does the attitude of the ego toward the psyche. The alchemists described this process with numerous complicated analogies about soaking, drying, mortifying, distilling, sublimating, and so on, to express the slow extraction of spiritual life from the unconscious and its effect on the personality when it is reintegrated as something new. We can see in this process that the ego learns to take a relative position to individuation, accepting the responsibility to focus energy toward emerging psychic life. The heroine, protecting her egg only after so many have followed the wizard's orders not to, shows us the profound transformation that can happen when a woman finally wakes up to the orthodox voice she has been obeying and instead follows her natural instinct to tend to her inner life as a holy mandate.

Nature Is Always the Mistress

When the ego first becomes aware that the unconscious exists, it faces a paradigm shift it couldn't possibly expect. The ego only slowly begins to realize that it is not the center of the personality and that conscious knowledge is not the only knowledge. Paradoxically, the ego needs the help of the unconscious to understand the unconscious. The seminal challenge behind these insights, especially in the beginning of the work, is to understand unconscious contents on their own terms, never assuming we already know the meaning of symbolic images.

Knowing that nature is the original source of his art, the adept doesn't only take the hen as a model, but from a larger perspective, Maier reminds his colleagues that "Nature is always the Mistress and art the Handmaid" (discourse 1). In other words, the alchemists' art, his artifice, is nature's handmaid, no matter how clever or valiant he may think he is. This consequential distinction is stressed in the emblem (illustration) for discourse 8, which depicts one of the philosopher's relatively well-known techniques—to "smite the egg with a fiery sword" (fig. 32).

This image marks the moment when the alchemist, almost ridiculously depicted as a soldier, apprehends the unconscious, or sees it as an objective reality and knows there is a life held captive within

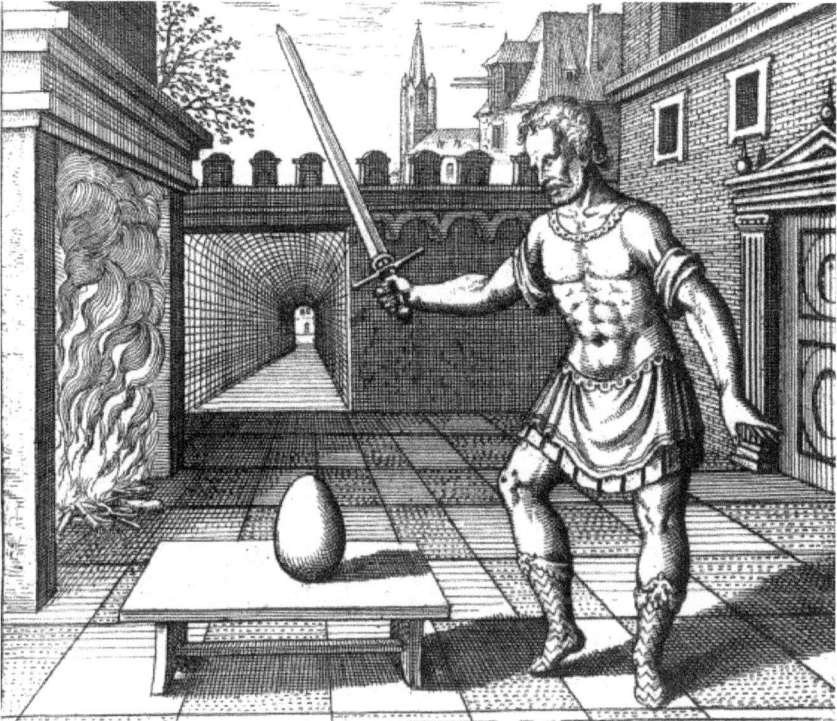

Figure 32. "Take the egg and pierce it with a fiery sword."
A warrior approaches the philosophical egg with a heated sword in order to divide it into its elements. Symbolically the warrior represents the courage and sacrifice required to approach the watery chaos of the unconscious. The image also may warn of the potential pitfalls of approaching an egg with a sword—to understand the natural, symbolic language of the unconscious with intellectual discernment and valor—which could kill new psychological life rather than foster it. The egg and the hallway behind it depict two forms of eternity, one found in nature and the other articulated by human consciousness. From Michael Maier (German, 1568–1622), *Atalanta Fugiens*, 1617, emblem 8; engraver Matthaus Merian (Swiss, 1593–1650).

its chaos. Now, this object, symbolized by the egg, must be divided into its parts so that the potential life inside may be organized, formed, and liberated. This is the beginning of the work which, in analysis, is identical to the initial step of realizing that an unconscious exists and that the unconscious must now be analyzed. Dividing the unconscious side of the psyche into its parts is the first step in determining the life purpose it wants to impart.

Approaching an egg with a fiery sword seems alarmingly aggressive compared to natural events. In the chicken coop, the hen provides just enough warmth to produce new life. In the alchemical laboratory (that is, in the alchemical imagination), a sword heated in fire is used to initiate this process—to meet inner heat with outer heat. We can easily see how a lack of care and an ignorance of nature's intentions could go terribly wrong. As he approaches the egg with a hot sword, the philosopher must be aware that he could kill or corrupt new life that has been incubating. Maier cautioned:

> The Philosophers do indeed smite their Eggs with fire, but it is not with an intent to mortify it, but that it may live and grow up. For, seeing that an animate and living chicken is thence produced, it cannot be said to be Corruption, but generation. (Discourse 8)

Maier is defending the work of the alchemist, saying that even though alchemy is an imitative art, and even though it looks strange, the goal of smiting an egg is not to kill the life inside but to encourage it. The proof of the method's effectiveness is that a chick does get born.

This egg in its original chaos must be divided, Sol and Luna separated from their original chaotic embrace so that a new world can be born. Jung said, "Dismembering the victim corresponds to the idea of dividing the chaos into four elements or the baptismal water into four parts. The purpose of the operation is to create the beginnings of order in the *massa confusa*."[145] In this sense, the alchemist in the image not only sacrifices the original egg, he sacrifices himself, which is to say, his heroic idea of himself.[146] In approaching the egg he knows that he will be divided from his original understanding of himself, now that he has objectified his own unconsciousness and has begun to divide it up. The philosopher-soldier also represents Mercurius and the sacrifice that he makes, transforming in the vessel. In the fairy tale, for example, the wizard as a representative of Mercurius ends up sacrificing his old way of behaving. No longer the arbiter of obedience, he faces intense transformation when he is forced to burn in his own house.

---

[145] Jung, "The Visions of Zosimos," *CW*, vol. 13, par. 111.

[146] Jung, in discussing the alchemical dividing sword, noted, "One finds in Christian symbolism the same 'circular' Gnostic thinking as in alchemy. In both the sacrificer is the sacrificed, and the sword that kills is the same as that which is killed." Jung, "The Visions of Zosimos," *CW*, vol. 13, par. 110.

In psychological terms, by dividing and understanding the contents of one's own unconscious, an old psychological matrix is killed off and a new one created from those same contents. The sword stands for valor and heroism as well as intellectual discernment, all of which can be used for good or for ill in approaching the precious life emerging from the imaginal realm. The image warns us about the dangers of our intentionality, once the unconscious and its images become visible to us. The stark contrast between hen and sword, and the hint against corruption, remind us that as human beings, our consciousness naturally wants to conquer heroically what it doesn't understand or doesn't like. We can easily find ourselves approaching the unconscious as we would an enemy and kill its meaning. Or, if we assume that we already know what we are looking at, we kill it through our tragic ignorance of its newness. Applying too much intellectual or emotional heat, or righteousness, or an ego orientation that remains unconscious of its ignorance, our rush to certainty can easily destroy the new life that nature's innovation is trying to engender.

This is true whether we are women or men: Consciousness, which is naturally masculine and discerning, can have a killing effect on symbolic life. The emblem portrays a man with a sword, referring to consciousness in a man. In a woman, he would represent the animus—a woman's fearless drive to understand. In both cases, it is one-sided consciousness, especially victorious rationality, that must become nature's handmaid and adapted to the humble work of the hen. We have seen how the rational animus can so easily kill wisdom and feeling trying to reach a woman from the depths of her soul as long as she remains enslaved to deadening mores. To be like hens, we refrain from automatically identifying a dream image as something we can reduce to a known fact. If we can allow a confusing psychic image to live and move in the imaginal world, warming it with our attention even though we don't yet know what it means, we have adapted our intellectual sword to the instinctual life of the hen, and in this sense our consciousness has become more feminine. We brood and we wait, allowing the life in the image to reveal itself in its own way—as we saw when Sandra allowed the image of the unknown infant to remain a mystery that needed her care.

As another example, the strange image of Fitcher's bird epitomizes the originality of a symbolic image, but its strangeness makes it vulnerable to the ravages of an intrepid intellect that would dismiss it because it is weird or illogical, or nothing but what we already know. The meaning of any dream image is so easily killed by the hubris of rationality or the pietist preferences of an old god-image that still grips our way of thinking and valuing. Under those influences, we may not realize that something very dark in our experience has profound meaning and needs our reflective capacity, not our judgment, if it is to heal psychic life with its newness. No one is immune to this inflation.

If we manage not to kill new life trying to emerge from the imaginal realm, then egocentricity is the thing that is killed or relativized—which is the appropriate meaning for the sword's killing action, dividing the ego from its illusion of creative ascendency. The *symbolic* meaning of a dream image is always surprising. Because it is always surprising, the symbolic dimension has a killing effect on our identification with rational assumptions and truisms. If we can sacrifice our righteousness, the sword of discernment in that case may kill off the ego's ignorant certainty (not the ego itself, but its centrality). Nurturing symbolic meaning over and over, eventually we may develop an appropriate level of henlike humility to relate to the realm of the nonego according to its transpersonal aim. In this case, our consciousness adapts to the unconscious, developing what the alchemists recognized as a feminine, lunar perspective—an ability to accept the paradoxes of the unconscious.

The Heat of the Yolk Can Be Evil

Of special interest to our discussion of the negative animus is the fact that the heat in the yolk of the philosophical egg has an inherently evil aspect. The fiery yolk contains the sacred life energy that drives the chick's development. But at the same time, the alchemists understood that the divine fire that impels life has a devilish side. In his commentary on Ibn Umail's *Ḥall ar-Rumūz*, Abt said,

> the egg is a symbol for successful integration of the yolk,
> fiery drive-soul (*nafs*), which has a direct relationship to evil
> (*Śaiṭān*). The stone is thus a two-oneness that is a symbol of
> the realization that consciousness and the unconscious always

belong together. The two are held together by the eggshell, symbol for the reality of the unique unity of the adept.[147]

In psychological terms, the yolk as "fiery drive-soul" refers to psychic energy from the germ of the self that pushes for new life and new consciousness with whatever it takes to awaken consciousness to its reality. At first, the drive-soul drives us unconsciously. Generally speaking (and my apologies for mixing two alchemical eras), men experience the fiery drive-soul through the anima in erotic fantasy, and women experience it through the animus in fantasy thinking, as expressed in the medieval illustration from "The Mortification of Adam and Eve" (fig. 33).

Figure 33. The Mortification of Adam and Eve

The hot drive energy of the psyche tends to affect women mainly in the realm of fantasy thinking, men in the realm of eros fantasy. The "mortification" refers to the work of containing the drive energy enough that it no longer controls the personality but instead is connected to the greater will of the self. Miscellanea d'alchimia, Ms. Ashburnham 1166 (14th century), Florence, Biblioteca Medicea-Laurenziana.

We have seen how this drive energy exists in the unconscious animus with its own moral criteria and has an evil quality when it motivates a woman without reflection—when it is not contained in

---

[147] Abt, *Book of the Explanation of Symbols,* 226.

a striving toward consciousness. The evil in the drive-soul is manifest when a woman is identified with it, when its relentless energy takes up residence in her system of thought in a way that pulls her out of life and relationship or blocks her from feeling nourishing meaning from the self. She still doesn't realize her "two-oneness."

We have also seen how much work it can take for a woman to build the awareness needed to catch destructive thoughts in action. Such a capacity requires that she extract the compelling quality of the drive from its unconscious condition, quelling its ability to carry her away. If she can realize the fiery thought as other and submit it to the vessel of her imagination, asking for an image to appear, its natural evil is at the same time contained in the reflective lunar waters of the psyche. The image then has a chance to produce new psychological life if it is understood in the context of individuation: No matter what it is, no matter how humble, unexpected, or distasteful, the image offers new wisdom when its symbolism is understood and integrated.

A 60-year-old analysand named Valorie told me during a therapy session that she woke up that morning obsessing over an old interpersonal problem. She realized that she was completely absorbed in her own fantasies about the situation the instant she woke up. She told me, with tears in her eyes, "I've been doing this my whole life. It's absolutely exhausting." As we worked with this insight, she could also see how her hellish fantasies had pulled her out of relationships in her life. Valorie was describing a sudden new awareness of the devilish energy *behind* her fantasy thinking. In that moment, the evil drive-soul of the autonomous animus was caught in consciousness. The hot obsession could be cooled and slowed down in her reflective capacity, which had been developing over the years through her work with the unconscious until it could contain this realization. In that moment of awareness, the psychic waters were prepared; yolk and white, the masculine and feminine aspects of Mercurius, could be brought together in a new kind of oneness. Without reflection, the drivenness of her fantasy-thinking cut her off from life and eros. With reflection, that drivenness could be contained and integrated as an aspect of individuation. She was able to work with the dynamism that she discovered in a creative process of painting.

The hellish drive in Valorie's unconscious fantasies finally provoked what seemed like a sudden awakening. Similarly, Pearl's devil-man seemed suddenly to pull her out of containment in his dynamism once she contained his dynamism in contemplation and allowed the unconscious to produce a picture. In fact, such a penetrating awakening is not as sudden as it seems but requires a period of requisite work through which the tricks of the animus are seen in action repeatedly, as we saw in Sandra's "caught in the act" dream. It takes time to build up enough familiarity with the animus (or the anima) to genuinely reflect on our naturally unconscious drivenness.

Knowing the unconscious drive has an inherently evil aspect, we can see how a woman's confrontation with her own fantasy thinking is comparable to dealing with the dark side and with evil, as the devil in Barbara Hannah's dream implored. We see how tending to our own dark thoughts stops them from reverberating into the world and how this simple and humble act could even keep war from breaking out. The evil side of the animus is for the most part transformed by being tended and contained, but we will also consider in chapter 13 how there may be some evil in the drivenness that cannot or is never meant to transform.

Sol and Luna in the Vessel

The alchemists considered the appearance of an image in the retort an achievement of the highest order, signaling that the work has begun according to the mysteries of Mercurius (fig. 34), or the "true imagination" as opposed to egocentric fantasies. In psychological terms, the appearance of an image in active imagination means the objective reality of the psyche has made an appearance and is contained to some extent in a relationship with consciousness. At the same time, the fiery drive-soul, finding receptivity in consciousness, is united with the lunar waters of the psyche. The image joins the opposites in a way that is unique to the moment.

In other words, as the ego becomes less identified with solar consciousness and tends to the images of the lunar unconscious, Sol and Luna in the background of the personal drama, in the archetypal realm, have a chance to come into relationship and create new psychological life there. The two appearing together in alchemical images indicate that both

Figure 34. Mercurius in the Philosopher's Egg

This picture is reproduced in Jung's *Psychology and Alchemy* (fig. 22, p. 66). Jung's caption reads: "Mercurius in the 'philosopher's egg' (the alchemical vessel). As filius he stands on the sun and moon, tokens of his dual nature. The birds betoken spiritualization, while the scorching rays of the sun ripen the homunculus in the vessel." The appearance of the sun and moon is an indication that the penetrating drive and reflective understanding have formed and are uniting according to Mercurius, according to the goal. Mutus Liber, in Joannes Jacobus Mangetus, ed., *Bibliotheca Chemica Curiosa, seu Rerum ad alchemiam pertinentium thesaurus instructissimus*, 2 vols. (Geneva, 1702), fig. 2.

sides of Mercurius are present—his masculine and feminine sides have found each other, thanks to the alchemist's humble efforts and indeed his eros in allowing new meaning to come forward from nature. It is almost impossible to convey the importance of this union, sometimes referred to as the first *coniunctio*, when the soul rises to the symbolic level of understanding. This phenomenon is also covered in chapter 12 and in the appendix.

In the philosophical egg, the yolk is compared to Sol and represents the fiery, solar aspect of Mercurius. It is called by various names, including the "sun-point," the infinitesimally small, invisible "dot" from which all being originates, the "fire-point," the "soul in the midpoint of the heart," the "quintessence," and the "golden germ."[148] The yolk contains the life energy that can become the chick, but the albumen is needed to bring that energy into form and substance.

The white of the egg is compared to Luna, the moon, and represents the receptive, cool, watery aspect of Mercurius. The lunar aspect is referred to as a receptacle, "mother and spouse of the sun."[149] The moon "secretes the dew or sap . . . of the water of life, which is hidden in Mercurius."[150] She makes what is hidden in the psyche real by receiving it into herself. Luna is represented by mercury, silver, and quicksilver. Sometimes quicksilver represents both the fiery and watery sides of Mercurius; like the moon, quicksilver itself is a union of opposites. Psychologically speaking, the solar aspect of the psyche is the life drive, libido, creativity, and the motivating energy of individuation, including its evil or driven quality. The lunar aspect is its reality, its continual gestation into form and substance, by which is meant its realization in consciousness.

It may seem strange that the masculine sun is seen as the soul and the moon as spirit, even though it is feminine. This is not because the alchemists were men but because they experienced the reflective, imaginal capacity of the spiritual realm as having a containing, quenching influence on the heat of the soul's drive energy. For men or for women, the fiery energy that drives the personality is soul energy (unconscious psychic energy). The soul is yearning, hot like the sun, driving us in ways we don't understand and often incorporating the ego in identification with

---

[148] Jung pulls these expressions of the yolk from several alchemical texts in "Paracelsus as a Spiritual Phenomenon," *CW*, vol. 13, par. 188.

[149] Jung uses this phrase but does not cite a specific reference in *Mysterium Coniunctionis, CW*, vol. 14, par. 154. His discussions of Sol and Luna in chapter 3, "Personification of the Opposites," bring important symbolic depth to the images.

[150] Ibid., par. 155, quoting Arthur E. Waite.

those drives. But when the soul's yearning is contained in the imaginal vessel, that yearning can be quenched through the creation of an image that expresses its deeper meaning and reality. The drive soul need not push so hard for recognition when it finds the symbolic containment it has been seeking. In every symbol that is understood, Sol and Luna are united.

We can revisit Pearl's work with the devil-man dream as an example of how this phenomenon occurs in the context of a single image. Pearl spontaneously framed her drawing of the nightmare scene in the shape of an egg, emphasizing the fact that when she brought consciousness and the unconscious together to contemplate the dream image, an imaginal vessel was created where the devil-man could be contained and reflected upon as a valid symbolic reality, not just an evil influence. Without putting an image of the devil-man in the imaginal container, neither he nor Pearl's consciousness would have changed; she would have gone on being tortured, and he would have continued to be seen as nothing but evil.

In the background of this process, Sol and Luna were brought together, fertilizing each other and bringing to life a symbolic solution that allowed Pearl's life to continue in a new way, the drive of the devil-man connected with meaning. This is the basis of the transcendent function, in which a third, symbolic possibility unites the opposites and at the same time moves psychic development from one stage to the next.

A steady lunar perspective in consciousness signals the second part of the work. It means that the ego naturally accepts the dual, paradoxical, and sometimes conflicting nature of the unconscious. In a woman or a man, a feminine, lunar attitude is needed to accept the bipolar nature of the psyche, including what the devil in Hannah's dream referred to as the darker side of life. Consciousness itself becomes dual, in other words, able to accept the irrational, ambivalent aspects of the psyche as valid, its strange images as meaningful, and the ambiguous drive-soul as an aspect of the divine.

The appearance of Sol and Luna in the alchemical vessel indicates that solar and lunar aspects of the psyche are reliably informing each other in the psychic realm, a result of the ego's steady relationship with the unconscious. The fiery soul and the watery spirit in the psyche can fertilize each other, inform each other, rather than existing in a split condition.

This is a remarkable achievement: the openness of consciousness to the unknown may help bring the whole psychic realm (the source of the god-image) into balance, where it may heal itself. We see this illustrated at the end of "Fitcher's Bird" when balance is restored to the family and the archetypal realm at the same time.

The Egg Has Everything It Needs

For a hen, tending an egg until it hatches is a completely natural process requiring no outside intervention, as long as the egg is fertilized. Ibn Umail, in *Ḥall ar-Rumūz*, emphasized that once an egg is fertilized, the transformation from yolk to bird needs nothing foreign: "The egg is like that: Without anything strange entering it, it transforms from one state to another, and is changed from one thing to another. Then it turns into a flying bird, like what was its origin and its beginning."[151] In psychological terms, the self may develop entirely and naturally through a development of the contents of the personality, as long as consciousness and the unconscious are fertilized with each other. The philosophical egg stands for the adept's own mix of psychic elements—his own soul and spirit, Sol and Luna, including any evil aspects. While everything needed is present, nothing is rejected. The heat of solar drive and the reflecting coolness of lunar waters fertilize each other, transforming "from one state to another," finally giving birth to a new form of themselves. The flying bird is the unique, new psychological life that emerges from the ego's devoted brooding over the self that "was its origin and its beginning." In other words, although the self may have given birth to the ego, that fact cannot be realized until the ego commits the crime of brooding over its origins and in doing so gives birth to the self.

The fact that every individual contains everything needed, including evil, for the inner divinity to become realized means that individuation needs not a perfect soul but an honest one. No matter who you are, individuation has its own divine mandate and comes with its own moral reckoning; no creed or philosophy foreign to the individual is

---

[151] Abt, *Book of the Explanation of Symbols,* 227. In his commentary of this 10th-century Arabic text, Abt summarizes the main message of *Ḥall ar-Rumūz* "as the creation of consciousness by continuously pondering over the symbols that emerge from the unconscious, gradually uniting the adept's soul with the divine into a two-oneness" (10).

required. The ability for an ordinary human being to observe and promote their own redemption according to an inner divine mandate represents a paradigm shift in religious life that we have only begun to fathom.

Nature Transforms Nature

Zosimos's axiom that "nature transforms nature" is another way to express the idea that nothing foreign is needed for the self to become realized.[152] Many people go through life without observing their relationship to the unconscious, and this is perfectly natural. But if we do see the unconscious and relate to it, we engage in a transformation that goes a little bit against nature. We may go against what seemed natural when we were unconscious, but individuation is also organized by nature. So through the development of consciousness, nature transforms nature. The self and the ego transform each other according to the chicken and egg paradox.

We can look at Pearl's experience with the devil-man from another perspective to illustrate this point. Her unconscious, torturous relationship with the devil-man was natural and familiar for most of her life. She could have gone on being tortured the same way for the rest of her life. But when the unconscious brought her a powerful dream image for that torture, the dream's intensity compelled her to explore its symbolic meaning and led her to a new understanding of her experience, a way to go against her original, unconscious nature. A way of thinking about herself that long had been unconscious and agonizing became the object of contemplation. In trying to understand the dream, she did not exclude the devil-man or assume that he should be conquered, whereas a conventional approach would have Pearl reject him. Thus, nature could transform nature without anything foreign entering the picture and without excluding anything from the picture. The very energy that tortured Pearl suddenly and naturally fueled her individuation.

In our tale as well, the heroine's awareness of her egg is a completely natural development—yet it indicates that she is acting against what had

---

[152] As cited in Jung, "The Visions of Zosimos," *CW*, vol. 13, par. 87, note 71.

been natural for her and her sisters and generations of maidens before them. The fairy tale expresses the sheer miracle of a woman getting outside the momentum of the unconscious, murderous animus. Then, seeing him objectively and trying to understand him instead of rejecting him, she accepts his dynamism as an aspect of her transformational fate that may be meaningful. In that sense, going against nature, she helps nature overcome itself. The tale doesn't give any reason for the heroine to become more aware or receptive than her sisters, except to say that she is clever and crafty, though in psychological terms, this means she is conscious, able to perceive invisible influences. As a woman begins to observe the orthodox animus seducing her into old emotional torment, and as she is crafty enough to contain the driven aspect of that energy and find its meaning, the hidden spirit of the unconscious will lead her into a world of new meaning.

We defy collective norms in order to pay attention to the unconscious in the first place. If we are clever according to the mandate of individuation, we may not seem very clever to the outer world, and this can be a paralyzing problem. Women need to be quite crafty, even devious, in finding ways to tend to their psychological opus in a world that expects them to prioritize the care of everyone else in their lives, obey organizational standards that ignore their personal realities, or participate in social niceties that suck up life energy. A fierce, henlike devotion to individuation requires that a woman turn her focus inward without apology, finding unconventional ways to fulfill her relationship to the inner world without neglecting life's essential responsibilities. I frequently tell my analysands that we have to schedule hidden time in our diaries for the inner work and then conscientiously take pencil to paper. Virginia Woolf's plea to women to claim their own room in the house is only the beginning. We need our own philosophical coop, with a lock on the door. From a worldly perspective, we may seem selfish, but the inner world demands that we be crafty enough to defy those standards and keep the process of individuation warm, by hook or by crook.

Sun and Moon, Cock and Hen

Discourse 30 of *Atalanta Fugiens* is fittingly entitled "The Sun needs the Moon, as the Cock needs the Hen" (fig. 35). Here, Maier pointed out the fact that fertilization occurs not only in the life of chickens but also, and by the same token, in the cosmos between the sun and the moon. This symbolism helps us understand the relationship between earthly and archetypal realms and how both are affected when consciousness and the unconscious come together for mutual development. Maier said:

> The Sun without the Moon is of no great Esteem, and the Moon without the Sun is of an abject condition and Vile Originall. But it is from her Husband the Sun that she receives Splendour, Dignity and Strength or Firmenesse both of Mind and Body. And the Sun obtains from the Moon the Multiplication of his Offspring and the Propagation of his Kind. Hence Rosarius says, if there were only one of them in our Stone the Medicine would never flow easily nor give the Tincture; nor if it did give it, it would not Tinge but for as much as was in it, and the remainder and Mercury would Fly away in Smoak, because a Receptacle of the Tincture would not be in it. (Discourse 30)

The need for both male and female in the production of new life is a basic, universal fact, expressed in the animal kingdom as well as the cosmic realm. In both worlds, the opposites need each other for life to continue. Fertilization here emphasizes the marvel of complementarity—how the opposites bestow meaning and purpose to each other *because* they are opposite. The sun is fertilized by the moon's reflection as much as the moon is fertilized by the sun's penetrating light.

Psychologically speaking, consciousness and the unconscious fertilize each other not only because they are opposites but also because they know they are opposites, which can happen when we know they are opposites. One opposite without the other would be "of abject condition," its qualities imperceptible even to itself. If consciousness and the unconscious weren't differentiated from each other, "Medicine would never flow easily nor give the Tincture"; no symbolic medicine could flow between them, and neither would be the wiser. Nothing psychically new could take shape. The onus is on the ego to recognize the difference between consciousness and the unconscious, as well as the personal and archetypal, because this capacity does not exist in the unconscious.

Figure 35. "The sun needs the moon like the cock needs the hen."
The author correlates instinctual and cosmic opposites, which mirror and inform each other. Psychologically they correspond to the opposites as they appear in personal and archetypal life. From Michael Maier (German, 1568–1622), *Atalanta Fugiens*, 1617, emblem 30; engraver Matthaus Merian (Swiss, 1593–1650).

The unconscious fertilizes consciousness the same way the moon fertilizes the sun—by reflecting it back to itself. Otherwise, in the bright light of day, consciousness (in a woman or a man) could never see itself. Solar consciousness can be arrogant and power-oriented, without eros, when it never reflects on itself or the shadow cast by its certainty. A woman identified with the orthodox animus often seems very sure of her way of thinking, especially when it comes to right and wrong. But in relationship to the unconscious, she may begin to realize that the light of the unconscious can be brighter, or wiser, than the light of her own solar thinking, no matter how brilliant she is.

The rhythm between the full moon and the dark moon as it reflects more or less of the sun symbolically expresses the connection between consciousness and the unconscious, naturally alternating between emptiness and fullness. At the full moon, the sun and moon are seen by the alchemists to reach a *coniunctio*, in which they are fully united, and the fertilizing wonder of their complementarity is most apparent. The moon receives from the sun its "Splendour, Dignity and Strength or Firmenesse," and the sun "obtains from the Moon the Multiplication of his Offspring and the Propagation of his Kind," according to the discourse above. Psychologically speaking, both solar consciousness and lunar unconsciousness are strengthened and given meaning when consciousness allows them to be in relationship with each other, so one is not dominating the other.

In the second part of the work, a stage is reached in which solar consciousness has accepted the lunar world of the unconscious and the dual nature of the psyche in a steady way, allowing the unconscious to be more present in life.[153] A receptive femininity, an eros quality in consciousness, develops as a result of relating to the unconscious over time. Consciousness becomes more flexible and less identified with truisms. Hard opinions lose their thrall. A person who can accept the paradoxical, "both-and nature" of the unconscious, at least in theory, is now challenged to bring that relationship into life, to live in relationship with the self and take up ethical demands that may go against precious assumptions. Otherwise, mercurial wisdom from the symbolic world of the self goes up in smoke, as if it didn't exist in the first place.

Maier is also implying that the earthly and cosmic realms need each other for the tincture of mercurial wisdom to have its healing, transformational effect. When the ego does become aware of the unconscious, it is also immediately in connection with the archetypal dimension of the psyche, and these two realms transform each other.[154] Going back to Pearl's example: Once she put the devil-man in a picture, thinking he was "just" a personal problem, Pearl could also see his objective reality, his archetypal dimension and his own way of being split. Inexplicably giving him wings, she realized he was both devil

---

[153] See Abt, *Book of the Explanation of Symbols,* 51.

[154] Jung explored the spectrum of psychic energy, from the "biological instinctual psyche" to the archetypal image, to the reality of the archetype per se, in "On the Nature of the Psyche," *CW,* vol. 8, par. 397ff.

and spirit—not only evil. She was confronted with his archetypal two-sidedness and his baffling, volatile autonomy. Mercurial wisdom from the cosmic dimension thus did not go up in smoke but fertilized Pearl's consciousness, sacrificing some of his autonomy to do so. Her ability to accept the paradoxes of the devil-man's archetypal dimension likewise had an effect on *him*, tempering his urgent drivenness and canalizing it toward individuation. The personal and archetypal realms had an effect on each other, tempering the solar tendency for trenchant, fatherlike criticism to take hold of Pearl and reject her suffering out of hand.

A "Specific Being Transmitted by the Stars"

We return to *Atalanta Fugiens*, discourse 8, where Maier described how each bird born to a hen is unique, in spite of the fact that every bird is made of the same elements:

> The external heat is the first mover which by a certain Circulation of the Elements and change of one into the other, introduces a new form by the instinct & guidance of Nature. For Water passes into Air, Air into Fire, Fire into Earth, which being joined together, & a specific being transmitted by the stars, an individual Bird is made of that kind whose Egg it was & whose seed was infused into it.

The opening statement reminds us that the egg of the self needs external heat in order to develop. Even though the yolk inside is hot, and even though the egg has everything it needs to develop into a bird, external heat is the "first mover." In psychological terms, even though the self has everything it needs to be born, ego consciousness is the necessary first mover, lending constant, henlike attention to the existence of the self and its symbolic messages.

Maier pointed out that each bird develops through a universal pattern. Just like every other bird, it goes through "a certain Circulation of the Elements." And yet, each bird is unique. The circulation of the elements informs the individual bird's development, as does the kind of egg "whose seed was infused into it," but so does the fact that it is "a specific being transmitted by the stars." In other words, the biological seed isn't the only thing that determines a bird's unique characteristics; the particular constellation of the stars in the moment the egg was conceived also has an influence. The circulation of the elements has a universal pattern, but the combination and proportion of elements is different in each bird, based on the cosmic moment of conception. Because of the stars that influence the elements and their origin, no two birds are alike. In psychological terms, the symbolic world into which we are born, not just the biological, makes us who we are; we are made of a certain constellation of archetypal phenomena. Knowing what those elements are and what they mean, we bring awareness to our symbolic birthright and begin to grapple with its moral implications.

Abt provided us with a psychological description of the circulation through the elements in his commentary on Ibn Umail's great vision, "The Silvery Water and the Starry Earth."[155] Turning earth into water (body into soul) psychologically describes the translation of emotion into image, through a dream or active imagination. When an image arrives, we see the soul of the emotion, its own way of portraying itself. Then, turning water into air (soul into spirit) describes the extraction of possible symbolic meanings from the image through amplification and ongoing contemplation. We may come up with several possible meanings for any dream image. Turning air into fire or light is about finding the one, unique meaning distilled out of the many possibilities—the meaning that shines the brightest in the context of one's individual cosmology. Then we know the meaning of a particular dream image for a particular moment in our particular life, as transmitted by our particular stars. The process emphasizes the importance of our understanding that in active imagination, we are in connection with the archetypal realm, with cosmic nous.

The overall process in which the true meaning of an image is finally understood and felt is often depicted in alchemy by the appearance of a bird and is called *sublimatio*; we could also call it "catching the bird." The bird at this stage is an image of achieved symbolic understanding, again, a union of soul and spirit.

Maier described the final step of this circulation when he said, "For Water passes into Air, Air into Fire, Fire into Earth, which being joined together, & a specific being transmitted by the stars." In this case, the final

---

[155] Abt, *Book of the Explanation of Symbols,* 25–58.

fire or the unique meaning of a symbol is turned back into earth, which means it is integrated into the earthly reality of the individual, contributing to their unique myth. In this way over time, the great bird—the bird of the self—is liberated from its unconscious condition and enters life as a constant presence.

The psyche continually tries to show us what is genuinely eternal in ourselves, in our specific lives as transmitted by our unique constellation of archetypes, even though we are ordinary human beings made of the same earthly, psychological elements and the same four functions as every other human being. What makes us unique is the singular life that is constellated in our archetypal, transhuman stars and how they are related to our earthly existence. If we never see that unique pattern or integrate it into our lives, the loss is not only personal, but an aspect of the divine is left in the lurch.

In the next section of discourse 8, Maier continued to describe the freeing of the chick into the world. Here he evoked the analogy of a human embryo:

> So an Embryo being freed from that human vegetable life which alone it enjoyed in the Mother's womb, obtains another, more perfect one, by his birth & coming into the light of the world. So when we shall pass from this present life, there remains for us another that is most perfect & Eternal.

When heat is applied to the egg successfully, the embryo inside is freed from the vegetative life it enjoyed in the womb. Symbolically, this means that the embryo of the self is freed from its unconscious, vegetative state. This can only happen when it is realized in the consciousness of the only person who, by birth, can bring its unique form into the light of the world.

The Bird as a Liberated Psychic Reality

In his interpretation of a case we now know belonged to Wolfgang Pauli, Jung included an important dream about the solstice (turning point). The dream included the image of a "large dark ring," which Pauli took into a series of active imaginations.[156] In the first vision, as he was

---

[156] Jung, *Psychology and Alchemy, CW*, vol. 12, par. 301ff.

focused on the ring by itself, an egg appeared in the middle of the ring. In the next vision, a black eagle emerged from the egg. Pauli reported that the eagle "seizes in its beak the ring, now turned to gold." In his discussion of the material, Jung commented on the symbolic meaning of a bird emerging from an egg:

> In alchemy the egg stands for the chaos apprehended by the artifex, the *prima materia* containing the captive world-soul. Out of the egg—symbolized by the round cooking vessel—will rise the eagle or phoenix, the liberated soul, which is ultimately identical with the Anthropos who was imprisoned in the embrace of physis.[157]

The "chaos apprehended by the artifex" refers psychologically to the apprehension of the reality of the unconscious—as illustrated in *Atalanta Fugiens* emblem 8 (fig. 32) of smiting the egg with a sword. The chaos or *prima materia,* the undifferentiated opposites, now need conscious attention in order to release the captive world-soul from its unconscious existence. Although we don't know the meaning of the black eagle and the ring for Pauli at what may have been a turning point in his life, his dream indicates at least the possibility for the unconscious to be apprehended, and subsequently the self to be realized as a living factor.

When spiritual meaning is liberated from an unconscious condition, even on the relatively smaller scale of a single dream image, this too can be understood as the liberation of the soul. Dream by dream, image by image, in each effort to understand the symbolic meaning of a chaotic situation, we liberate a bit more of the self, gradually building up its wholeness and integrating its reality into our lives.

The differentiation of the opposites, a necessary first step to their reunion, is symbolized in these alchemical pictures by the appearance of Sol and Luna (as we've already seen), or a king and queen, or by solar and lunar birds, such as the eagle and swan or dove that emerge from the retort (fig. 36). These images indicate in yet another way that as the ego apprehends the opposites in the unconscious, those opposites become differentiated in the unconscious on the transpersonal level. It marks a critical turning point in the opus when the opposites are separated

---

[157] Ibid., par. 306.

Figure 36. "Sublimatio," from *Philosophia Reformata*

The king holds an eagle and the queen a swan, representing the philosophical gold and silver extracted from their common or vulgar form in the alchemical furnace. Outside the furnace, their symbolic value has been made conscious and will be united in the "mystical marriage" to form the *rebis*, the *filius*, or Mercurius as a union of two. From Johann Daniel Mylius (German, ca. 1583–1642); engraver Balthazar Schwan (d. 1642).

enough that they may begin relating to each other. Whether Sol and Luna, king and queen, or airy and watery birds, the images of the opposites are identical with the two sides of Mercurius, who has initiated this process in order to renew himself. Like the sun, the eagle is associated with philosophical sulfur and gold; like the moon, the swan or dove is associated with philosophical mercury and silver. The fact that the birds come out of the alchemical oven or vessel indicates that at this stage of the work, after a period of heated containment and transformation, the opposites have become psychically real and may unite, bringing both sides of the self together, a consummate healing event sometimes referred to as the first coniunctio that eventually may lead to the realization of the self in the second coniunctio (see chapter 12 and the appendix).

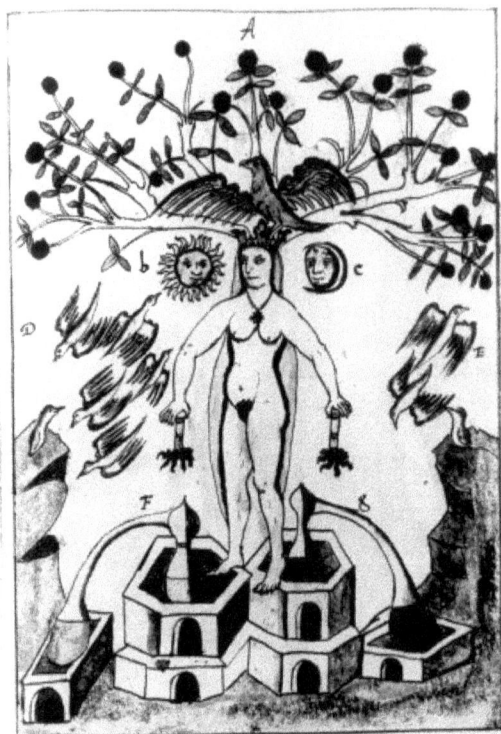

Figure 37. Mercurius as World Virgin or *Anima Mundi*
The virgin stands on two alchemical vessels, holds plants in her hands, and has a bird perched on top of her head. The sun and moon are on either side of her, and she is surrounded by birds. The ascending and descending birds symbolize ongoing transformation. From H. Reusner, *Pandora*, in Julius Ruska, ed., *Turba Philosophorum* (Berlin, 1931).

Mercurius as a representation of the self in its various aspects is the eagle and he is the swan; he is the sun and he is the moon. He is their differentiation, their transformation, and he is their reunion and rejuvenation. Once reunited, the two sides of Mercurius become the *rebis* (literally a "two-thing," derived from Latin *res*, "thing," and *bīnī*, "two" or "pair"), a hermaphrodite, as we saw in fig. 25.[158] In other images depicting his two-ness, Mercurius is depicted as virgin of the world or *anima mundi 9* (figs. 37 and 38). These too are images for the union of opposites, even though Mercurius appears as primarily feminine. As a

---

[158] See Read, *Prelude to Chemistry,* 238.

Figure 38. Another Version of the Symbols for Mercurius as *Anima Mundi*

The virgin stands on the conjoined sun and moon, another version of which she holds in her left hand. In her right hand is a chalice containing five serpents. She is surrounded by wings and has a bird perched on her head above her crown, symbolizing the completion of a spiritual transformation as well as ongoing transformation. From *Turba Philosophorum*, fol. 16, H. Reusner, ed., *Pandora* (Basel, 1588).

feminine being, Mercurius is an image for the soul of the world that holds everything together, materially and psychically. The images emphasize the wholeness and interrelatedness of the psyche as a phenomenon of nature, overall a feminine, yet spiritual reality—an entity that is still trying to penetrate our collective solar consciousness.

In psychological terms, Mercurius represents the objective self. At the same time, he is the wholeness of nature, of the psyche, and its intricate interrelatedness, including life and death, fire and water, spirit and soul, his two sides differentiated and then reunited, related to each other in a new way for the purpose of creating new life. The predominance of birds or wings in these images signal the psychic nature of Mercurius, and the fact that he transcends consciousness. The birds are ascending and descending, symbolizing the ongoing circulation taking place by way of the self, a psychic event that is continually renewing itself and needing to be reintegrated into conscious life. Nature transforms nature, the psyche transforms the psyche without end, but needs the individual to realize its renewal consciously and to make it real in their life.

I would submit that the unique image of Fitcher's bird at the end of the fairy tale also symbolizes a liberated psychic reality with an overall feminine cast—an expression of the unifying soul of nature, renewed and realized through the work of one human being. Although not an elaborate creature, the heroine in her bird regalia nevertheless is described as wondrous. She may be considered a feminine version of wholeness made from elements of nature—honey and feathers—each of which in its own way expresses the reality of the psychic realm. Honey and white feathers are important alchemical images that bring rich meaning to the relationship between the opposites. The fact that the heroine is completely immersed in them invites us to look closely at the symbolism.

12
The Significance of Honey

As we near the end of "Fitcher's Bird," the heroine has cleaned the wizard's house and prepared a feast for her supposed wedding. But instead of dressing in a wedding gown before the guests arrive, she disguises herself as a creature called Fitcher's bird. The fairy tale says, "When all was ready, she got into a barrel of honey, and then cut the feather-bed open and rolled herself in it, until she looked like a wondrous bird, and no one could recognize her." In the previous chapter, we explored the meaning of the bird as an image of spiritual realization. To understand the symbolic meaning of Fitcher's bird in particular and the fact that the heroine makes herself appear as such a distinctive creature, we will review the motif of special garments in fairy tales and explore the important psychological meaning of honey.

Garments and Disguises

Special garments and disguises ranging from animal hides to fine dresses are worn by heroines in many fairy tales of feminine redemption, signaling stages in a metamorphosis.[159] The father-daughter tale "Allerleirauh" (sometimes titled "Thousand Furs," literally translated "all kinds of roughness") may be the only tale in which the heroine employs a full range of disguises, from coarsest to finest. In the beginning of the tale when she has to escape from her father who wants to marry her because

---

[159] The worldwide motif of a heroine donning successive dresses occurs in Cinderella tales (Aarne-Thompson-Uther Tale Type 510A, Persecuted Heroine, and 510B, Unnatural Love). The motif appears in various collections; tales include "Donkey Skin," "Catskin," "The King Who Wished to Marry His Daughter," "The She-Bear," "Tattercoats," "Cap o' Rushes," "The Princess That Wore a Rabbit-Skin Dress," The Bear," and "Mossycoat." Thanks to Douglas Graves for referring me to the feather dress motif in "Catskin."

she looks like her recently deceased mother, she conceals herself under a cloak of animal skins made from the fur of a thousand animals and hides in the forest of another kingdom. The prince of that land eventually discovers her sleeping in a hollow tree, so dirty and matted he can't tell if she is human or animal. But he takes pity on her and brings her to his palace, where she works as a lowly kitchen maid, covered in ash.

Secretly, Allerleirauh attends three of the prince's grand balls and, like Cinderella, she wears a different magical dress to each ball, piquing the prince's interest in her. For the first ball, she wears a dress as golden as the sun, the second a dress as silvery as the moon, and the third a dress as bright as the stars. After the third ball, the prince finally recognizes her as the same creature he rescued from the forest, and soon they are married. From the animal fur to the star dress, Allerleirauh's garments symbolize a psychological transformation in the feminine realm, one that brings the masculine along.

The heroine hiding in an animal skin can indicate a deeply wounded state of femininity—a near-animal state in which eros is hardly recognizable.[160] A woman overwhelmed by the father complex or the animus barely can feel who or what she is, or how to extend herself into the world. We remember Pearl sewing a heart to her chest as a way to claim some semblance of her reality as she suffered in a state of deep isolation and loneliness. I have seen women who are so inundated by the threats of negative animus projections that their eyes furtively dart like those of a vigilant animal of prey.

Remembering that the heroine of a fairy tale represents an ego connected to the self, however, we know that hiding under an animal skin and escaping into another forest may also have a redemptive aim; that Allerleirauh doesn't spend her life in the forest but eventually is found by a prince tells us that her solitude has led to a new development between her and the masculine. Likewise, a woman who enters a depression at first involuntarily may over time engage her depression more deliberately as an introverted encounter with the unconscious, and this brings the animus around to her so that she can realize her suffering as a way toward

---

[160] See von Franz's discussion of the symbolic meanings of animal skins and garments in *The Feminine in Fairy Tales,* 126.

grace. The fairy-tale encounter between the lonely, dejected maiden and a new prince represents a potential new recognition between a woman's suffering soul and her own way of understanding that suffering. One day, her animus sees her struggle as if for the first time and doesn't condemn it, but wonders what it is. She can realize for herself that her solitude is meaningful; her introversion has led to a potential new relationship between masculine and feminine realms in her own psyche. Allerleirauh's ensuing work as a kitchen maid in the prince's palace, like our heroine's work in the wizard's house, represents another level of relationship with the unconscious, in which the daily toil of understanding hints from the unconscious is taken up in a consistent way as part of life. A woman devoted to her work in the inner kitchen over time begins to feel herself and her world in a new way.

The sun, moon, and star dresses in the fairy tale represent psychological transformations from solar to lunar to stellar orientations as a woman develops a more and more individual relationship with the animus; these are similar to the transformations that we observed in the philosophical egg texts. A woman's solar orientation is the most collective, most in line with the philosophies of the day. Her lunar orientation is more feminine, more related to the unconscious, a result of ongoing reflection and work with symbolic life. A stellar orientation, wearing the dress as bright as the stars, would mean that individuation according to her own archetypal alignment has become a way of life. In an English version of this tale, "Catskin," the third dress is made from the feathers of all the birds, a costume closer to the one in our tale, the feathers indicating an orientation to the psychic realm.

The prince puts two and two together. Realizing that the beautiful princess he found so intriguing is also the kitchen maid he rescued from the forest, he expresses an important integration in the personality as a whole. In a woman, the lowest and the highest, the dejected and the holy in herself, can be seen as one. She is not either/or but both, and, in fact, neither without the other because her lowest experience of life leads her to the self.

By the time the heroine of "Fitcher's Bird" creates her bird regalia, she has done her housework, so we can understand her appearance as a wondrous bird to express an achieved psychological transformation and soon discover that her garment, though not a beautiful gown, expresses a connection to the self. Her garment is not finely made as in the other tales but fabricated of raw materials, not delivered magically but created by herself, emphasizing how closely now her impulses are assimilated to the self. Consistent with alchemical symbolism, the costume focuses our attention on the nature and quality of its substances and the way they are joined together as a union of opposites. Honey—a sticky, sweet, earthy, moist element—is joined with feathers—a subtle, airy, dry element. Together, honey and feathers symbolize the opposite qualities of any psychic image, which can sweeten and refresh life with its wisdom or disappear in a moment if its symbolic meaning is not understood and anchored in felt reality. Symbolic honey—the eros of nature—is the requisite goal in this combination and makes the image an expression of the self not just as a concept but as a felt reality.

The Self as a Work of Nature

The strange final image of the crowned and winged hermaphrodite in the *Rosarium Philosophorum* pictures is another image that depicts the self as an odd combination of animal, elemental and spiritual elements. Jung explained how such an image represents the self:

> The self too is both ego and non-ego, subjective and objective, individual and collective. It is the "uniting symbol" which epitomizes the total union of opposites. As such and in accordance with its paradoxical nature, it can only be expressed by means of symbols. These appear in dreams and spontaneous fantasies and find visual expression in the mandalas that occur in the patient's dreams, drawings, and paintings. Hence, properly understood, *the self is not a doctrine or theory but an image born of nature's own workings, a natural symbol* far removed from all conscious intention. [161]

The image of a woman covered in honey and feathers expresses a union of ego and nonego, subjective and objective, individual and

---

[161] Jung, "Psychology of the Transference," *CW*, vol. 16, para. 474., emphasis added.

collective. Immersed in the marvels of nature's birds and bees, the heroine as Fitcher's bird shows us an entity born of nature's own workings, an anomaly, like the alchemical bird or hermaphrodite with wings, that is far removed from all conscious intention—in this case with an overall feminine cast.

White Feathers

The fairy tale doesn't make it clear exactly who or what Fitcher is.[162] The name "Fitcher" most likely comes from the German *Feder*, "feather," or *Fittich*, "wings." The Grimm brothers suggested that the name "Fitcher" derives from the Icelandic *fitfuglar*, a legendary bird that was web-footed and "looked as white as a swan."[163] The webbed foot of the *fitfuglar* would make it a water bird and distinguish it from birds with talons or claws (like chickens or eagles) that don't swim. Since the heroine rolled in the feathers of a bed, they are probably from a goose, another white water bird with webbed feet. Whether from a *fitfuglar*, a swan, or a goose, feathers themselves stand for the bird as a whole, as von Franz pointed out. She said, "birds in general represent psychic entities," as we have discussed in the context of the philosophical egg.[164] The feathers are symbolic of the psyche's airy, spiritual side, which can make its imagery so difficult to pin down or experience as real. They emphasize the subtle-body aspect of symbolic life.

These details tell us that Fitcher's bird is not a solar bird like the eagle or phoenix in some alchemical pictures that soars into the heavens alone, representing an unfettered spiritual phenomenon. She is more feminine, like a goose that can go from water to earth and flies in a skein, in constant connection with the whole flock. Geese can migrate thousands of miles between exact locations by staying in touch with each other and the lay of the land. Symbolically, geese are the birds of the Great Mother, constantly harkening to her presence through their incessant honking.

---

[162] Maria Tatar, in *The Annotated Brothers Grimm* (201), assumes that the wizard is Fitcher. But the wizard doesn't recognize his own bird and addresses it as "Fitcher's bird," as if Fitcher were someone else. One never knows, however, how such expressions arrive in fairy tales.

[163] Grimm and Grimm, *Grimm's Household Tales*, 1:237.

[164] Von Franz, *The Interpretation of Fairy Tales*, 67.

Perhaps most important from our symbolic perspective, a mother goose or swan does enormous work brooding her eggs for a term of up to 35 days.

In alchemical images, the whiteness of the bird signals the *albedo*, or whitening, another alchemical term like the *sublimatio* for realized spiritual meaning, also denoting a steady, abiding state in which the personality is mostly detached from the drivenness of the unconscious after a long period of work in the black, *nigredo* phase. In some alchemical texts, the *albedo* is called the white swan. Jung quoted one alchemist regarding the *albedo*:

> The old masters were wont to call this work their white swan, their albification, or making white, their sublimation, their distillation, their circulation, their purification, their separation, their sanctification, and their resurrection, because the Tincture is made white like a shining silver. . . . They call it their resurrection, because the white rises up out of the black.[165]

We sense the miraculous nature of the white swan of resurrection as one in which a clarity of understanding and feeling finally release an individual from a long, dark period of struggle through which unconscious identification with the self is mortified. The swan symbolizes a moment of grace: "the white rises up out of the black" when symbolic meaning finally achieves its healing aim and a person feels creatively and legitimately connected to her life work.

Honey and the Eros Quality of the Self

To make a pound of honey, a hive of worker bees flies about a thousand miles. They collect pollen from flowers in peak bloom and bring it back to the hive, using the angle of the sun as a guide to find their way. They store their honey in combs, deep interlinked hexagonal cells—

---

[165] Jung, "Psychology of the Transference," *CW*, vol. 16, par. 515. Jung quotes John Pordage, apparently writing to his *soror mystica*, Jane Leade, in 1698. The footnote to paragraph 515 reads: "The letter is printed in Roth-Scholz, *Deutsches Theatrum Chemicum*, I, pp. 557–97. The first German edition of this 'Philosophisches Send-Schreiben vom Stein dei Weissheit' seems to have been published in Amsterdam in 1698." The editors note that they were not able to find the manuscript in British or American libraries at the time volume 16 was published.

the most efficient shape possible for liquid storage—made of wax that they produce themselves. They keep the hive meticulously clean, at a constant temperature of 95 degrees Fahrenheit (35 degrees Celsius), and are continuously engaged in producing a new brood. Their tireless, daily work is organized around the queen as their central ruling figure, who outlasts many generations of workers.[166] When we put honey in our tea, we may enjoy its sweetness even more when we realize the sheer amount of life energy that goes into producing it or the fact that we are taking in nature's interwoven mysteries.

In these ways, honey is a symbol for the psyche itself, an intricate, natural phenomenon that has evolved over millions of years through the detailed labors of nature. We depend on the psyche and live from its energy without knowing how the psyche produces itself, binds itself to us, nourishes us continuously, or how it drives development, and rarely do we think to ask. When we do pay attention, we find that individuation is meticulously organized as if by a beelike intelligence, in such minute detail that no psychic grain is left unturned. With this in mind, the heroine's immersion in honey expresses a woman's saturating experience of the psyche as a "substance" that mysteriously and intricately supports life through the generosity of nature.

Von Franz gave us a powerful example of the symbolic meaning of honey in her essay "Transformed Berserker," about the great vision of the Swiss saint Niklaus von Flüe.[167] Brother Klaus, as the saint was called, suffered deep depression and inner conflict in his quest to become close to God but kept his troubles mainly to himself. His inner world burdened him with dark visions and forced him to make impossible life choices, including leaving the home of his wife and 10 children to live as hermit (though in the end he didn't go far). In one of a series of numinous visions he had while in seclusion, Brother Klaus was walking in nature when he encountered a pilgrim, who held out a cup for alms. When Klaus dropped his coin into the cup, he saw under the pilgrim's robe the fur of

---

[166] See Luton, *Bees, Honey and the Hive.*

[167] Von Franz, *Archetypal Dimensions of the Psyche.* In this essay, von Franz describes four levels of eros development.

a bear glittering with gold. He knew then that this pilgrim was both bear and God.

Von Franz understood Klaus's vision to represent a new god-image that unites Christ, the god of love, with Wotan, god of berserkers, warriors who dressed in bearskins and stirred themselves up emotionally and physically to go into war. Through Brother Klaus's introversion, through his deep contemplation of his own darkness, Christ and Wotan came together, uniting light and dark, Christian and pagan, loving and warring aspects of the god-image, aspects that long have been split apart. Klaus's vision of the pilgrim came to a profound end, suggesting that the unification of God-images can have a profoundly healing effect on humanity by reminding them of the love they have for each other. Klaus described the pilgrim in the bearskin as pouring out great love like "a vessel that is filled to the brim with honey."[168]

Von Franz explained that if, like Brother Klaus, "we suffer the problem of the opposites to the utmost and accept it into ourselves, we can sometimes become a place in which the divine opposites can spontaneously come together."[169] By taking his own conflict about God into deep introversion and conscientiously refusing to project it outward, Klaus became a place where a profound reconciling image could come into being. Von Franz even went so far as to say that his vision produced an "unofficial development of the Christ image."[170] The symbolic image coming from the psyche of this individual man moves the god-image forward by circling back to the nature god Wotan (one of the gods that Mercurius encompasses) and unifying that pagan image with Christ. This unification produced what von Franz identified as the highest form of eros, which "heals humanity in all of its imperfections . . . a redeemer of the whole of nature,"[171] as the alchemists saw in Mercurius.

To help amplify the symbolism of honey in Brother Klaus's vision, von Franz turned to the Brihadaranyaka Upanishad, where the individual

---

[168] Ibid., 40. It is best if readers go to von Franz' account to read the details of the vision.
[169] Ibid., 48.
[170] Ibid., 46.
[171] Ibid., 49.

realization of self as a unifying wonder is compared to the sweetness of honey:

> This self is honey for all beings. For this self all beings are honey. And that which in this self is that ātman—that is, that purusha that arises out of light energy, out of the deathless— is that very primordial Ātman, Deathlessness, Brahman. It is the universe. And verily is the self the lord of all beings, the king of all beings. And just as all the spokes are held in the axle and the rim of a wheel, so all beings and all these selves (of the earth, of the waters, etc.) are held in the self.[172]

In this beautiful verse, the Hindu experience of Brahman, the collective dimension of the self, is described in terms of its numinous uniting quality, which can be realized when an individual becomes aware of Brahman through *ātman*, the individual experience of the self. The experience of a unified, transcendent reality that lies hidden behind perceived reality is replete with eros, "honey for all beings."

The *Coniunctio*: Honey Binds without Corruption

Honey was held in high regard in the alchemical imagination as a unifying agent. The power of Mercurius to join things together was compared with honey, and in his capacity as world soul, he was described as the "'glue of the world' (*glutinum mundi*), the medium between mind and body and the union of both."[173] Gerhard Dorn considered honey to be the appropriate binding substance in the crucial, penultimate stage of transformation called the second *coniunctio* depicted in the *Rosarium Philosophorum* picture series. We've noted that the king-queen or brother-sister hermaphrodite in this series endures a long transformation that involves their death and resurrection. The second *coniunctio* marks

---

[172] Ibid., 116; von Franz quotes from the Clarendon Press edition (1900). Another version of this section of Brihadaranyaka Upanishad (2.54), from an edition translated by Patrick Olivelle, reads: "This is very self (*ātman*) is the honey of all beings, and all beings are the honey of this self. The radiant and immortal person in the self and the radiant and immortal person connected with the body (*ātman*)—they are both one's self. It is the immortal; it is the *brahman;* it is the Whole" (32).

[173] Jung, *Psychology and Alchemy, CW*, vol. 12, par. 209. He quotes from "Aphorismi Basiliani" in *Theatrum Chemicum*, 4:368.

the moment just before the resurrection, when the soul returns to the body of the hermaphrodite and revives it in a new way.[174] Both soul and body have gone through a purification process, and their reunion culminates in the newly alive, crowned hermaphrodite, a symbol for the newly realized self. According to Dorn, honey is the perfect substance for this reunion because its purity prevents body and soul from become recontaminated.[175]

In psychological terms, the purified body of the hermaphrodite represents a personality that has gone through a long opus with the unconscious, has died to old ways of being driven by the unconscious, and may now join in relationship with the unconscious in a new way, according to the inner living spirit. At the deepest level of the personality, the female and male sides of the hermaphrodite represent eros and logos that have transformed each other, bringing about a new realization of the self. In other words, this healing process may come about through the suffering of a deeply held split. We have, for example, seen how the negative animus may convince a woman that her life or the people she loves are somehow wrong for her. Eros, or her feeling for her life, and logos, her understanding of her life, are contaminated with someone else's ideals. She may think she should have a different husband or a different kind of suffering, that she deserves to be better respected, etc. If she is able to suffer through the enormous work involved in healing such a split between her life as it is and what she thinks it should be, she may find herself in a deeply healing experience of the self. She wouldn't feel the least coddled, but she would experience grace. In such a moment of deep healing it is crucial that the ego is in relationship with the self through a natural, honeylike eros that cannot be contaminated by power or subjugated to the old opinions that were so powerful before. It is honey, the natural eros of the self, that can reliably help her avoid inflation and stay connected to the self in her own way.

---

[174] A psychological interpretation of the first *coniunctio* and second *coniunctio* in the last half of the *Rosarium Philosophorum* pictures from the point of view of women's individuation appears in the appendix.

[175] According to Paracelsus, however, in certain alchemical operations involving honey, its sweetness can become dangerous because it contains "Tartarum," which can tempt the alchemist back into a sensory or ego-centered orientation. See Jung, *Mysterium Coniunctionis, CW*, vol. 14, par. 687 and note 81.

In *Mysterium Coniunctionis,* Jung reported how Dorn chose honey as the right substance to symbolize such an enduring union:

> Dorn, in order to describe the union of the *unio mentalis* with the body . . . was illustrating his fantasies by chemical procedures. For this purpose he chose the most suitable substances, just as the painter chooses the right colours. Honey, for instance, had to go into the mixture because of its purifying quality. As a Paracelsist, Dorn knew from the writings of the Master what high praises he had heaped upon it, calling it the "sweetness of the earths," the "resin of the earth" which permeates all growing things, the "Indian spirit" which is turned by the "influence of summer" into a "corporeal spirit." [176]

A corporeal Indian spirit symbolizes a union of spirit and matter in which the purity of the spirit remains intact and preserved, even though it has become corporeal, or stabilized in reality. Honey made from the pollen of lavender flowers retains the lavender fragrance, or spirit, in its substance. Similarly, baptismal ointment is said to hold in its materiality the purity and force of the spirit of Christ. In psychological terms, a corporeal Indian spirit retains the spirit or atmosphere of the self and can't be mistaken for anything else, such as a philosophical idea. Its potency continues to renew life through natural means.

In the final picture of the alchemical series, *De summa et universalis medicinae sapientiae,* the image of honeycomb appears to be left behind in the egglike vessel after the bird, or the *filius,* is born and has projected itself out of the container (see fig. 30 p. 250). The wax is an image for *ceratio,* or softening, which takes place as the bird of Mercurius has been developing and is finally liberated. Psychologically speaking, the wax represents how malleable the personality becomes as the self makes its way into life. The ego is softened, eros integrated to such an extent that one-sidedness simply cannot take hold. Such a rare person in whom the Indian spirit lives is naturally immune to unconscious power motivations.

Abt pointed out that in Ibn Umail's *Ḥall ar-Rumūz,* honey is equated symbolically with chrysocolla, a substance that was once used to

---

[176] Jung, "Psychology of the Transference," *CW,* vol. 16, par. 687.

weld gold. Honey is likewise a gold glue, "which is the thing that grasps all the things . . . one of the actively unifying aspects of the white or second stone."[177] In psychological terms, the self is the thing that actively grasps all things that it is or that it can be with a kind of magnetic or sticky eros. The hope is that the ego has softened enough for that eros to be felt in its unifying capacity.

The Honey of Eros in Life

A dream came to me while I was working with the motif of honey that helps describe the permeability of the moist, quickening wisdom of the self that can penetrate life when the psyche has developed enough receptivity to absorb it. Here, egg yolk, rather than dew or honey, is the refreshing moisture. It penetrates life and, like a golden glue, attracts all the senses to it, overcoming resistance:

> *I am sitting at a table with a very wounded woman, an analysand who has never felt confident in life. I have a large metal bowl filled with a rice and vegetable salad. I have added an egg yolk to the salad and am mixing it in with my hands. As I mix, I bring the rice up from the bottom of the bowl into the vegetables and the bright, yellow-orange yolk. As I do this, the yellow penetrates the dull white rice, bringing it alive with color.*
>
> *I am thrilled by this and say to the wounded woman, "Yellow really is so much different than white." The woman also has a bowl in front of her, and as I mix my salad, hers also turns from white to yellow. She sees the beautiful yellow forming in her bowl, and then she begins to eat. Her appetite has returned, and she is so glad to be eating again. I can see that the food is delicious for her. The food is penetrating her the way the yellow penetrated the rice.*

The dream-ego has a strong feeling connection with the saturating power of the yellow yolk, and the yolk permeates her senses to such an extent that it reverberates to the wounded woman, inspiring in her an appetite for its nourishment. I saw the wounded woman in this dream as

---

[177] Abt, *Book of the Explanation of Symbols*, 110.

a deep shadow aspect, so injured by trauma that she had not yet been able to connect with symbolic life in a way that felt healing. This yellowing is an image for the alchemical *citrinitas,* which in some texts is a step between the *albedo* and the *rubedo,* and in others takes the place of the *rubedo.* The yellowing and the reddening refer to the penetrating potency of the self when it meets an absorbent, receptive individual (a whitened or purified body). Considering the symbolism of the yolk as the fiery drive of the soul, this dream helps us see how through the psychological opus, drivenness itself is the original source of the healing balsam, the penetrating reality of the self. When realized symbolically, this wisdom accrues a strong, yellow staining power that can bring the personality along. We can see in this staining power the alchemical *multiplicatio,* how the self multiplies itself, coloring new areas of the psyche with the penetrating citrus of its wisdom.

Sylvia described a similar development in herself as a realization washing over her that she has never not been on the path of individuation, even in the darkest times. She had become open, whitened, to a new kind of wisdom that could then be penetrated by the self and its symbolic meaning. In that moment, the psychic honey or eros of the self was strong enough to protect her from doubting her genuine feeling for the value of her experience. She didn't any longer feel the contaminating need to condemn her own suffering.

Felt Meaning, Loving Understanding

Jung took special effort to emphasize that bringing the symbolic realm of the self into life is more than an intellectual or conceptual process, which would consist of thinking and intuition. Here he compares the goal as it appears in alchemy and in analysis:

> Both disciplines, it is true, are aiming at a "spiritual" goal: the alchemist undertakes to produce a new, volatile (hence aerial or "spiritual") entity endowed with *corpus, anima, et spiritus*, where *corpus* is naturally understood as a "subtle" body or "breath body"; the analyst tries to bring about a certain attitude or frame of mind, a certain "spirit"

therefore. But because the body, even when conceived as the *corpus glorificationis*, is grosser than *anima* and *spiritus*, a "remnant of earth" necessarily clings to it, albeit a very subtle one. Hence an attitude that seeks to do justice to the unconscious as well as to one's fellow human beings cannot possibly rest on knowledge alone, in so far as this consists merely of thinking and intuition. It would lack the function that perceives values, i.e., feeling, as well as the *fonction du réel*, i.e., sensation, the sensible perception of reality.[178]

Sensation and feeling, the perception and valuing of reality, are the functions that demand an adaptation of life's tenets to the ethics and goals of individuation—bringing new consciousness not just to the mind but also infusing the *corpus,* the subtle viscera of the personality. If feeling and sensation weren't involved, as Jung went on to explain, individuation would be much easier, requiring only relatively lightweight insight and demanding little or no ethical reckoning of values. For a woman who struggles with a negative animus, a new experience of inner value involves finally assimilating the fact that *the self wants and even needs her existence*—that with all her flaws, or even because of her particular flaws, she is the medium for a world-redeeming transformation.

After Sylvia realized that she had never not been on the path of individuation, she continued with her active imagination and writing. Even though intensely depressed at times, the experience of the self as a fount of wisdom became further alive and real to her. In her writing and pondering about the dream, we sense how permeable her personality has become to the eros of the self, and how she is understanding what is happening symbolically. She wrote:

> This is the first time in a very long time that I have felt connected to the Source, the God, the Self—actually felt it rather than thought about it. I have dutifully written and attended to my dreams, but I have not known/felt that they came from somewhere other than my brain.
>
> I realize now that I have felt pursued, terrified of being caught. I know that I must surrender to something

---

[178] Jung, "The Psychology of the Transference," *CW*, vol. 16, par. 486.

that scares me almost to death. But I am not powerless, helpless. I can turn and face this awesome power. I can see it as something other than the enemy. It is: what I was born to know. It has been my fate to suffer, but my suffering has not been without a purpose. I see it—vaguely, faintly—*that the thing that pursues me needs me to see it, know it, and in a sense to serve it.* (Emphasis added)

In this passage, we see Sylvia's acceptance of the dark and light sides of her experience—her feeling for its value, and her understanding and integration of its meaning. She experienced a new perspective of her own worth in a way that saturated her feeling life, the subtle earth of her being. Shortly after writing this passage, Sylvia had a dream of a copper frog that at first was "lifeless and flat," though "beautiful because it was made of copper and a bit shiny." She took this image into active imagination:

As I focus on the frog, it gradually changes, begins to breathe, takes on the appearance of a living being. In the beginning it continues to face away from me and stay very still on the floor.

The frog is still made of copper, but it is alive and begins to move. It turns to face me. Everything changes. The room itself is transformed by the light emanating from the frog. I feel . . . lit up! I feel seen by the frog. I ask . . . no, I express my gratitude for this visitation. For long moments there is just the frog and me and the light and the Observer. I think that I will ask the frog whether it is male or female, but then the question seems trivial in this moment. Time means nothing now. It is as though the frog and I have always existed, and that we will always exist. (Tears.)

The sense of timelessness is the answer to a question I cannot put into words. Until this moment, I didn't know the question was in me. It has to do with my reluctance to live in this world, my reluctance to be in my own body. My body is not timeless! It exists very much in time-limited reality. But the frog is so very much alive and embodied. She comes from the muddy, wet, stinking environs of the pond or lake or swamp. This frog is here to remind me that this is also where I originated—in the most basic elements of earth. And yet there is this light, this timelessness, this mystery. Perhaps the question is "What am I? Really?" I am my body, which is not timeless. But I am also this light, this mysterious energy that is eternal.

Words seem inadequate now. I simply sit in the silence. I gaze into the eyes of the frog; she gazes into my eyes until it seems that we are one. And then there is just the light, still contained in the sacred space of the cave/room, secreted in the round, dark space, in the presence of something I cannot name—the self, the God, the Infinite? My mind is blown! My life is reenchanted! So many things make sense and have meaning in a way I have never realized. I see now why writing, painting, music—all art forms—are ways of trying to communicate the great mystery. I see why images, stories, metaphors are ways of trying to express the inexpressible. It is a language that speaks to us all—tries to speak to us; wants to be known; lives in the collective unconscious, waiting to be made real, waiting to be real and realized.

This is the thing that has pursued me all of my life.

This beautiful passage describes the integrated feeling and the meaning of an enduring connection to wholeness and how it might sink into Sylvia's *corpus* in a lasting way. She is vitalized by her experience of the unconscious, without needing a forever kind of bliss. The frog, symbolizing the impulse to consciousness that is born in the depths of the nature psyche, is coming to life in the reality of Sylvia. The frog was originally copper, the metal of Venus and of eros. In Sylvia's care, this eros metal, which the alchemists considered to contain a living spirit, has come alive in her, felt and understood as meaningful and real. The frog helped her accept how natural and humble an offering from the self can be and how such a small, humble being can renew life; in this sense the frog is related to the homunculus, the little soul that reanimates life after a long purification process. I cannot begin to describe how much Sylvia suffered from a torturing animus, but here she has reached a moment of redemption when she genuinely absorbs the honey of the self and feels in her bones the value of her unique connection to the living psyche.

13
The Bird and the Fire

As "Fitcher's Bird" ends, the wizard still assumes that he will marry the heroine, but she is fully prepared to keep that from happening. She has prepared the wizard's house and arranged a wedding feast as if she were getting married, but she has also disguised herself in her costume and sent for help. The wizard doesn't recognize her when he arrives; instead, he kindly greets the grinning skull that she decorated as a bride and placed in the attic window as a decoy. Once he and his guests are inside his house, the heroine's brothers and kinsmen lock them in and set the house on fire, forcing the wizard, his guests, and the skull-bride to burn.

Psychologically speaking, the heroine makes it clear that when a woman is connected with the self via its honey, its sticky and penetrating eros, she has at her disposal the resources she needs to handle the most destructive vestiges of the negative animus and any residual power he may have to take her over. She knows how to subject the animus to his own fire, keeping herself out of his possession. Of course, there will always be setbacks, but knowing how to objectify the destructive voice of the animus and how to work with it brings a stability to life that is difficult to thwart.

Unlike most fairy tales of feminine redemption, many of which end in a beautiful wedding, this one ends in the avoidance of a terrible one. Masculine and feminine are united, however, in images that belong to the symbolic world of alchemical elements and energies.

Mercurius Is the Fire

In alchemical terms, the fire in the wizard's house reminds us that the wizard is after all identical to the highly sulfuric, autonomous

Mercurius, who is said to be the fire in some alchemical texts.[179] As we saw in Zosimos's vision, Mercurius is the god "burning yet alive," enduring a transformation that may or may not be realized in conscious life. According to his dual nature, Mercurius is sometimes the evil aspect of the fire, the evil in the drive-soul, and sometimes the divine light of nature, the *lumen naturae* that guides the alchemist in his work, depending on our relationship to him. Likewise, Jung pointed out that "the revelatory light of nature is also hell-fire, a rearrangement of heavenly spiritual powers in the lower, chthonic earth."[180] Mercurius needs these opposites to be reconciled through our consciousness of them in our own lives.

As we've seen in alchemy and in women's lives, the fiery nature of life energy seems to have an evil quality when it drives us uncontrollably, even toward love. But in this drivenness is hidden the psyche's burning desire to be known for its phenomenal reality—as the divine force of transformation in nature and in the psyche. The alchemists saw this paradox personified in Mercurius, who works invisibly as hellfire when he is ignored or rejected and yet makes himself known spiritually to those willing to have an encounter with him. He is evil with those who are unconscious of him or those who appropriate his fire to their own purposes, and good with those who somehow manage to recognize and respect the objective autonomy of his fire.

After suffering in the fire, Mercurius emerges with a crown on his head and takes on the characteristics of a world redeemer, as discussed in chapter 10, able to save the world if enough individuals become conscious of his autonomy and engage with him—contain his fire in a relationship with it (fig. 39). As a redeemer he is described as "crowned with his diadem, radiant as the sun, shining like the carbuncle . . . constant in the fire."[181] A crowned Mercurius is an image for the spirit of the unconscious that may once have driven the personality unconsciously but is now constant—recognized as the divine will in an individual soul. That will can be brought into consciousness and oriented toward individuation. The heroine's deft ability to put the wizard

---

[179] In *War of the Ancient Dragon,* I trace the transformation of a 6-year-old's violent impulses through his work with fire and war.

[180] Jung, "The Spirit Mercurius," *CW,* vol. 13, par. 257.

[181] Jung, "Paracelsus as a Spiritual Phenomenon," *CW,* vol. 13, par. 183. A carbuncle (from the Latin *carbunculus,* "small coal") is a bright-red gem, like a ruby or garnet.

Figure 39. The Transformation of Mercurius in the Fire

Mercurius, transformed in the fire, is now fixed, or constant, no longer volatile, having been redeemed as the *filius philosophorum*. He is wearing a crown and holding a crown, indicating the union of temporal and spiritual power. From Barchusen, *Elementa chemiae* (1718).

in his place shows us that a woman in whom the spirit of the unconscious has become constant is no longer vulnerable to his drivenness. We have an example of how this happens in Sylvia's work below.

Subjecting Fire to Fire in Active Imagination

Several months before Sylvia had the remarkable realization that she had never not been on her individuation path, she went through an intense depression, feeling resentful and rebellious toward the demands of the unconscious on her life. At a trying turning point, she had a nightmare about a frightening, devouring monster that was chasing her relentlessly. Her dream had similar dynamics as Pearl's dream of the devil-man, but Sylvia was at a later stage in her analysis. She came to my office convinced that the dream proved she was hopeless and that after all these years, analysis had gotten nowhere. Daring to confront her

Figure 40. Sylvia's Monster

Sylvia's tree-shaped monster came from a nightmare. The tiny figure in the lower right corner represents Sylvia. Artist's photo.

resistance and knowing she was stronger than she felt in that moment, I insisted that she make a picture of the monster during our session. The drawing was coarse, smeared resentfully in crayon (fig. 40). But crude as it was, the image of the monster engaged Sylvia in a way she didn't expect. Her attitude toward him changed from helpless fear toward curious interest. His threatening energy was immediately tempered and so was her relationship to it—a result of containing his energy in the vessel of her imagination, where he could meet himself in an image. Bringing the monster into the world was a relief, not the least because he was seen and accepted as real. His enormous thirst to be acknowledged was quenched partly because Sylvia's many years of work in individuation made her that much more receptive to his reality and his symbolic meaning.

Figure 41. Sylvia's Tree of Individuation

Sylvia's tree of individuation transformed over time from the image of a tree-shaped monster to a tree with a crowned bird in its branches. The figure depicting Sylvia is now larger, and reverent instead of fearful. Author's photo.

Sylvia continued to be curious about the monster and his effect on her through the following weeks and months. She began regularly to consult him—even briefly asking what he looked like in the moment she was feeling she could be taken in by despair or disappointment. If she felt the temptation to indulge in resentment about her life, she would ask the monster about his state of being and draw a picture of whatever came to her, or she would write about it. The creative work helped contain the monster's energy, keeping a destructive mood out of his reach. Instead of feeding the monster her emotional distress, she offered him—an archetypal reality that was clearly pursuing her—a reflective heart and mind, a lunar receptivity. In this way, Sylvia submitted the destructive side of the animus to his own fire, inviting the individuating side to make itself known to her.

One day, when Sylvia was engaged in this ongoing process, drawing a picture of the monster's current state, she found to her surprise that the tree-shaped monster had transformed into an actual tree with symmetrical branches and roots (fig. 41). Then she discovered that a wide-eyed bird wanted to perch itself in the branches—and that it wore a crown. Sylvia portrayed herself bowing in reverence to this tree. The destructive monster had transformed into her own tree of individuation.

The capacity in Sylvia's imagination for this touching and humble image to appear developed one step at a time, through creative work with the very fire that threatened her. Through that process, the drivenness of the monster-animus could be realized for its spiritual aim. The crowned bird suggests that some part of the drivenness had become a watchful, spiritual entity living in the tree, "constant in the fire," no longer wreaking so much emotional havoc. Sylvia could continue to relate to the guiding will of her inner spirit as he sent her images in dreams and active imagination. The tree and the bird represent opposite aspects of the psyche involved in individuation—the tree slow, patient growth according to the bounds of earthly life, and the bird the lively quest to liberate spiritual meaning from the unconscious. These earthly and spiritual opposites, united in an image, contributed to Sylvia's stabilized feeling for the self as a reliable, nourishing reality.[182]

I would emphasize that Sylvia was not trying to confront evil per se, and certainly not trying to correct it, but engaging the images and impulses that the animus-monster was trying to impose on her before they had a chance to do any damage—especially the impulse to be duly disappointed in her own work with individuation. In submitting a potential mood to containment, she put the demon animus in the fire—an enormous sacrifice of the emotional indulgence he was after. She removed his object

---

[182] In "The Philosophical Tree," Jung discussed the tree as it appears in alchemy as an image for the world soul that permeates and animates life on a collective, unifying level. He provides several examples from his patients of tree drawings and paintings that spontaneously illustrate qualities of the long, nourishing process of vegetative psychic growth. The unique character of each tree indicates the very intimate development that an individual experiences in his or her own organic life span. Yet our shared experience of psychic development on a symbolic level seems to demonstrate the existence of a psychic world tree, a collective body of growth and soul development to which each of us contributes. See Jung, "The Philosophical Tree," *CW*, vol. 13, par. 304–482.

(her own emotional life) from reach and instead helped give form to his deeper aim. Soon after the tree and bird appeared, Sylvia had the dream of the dancing corpse and her active imagination of the copper frog that came alive. Although there were bumps along the way, she began to feel the reality of the self as a more constant presence in her life, mainly in her capacity to love.

The fact that the fire in the fairy tale is side by side with the soul-image of a bird may also remind us that work with the unconscious is never done but that the possessive fire must be continually subjected to containment and connected with psychic meaning. The death aspect of the animus is submitted to death, nature is allowed to transform nature, and what can be adapted to human life may continue as the principle of individuation. Knowing that the animus is always dual, a woman may at least save herself from the priggish expectation that somehow he will become an angel or a hero who rescues her from her own calling.

Sylvia's work shows us that an ongoing confrontation with the animus may gradually reveal the fact that he has been offering her the balsam, the central psychic fire, all along. He may be realized as the *spiritus rector*, renewing life daily when engaged in a sustained quest for meaning. There is no cure for the animus, but relating to him on a daily basis allows him to be recognized in his depth as the inner daimon of individuation. This is how we can understand the transformation of Mercurius in a woman's psychology from a devil to a crowned, guiding spirit: His sulfuric energy slowly transforms from an unconscious dynamism that would devour her individuality into a constant, guiding light, a *lumen naturae,* that leads her toward the meaning of her unique life. Not only does she need Mercurius to see her, but Mercurius needs her to see him, as a transpersonal spirit interested in her life. We can feel the eros that develops between them is something that heals not only them but the world they inhabit.

The Evil That Cannot Be Transformed

The wizard has transformed to some degree since his first appearance as a murderous demon. He has returned the sisters to their home and lost his dominance over their lives. But the wizard's attraction to the decorated skull in the attic window proves that some portion of him is still naturally attracted to death. Von Franz warned of a connection between death and evil in her interpretation of "Vasilisa the Beautiful":

> So, in a way, evil *is* a skeleton. It is that spirit of "no life and no love" which has always been associated with the essence of evil. It is destructiveness for its own sake, which everybody has in himself to some extent. But some people are completely possessed by it. . . . This kind of death-devil is best simply starved to death. One hands back what the person is, what he or she does, and one gives no life. One stretches out a skeleton hand to shake the skeleton hand; one gives no blood, no warmth, nor life, and that makes the devil turn back to where he came from.[183]

Someone possessed by a death-devil kills any warmth that is extended to them, perhaps not even noticing that such warmth exists. They are like hungry ghosts in Buddhist psychology, under the impression that they never have enough of anything. We experience an animus-possessed woman or an anima-possessed man as someone whose need for constant attention and validation sucks up an incredible amount of energy from their environment.

A woman possessed by a negative animus that springs from a negative father complex may remain impervious to even the most beautiful, compensating dreams. The situation is worse if she also suffers from a negative mother complex. In the psyche, a secret partnership forms between the death-devil and the devouring mother, making the influence even more difficult to objectify. One can pour one's energy into such a person and end up feeling completely exhausted and befuddled by their inability to feel the beauty or the meaning of the psychic images generously offered to them. The death couple devour all of it—the love and the meaning—trapping the ego in an addictive identification with victimhood. One has the sense that there is no vessel in which a fire can

---

[183] Von Franz, *Shadow and Evil in Fairy Tales,* 173. Von Franz, just before this quote, tells the story of one of her own analysands whose "demon was eating everything she was given so that one couldn't get anything into her, neither human feeling nor psychological food."

be contained, and that analysis simply may not take hold. In such a case, von Franz's advice is well taken.[184]

Knowing well the wizard's evil side, the heroine knows that the skull-bride naturally will lure him into his house. The evil side of the animus (or the anima)—the thread that cannot be humanized—in its essence belongs to death; this is partly how the archetype puts us in awe. We have seen the archetypal death orientation in several of the dreams that we have reviewed, including Pearl's dream of the devil-man who can't be killed, Sarah's dream of the butchered singing woman, and Sylvia's monster. These energies could have been quite dangerous if not contained in conscious work, suggesting to each of these women that it would be easier to commit suicide than go on feeling the worthlessness that the animus inflicted on her.

Von Franz in the quote above suggested that if we see evil in others, we not give it any energy at all. If we see it in ourselves and cannot work with its energy or find an image, she again advised against confronting it directly, referring to the alchemical view of *terra damnata*:

> One alchemist observed that in the *prima materia* there is a certain intractable amount of *terra damnata* (accursed earth) that defies all efforts of transformation and must be rejected. Not all dark impulses lend themselves to redemption; certain ones, soaked in evil, cannot be allowed to break loose and must be severely repressed. What is against nature, against the instincts, has to be stopped by main force and even eradicated. The expression "assimilation of the shadow" is meant to apply to childish, primitive, undeveloped sides of one's nature, depicted in the image of the child or the dog or the stranger. But there are deadly germs that can destroy the human being and must be resisted, and their presence means that one must be hard from time to time and not accept everything that comes up from the unconscious.[185]

---

[184] Interestingly, some of the most intractable cases in my experience have been under the influence of new age, Christian-oriented spiritual groups that are oriented around a state of bliss as the main goal of spiritual life. They have no way of honoring the dark aspects of the psyche or allowing an unpleasant experience to have a meaningful aim.

[185] Von Franz, *The Interpretation of Fairy Tales*, 132.

The fact that the wizard sees his betrothed in a decorated skull is a sign that in the end he contains a kernel of permanent damnation. A woman who realizes how close to death the destructive side of the animus truly is—how it could even kill her—may leave the irredeemable aspect of the animus burning in his own fire, either by confronting him in image or by ignoring and repressing him as best she can. Through analytic work and practice, we learn to differentiate between what can be submitted to the transformative fire through our effort, and what must be repressed.

Expressions of Wholeness

Abt noted that in Ibn Umail's *Ḥall ar-Rumūz,* one of the many images signaling the second part of the work is the appearance of the peacock with the fire or in the fire (fig. 42). The peacock is sometimes called the red bird, which is said to be inside the white bird—another image for psychic fire contained in spiritual meaning. Abt said:

> The white peacock emphasizes its symbolic nature. It is a container that unites the different colors. As a symbol it shows that the goal of the work is attained when the different emotional impulses are replaced by a colorless constancy that is able to contain the fiery red bird that is the soul.[186]

Further, Abt explained the whiteness as symbolizing how "one emotion or the other no longer dominates, and the wholeness of the personality becomes balanced."[187] As this happens, an individual realizes (is colored by the fact) that she or he is the container for the eternal fire of the self.

In a woman, the "colorless constancy" would mean that the power of the animus no longer dominates her emotional life unconsciously but is oriented toward individuation or some form of creative life. At the same time, she may be colored (or saturated) by the meaning and value of images offered to her from the self because symbolic life has become real to her through that very work. Like honey, the colors of the peacock signal

---

[186] Abt, *Book of the Explanation of Symbols,* 120.
[187] Ibid., 119.

Figure 42. Peacock and Alchemical Retort

The image of the peacock and the alchemical retort depict a constancy in the fire, psychologically indicating that the heat of emotion or fantasy is contained in an individual's relationship to the symbolic realm and no longer dominates life unconsciously. The peacock is a sign of the rubedo or reddening, in which the reality of the self and the splendor of all its colors is brought into life in an enduring way. It is synonymous with the symbolic honey that unites the transformed personality with the psychic reality of the self. From Muḥammad ibn Umail, *Aurora consurgens*. Zürich Zentralbibiothek, Ms. Rh.172: Aurora Consurgens.

the *rubedo,* meaning that the presence of the self colors the personality with a kind of permanent dye.

The fire and the bird are a pair of opposites that resemble Sol and Luna, showing us an image of the archetypal opposites that have come into relationship with each other. Sylvia had a dream with a touching image that depicts her own experience of this union:

> *I am in the woods alone, standing knee-deep in a gently*
> *flowing river. A leopard runs toward me, splashes into the*
> *water and jumps up, placing his front paws on my shoulders*

and nuzzling my face with his head. Surprised, I hug the leopard and delight in this amazing event.

The leopard symbolizes primal energy, wild, fiery intensity from the lower, chthonic realm that once felt threatening to Sylvia. Here, he joins Sylvia in the cool, flowing water, grateful for her receptivity. She said in the dream she felt she was being "hugged by God." The experience reminded her that as a girl she experienced herself as a child of the forest, when she could feel the animus as her own instinctive urge to explore nature.

Quaternity of Elements

The ending images of the fairy tale—the fire, the heroine's costume, and the relationship between the fire and the bird—each unites the opposites in its own way. In the fire, the wizard's death aspect is united with a death-bride. In her costume of honey and feathers, the elusive quality of spiritual life is grounded in the eros of honey. The opposites in the bird and the opposites in the fire are united by virtue of the relationship between them; together they express a quaternity in which all aspects of the self are present—everything that belongs to Mercurius as a union of

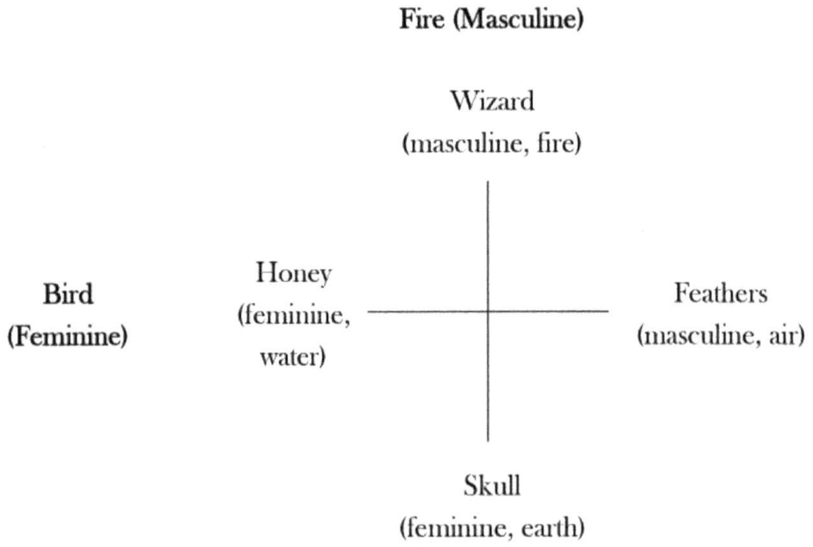

Fire (Masculine)

Wizard
(masculine, fire)

**Bird
(Feminine)**
Honey
(feminine,
water)
Feathers
(masculine, air)

Skull
(feminine, earth)

Figure 43. Quaternity of Elements in the Fire and the Bird
Author's diagram.

masculine and feminine, life and death (fig. 43). We can even find the four elements.

In this image of wholeness now present in the depths of the wizard's realm, death no longer holds sway—neither over the masculine as aggressor nor the feminine as victim. In fact, the new feminine presence has proved to have as much power to reflect as the masculine has to compel.

The Redemption of Eros in Human Life

The overall goal expressed in "Fitcher's Bird" is the redemption of the archetypal feminine, especially the Kore, from a worldview that is inured to its absence. We see how girls and young women carry the Kore or feminine spirit, the eros development that is trying to come forward and be realized as a divine value in our age. This value, so deeply and unconsciously treasured, is in part projected and adored in a young girl's beauty, as if physical beauty itself were the treasure. A woman's value thus can easily be reduced to her perceived beauty, her life to the appeasement of aesthetic ideals. Or eros is grasped materialistically as a sexual quality.[188] A woman who intuitively picks up on a man's need to possess her as a beautiful bauble or an innocent servant to his vanity may not have the capacity to resist such flattery if she is disconnected from the self and from her instincts. She unwittingly neglects her own development and abandons real eros. The fairy tale shows us through the murder of maidens what a deeply tragic event this is.

On the other hand, as our tale seems to indicate, a woman who wakes up to the old modus vivendi and becomes curious enough about its darkness may challenge the collective state of affairs. She may differentiate between herself as an individual and the value that is being projected onto her.[189] She may find the courage to enter introversion in a deliberate way and feel for herself who she really is, disobedience, darkness, loneliness, and all. As a result, she may find herself in a full-bodied experience of the very natural eros quality of the self that is missing from the world. If eros

---

[188] Von Franz discusses this problem in *The Cat*, 75ff.

[189] Marilyn Monroe was a tragic example of a woman who received a projection that put her on a pedestal but had nothing to do with who she really was.

does come alive in her in its transhuman form, she returns a measure of its divine value to human life.

Entering nature, quite literally, can help a woman suffering from inner uncertainty find refuge in the magnitude of her own nature and in her genuine connection to the nature psyche. How she feels in nature may help her discover the original, unfeigned relationship to the inner world she felt in childhood. Von Franz wrote of the healing effects of being alone in nature in her work with "The Girl without Hands," in which, like many tales of feminine redemption, the heroine finds herself alone in a forest. I read this passage aloud to analysands who are beleaguered by the negative animus, insisting that their loneliness is wrong, punishing, or undeserved.

> [The handless maiden] is driven into nature where she has to find the connection with the positive animus within, instead of functioning according to collective rules. She has to go into deep introversion. The forest could equally well be the desert, or an island in the sea, or the top of the mountain. She is cut off in the stillness of virgin country, which would imply that she has to retire into her own loneliness and must realize that, for though it looks as though she had a husband and children, or a job, she is not yet really alive. Most women, since they depend so much on relationship and long for it, have a great difficulty in admitting to themselves how lonely they are and in accepting that as a given situation. To retire into the forest would be to accept the loneliness consciously, and not to try to make relationships with good will, for that is not the real thing. According to my experience, it is very painful, but very important, for women to realize and accept their loneliness. The virgin soil would be that part of the psyche where there was no impact of collective human activities, and to retire to that would be to retire not only from all . . . opinions and views of life, but from any kind of impulse to do what life seems to demand of one. The forest would be the place of unconventional inner life, in the deepest sense of the word. Living in the forest would mean sinking into one's innermost nature and finding out

what it feels like. The vegetative is also spontaneous life and offers healing to the woman destroyed by a negative animus or negative mother complex. It is a question of going back to the hurt virgin ground in her soul.[190]

Our heroine, too, finds herself alone in the forest at the wizard's house, in fact, for nearly all of the fairy tale, taking care of her egg, resurrecting her sisters, cleaning the house, preparing for a wedding, and covering herself in honey and feathers. Taking all of the symbolic meaning of these images to mind, the fairy tale shows us the detailed effort—the full opus involved in a woman sinking into her innermost nature. Sinking into herself is the core of a singular development in which the spirit of the unconscious and the divinity of eros are redeemed out of darkness together.

For a woman, the great work, the result of her confrontation with the old god-image in herself, is to bring home love that possibly nobody knew was missing. In her personal life, she discovers that love rooted in her connection with the transpersonal realm brings her life profound value. A dream from Sylvia marks this achievement in no uncertain terms:

> *I am in Küsnacht, Switzerland, and I have been staying in the home of Emma and C. G. Jung. I came to Küsnacht to study and write, and I have been deeply engaged in this for an extended period of time. Emma, C. G., and I are sitting around the dining table, engaged in conversation. Emma indicates that I should stand up with her, and she embraces me tightly. Her strength and enthusiasm surprise me.* [In the dream, she is middle-aged and sturdy like a Swiss farmer.] *"You have been working so hard. It is a great pleasure to encourage and support you." C. G. is still seated, and he opens his arms, offering a hug. His embrace is less strong and energetic than Emma's, and I am reminded that he seems older and somewhat frail. In a fatherly way, he quietly and kindly complements my efforts. I sense that it is time for me to leave Küsnacht, but I have no idea where I will go or what I will do.*

---

[190] Von Franz, *The Feminine in Fairy Tales*, 84–85.

Emma Jung represents the feminine side of Carl Jung in terms of hearth and home in this dream. She is the eros to his logos, and in Sylvia's dream, she is the stronger and more vital of the two. Reminding Sylvia of the farm women she saw in Switzerland pitchforking hay in Alpine meadows, Emma is down to earth like the nature mother, absolutely straightforward, and conveys an abundance of soulful intensity.

Psychologically, Emma and Carl Jung symbolize the royal couple of the depths. In Sylvia's psychic life, they have become manifest in a way that emphasizes eros as the strongest attribute between them. Emma's stronger presence gives the pair a feminine emphasis overall, with Carl symbolizing the orienting logos. In acknowledging Sylvia's hard work, which we can understand as her opus with the psyche, Emma offers warmth and support, helping Sylvia to feel the reality of the redemption she has brought about—this feeling was as strong in waking life as it was in the dream. Not knowing where she will go next, Sylvia isn't fearful but open to her next life journey. She entered a phase of her life that was more peaceful and full of love than she had ever experienced.

We should consider one more motif from the tale that we touched upon earlier. The heroine's bird habiliment does not arrive by way of a magical animal, clever maidens, or a fairy godmother, as happens in other tales. She creates her garment using her own body and natural, everyday elements, through what seems to be an instinctive impulse from the depths. Yet the image symbolizes a woman's profound connection to the mysterious eros of the self. It shows us that a woman needs nothing outside herself, and leaves nothing of herself out, to redeem the divine value of her life.

Epilogue
Refuge for Feminine Development
in Fairy Tales and Legend

In the "Golden Legend of Mary Magdalene" and other medieval legends, Mary lives in the wilderness for 30 years, taking no food or drink and growing her hair so long that it covers her entire body (fig. 44). After years of ascetic penitence, she becomes so spiritualized that, as light as a feather, she levitates at each canonical hour to hear the heavenly angels sing. *The Golden Legend*, a collection of European hagiographic tales, was written in the 13th century, when fairy tales were still developing in Europe. The authors of Mary Magdalene's legendary life picked up on certain motifs from fairy tales of feminine redemption. In the fairy tale "Our Lady's Child," a Christianized version of "The Black Woman's Castle," the heroine's hair, like Mary Magdalene's, grows long enough to cover her body and helps protect her during her exile in the forest. Mother Mary has banished her there, ostensibly for lying (fig. 45).[191]

The Christianization of fairy tales is another example of how the development of the feminine principle is sent underground, even in recent times. Christian tales such as the Golden Legend do not derive from oral tradition, in which the unconscious spontaneously insinuates itself into the story, but instead are written by a priest or clerk, who consciously imposes dogmatic motifs into the stories to promulgate Christianity. Nevertheless, religious legends accidentally retain motifs with more natural and psychological truths than the authors may have realized.

On a symbolic level, such long hair represents how living in an introverted way for a long time with the stuff that comes out of her head, a woman may become familiar with her thoughts—conscious of them,

---

[191] Von Franz interprets "The Black Woman's Castle" in *Archetypal Dimensions of the Psyche*.

Figure 44. *Saint Mary Magdalene*, by Quentin Massys, 1520–1530
Philadelphia Museum of Art, John G. Johnson Collection, cat. 367.

so that they lose their obsessiveness and develop into a protective layer that naturally safeguards the naked soul. Thus, what may seem like an exile becomes a welcome introversion in which she gains protective, healing contact with the archetypal feminine realm. Legends and fairy

Figure 45. Heroine in the Forest
Illustration by Josef Scharl from "Our Lady's Child," a Christianized version of "The Black Woman's Castle." From *The Complete Grimm's Fairy Tales* (New York: Pantheon Books, 1944), 25.

tales retain these redemption motifs and have long provided refuge for feminine development. It is vital and even world redeeming, that we not only recognize that development but continue bringing it into life.

Appendix
A Psychological Interpretation of the
Unio Mentalis (First *Coniunctio*) and the
Second *Coniunctio* in the *Rosarium Philosophorum*
from the Feminine Point of View

The steps involved in the first *coniunctio* and second *coniunctio* are depicted in pictures 6–10 of the *Rosarium Philosphorum* series, which we will explore in terms of women's psychology.[192] First, we must orient ourselves in the *Rosarium's* first five pictures, which express an original, unconscious union between conscious and unconscious from the point of view of individuation.

<u>Summary of Pictures 1–5</u>

The first five pictures of the *Rosarium Philosophorum* are introduced by an image of the mercurial fountain (fig. 46, picture 1), another analogy, like the philosophical egg, for the psychological vessel that is a container for transformation. The five stars in the image, the divine water in the fountain with its three spigots, the two snakes, and the overall unity of the picture express the mysteries of the opus and tell us that the transformation we are about to see can only take place under the auspices of Mercurius.[193] In psychological terms, we know that although we are anchored in an individual process, we are also in the archetypal realm and guided by the self.

---

[192] Jung, "The Psychology of the Transference," *CW*, vol. 16, par. 402. A thorough interpretation of this profound symbolism cannot be fully explored here, but we will try to understand how the pictures inform a woman's empirical process of individuation. I highly recommend reading Jung's essay for a much more in-depth review of the symbolism.

[193] Jung discusses the motifs in "The Psychology of the Transference," *CW*, vol. 16, par. 402.

Figure 46. Pictures 1–5, from the *Rosarium Philosophorum*

These pictures depict the original union of opposites in the personality in the context of individuation, or from the point of view of the self, the goal. Their union is unconscious, and yet meant to be brought into consciousness, bringing about a transformation in the personality and a realization of the archetypal participation that was present from the beginning. The archetypal dimension is expressed by the mercurial fountain and the presence of the sun and the moon. The dove indicates a spiritual presence as the couple undress, revealing their respective souls, and descend into the waters of the psyche with Sol and Luna. From *Rosarium Philosophorum: Secunda pars alchimiae de lapide philosophico* (Frankfurt, 1550).

In the next four pictures, the royal couple greet each other, disrobe, and descend into the mercurial bath (picture 4), where they engage in sexual intercourse (picture 5). Psychologically, they depict the inner dynamics that occur when a person descends into an unconscious situation and is completely gripped by it, as happens in a transference or projection, or when we are subsumed in a complex. The king and queen in the simplest terms represent the ego and the unconscious of one person. For this reason, as we saw in chapter 9, they are sometimes called brother and sister.

For a woman, the queen represents the ego to the extent that her own feminine side is relatively more conscious and engaged in life than the masculine, even if she has fallen into identification with the animus.[194] But the queen also represents the ruling feminine eros—the usual way of valuing herself and her life—that goes along with the ruling logos of the animus. If a woman is caught in a judgmental animus, her eros is caught too. For a woman subsumed in a projection, the intercourse depicted here reflects the depths of her unconscious participation—for example, the way Pearl was so ensnared in her professor and the hope that he could validate her. Her own eros and logos were completely entangled with each other in this illusion until she began to see how she had been taken in. *In that moment of awareness, she could see her unconscious situation.* That crucial awareness of an unconscious condition is implied in the very fact that the alchemical image exists. When a projection finally becomes even somewhat visible, a woman begins to see her inundation, how she is in the hot water of the mercurial fountain with her own desire for validation. The next six pictures describe the changes that occur as consciousness becomes a more active part of the equation.

The Death That Signals New Life

In picture 6 of the *Rosarium* series, the king and queen/brother and sister pair lie in a tomb, apparently dead (fig. 47). They no longer inhabit two discrete bodies as they have in the first five pictures. Having engaged in sexual intercourse, the two are now also one.

The title, "Conception. Putrefactio," tells us that both conception and decay are taking place at once. Psychologically, this picture represents a situation in which one realizes one's unconscious attitude (conception), and in that conception the change begins (putrefactio). An insight awakens us to how unconscious we have been, and in that moment, the ruling principles that have been guiding us suffer a little death. The caption

---

[194] Jung delineates the many psychic aspects of relationship represented by the king and the queen in these pictures (ibid., par. 421ff). In one relationship, a woman is relating to a man, the man's anima, and her own projected animus. A man is relating to the woman, her animus, and his projected anima. King and queen on the archetypal level represent logos and eros—aspects of the self that become more consciously related to each other through the process.

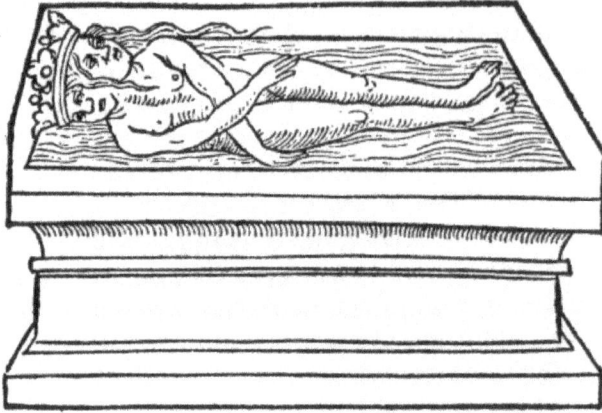

Figure 47. *Conceptio, Putrefactio*
Rosarium picture 6, "Conceptio. Putrefactio," depicts death but hints at the potential for new psychological life to be conceived, the way new life sprouts from the death of a seed. From *Rosarium Philosophorum: Secunda pars alchimiae de lapide philosophico* (Frankfurt, 1550).

for this picture reads, "Here lie the King and Queen dead. The Soul is separated with great grief."[195] We lose soul, in the sense that we are no longer able to live with the royal illusions that have sustained us, and we don't yet feel a new animating energy. We feel grief not only for the passing of an old, more naïve way of life but for the fact that we have been unconscious.

The hermaphrodite as a single body represents a personality that now conceives of the fact that it is two—both conscious and unconscious. In terms of a woman's psychology, for example, she knows that the animus has been driving her unconsciously, projecting himself onto others as if he were a second personality, gripping her feeling for herself. As this dynamic becomes more and more conscious, the energy of the original, unconscious union immediately begins to wane, and a new relationship with the animus starts developing in accordance with her new consciousness. In the fairy tale, such a moment of realization is depicted when the heroine sees the murders that have been taking place in the wizard's secret chamber. For a woman, this horrible insight would

---

[195] Smith, *The Rosary of the Philosophers,* 37.

represent a moment when she can finally see the reality of a murderous union in herself, a cooperation with a devilish animus that has killed off developing eros. We have seen this happen when a conventional attitude makes it impossible for a woman to take in eros from the self that is trying to value her or her life just the way it is. If individuation continues, the murderous union itself can begin to die and itself become the object of conscious dismemberment.

This conception/putrefaction reflects the end of a way of being, the end of a certain united front of thinking (king) and valuing (queen). A woman in a certain stage of understanding may realize that the end of a way of life is forming, even if she is in a deep state of confusion or depression. The psychological death that takes place at the end of an unconscious projection or identification is referred to in some alchemical texts as the death of the first body, the rotting, the *nigredo,* or the first blackening, signaling the necessary mortification of the original "incest" (unconscious identification) between ego and the unconscious, as well as the egocentricity at its core. Seen from the point of view of the self, life simply cannot go on in the old way. We may feel this quite clearly, but the death of the old way takes time and can be very painful; there is a reason the alchemists call it putrefaction or mortification, and insist on so many images of washing, rinsing, and burning, etc.

In his commentary for this picture, Jung compared the death of the hermaphrodite to that of a seed whose demise eventually brings about a new life. A seed, like an egg, needs to be tended if it is to produce new life.[196] If we are committed to individuation, we tend to the new life that we know will eventually sprout, even if we are suffering through a dreadful realization about ourselves. The pair in picture 6 that seem dead will, in picture 10, become the revived, winged hermaphrodite, the *rebis* standing on the sun or the moon signaling a new, living relationship between the opposites and a constellation of wholeness. In this final image, masculine and feminine archetypes are united in a way that reliably serves life (fig. 48). *But until that moment, the pair in pictures 6-9 remain in a coffin.* Jung said of the lifeless hermaphrodite: "Since the *hermaphroditus* turns out to be the long-sought *rebis* or *lapis*, it symbolizes that mysterious

---

[196] Jung, "The Psychology of the Transference," *CW*, vol. 16, par. 512.

Figure 48. The New Hermaphrodite
The new hermaphrodite, *Rosarium* pictures 10 and 20, symbolizes the paradoxical wholeness of the self. The version on the right (picture 20) is from the second cycle of pictures, which Jung attributed to female psychology. Its tree is made of suns rather than moons, which may mean that for a woman, the solar world is the main source of unconscious energy, and leads her to realize the godlike reality of the animus. From *Rosarium Philosophorum: Secunda pars alchimiae de lapide philosophico* (Frankfurt, 1550).

being yet to be begotten, for whose sake the *opus* is undertaken. But the *opus* has not yet reached its goal, because the lapis has not come alive."[197] The suspension of the old way, the rotting and mortification continue, even as a new relationship with the self is gathering strength.

Suspension and the Transcendent Function

A person in this state of suspension may have some sense that the self is guiding a new development, but to feel enlivened by that fact, to actually feel the honey of an eros connection to the self, could take a long time. Some aspects of life may seem to come to a standstill and feel quite disorienting, but an ongoing devotion to individuation keeps the psychic stream moving.

The heroine in "Fitcher's Bird" gives us another image for this suspension when she remains in the wizard's house, cleaning it from garret

---

[197] Ibid., par. 468.

to cellar. She doesn't return home with her sisters but stays in the forest, devoted to her work. Psychologically, we've noted that the housecleaning represents a detailed confrontation with the animus-related shadow; it is an ongoing process that facilitates the putrefaction, the rotting of the old way and encourages the slow evolution of a new way.

A woman who can sustain this suspension remains connected to animus dynamism in an introverted way, brooding over her dreams and holding back her desire to act out her projections. She learns when to withhold words of judgment. She focuses on her creative work. She is constantly reminding herself that she is in the egg, in the mercurial fountain with her old ideas about herself and the world. At times of deep frustration she may be helped by remembering that she is involved in a process that is slowly relativizing her egocentricity and that there is virtue in her suffering, exactly as it is appearing in her life.

Interestingly, Jung saw that this suspended state is rare in religious practices and that most meditation exercises do not invoke anything like the fountain of Mercurius, where a long process of dismemberment takes place, but instead are designed to protect the ego from such a painful process:

> If the ancient art of meditation is practised at all today, it is practised only in religious or philosophical circles, where a theme is subjectively chosen by the meditant or prescribed by an instructor, as in the Ignatian *Exercitia* or in certain theosophical exercises that developed under Indian influence. These methods are of value only for increasing concentration and consolidating consciousness, but have no significance as regards effecting a synthesis of the personality. On the contrary, their purpose is to shield consciousness from the unconscious and to suppress it. They are therefore of therapeutic value only in cases where the conscious is liable to be overwhelmed by the unconscious and there is the danger of a psychotic interval.[198]

---

[198] Jung, *Mysterium Coniunctionis*, *CW*, vol. 14, par. 708.

Suppressing the unconscious may make a person feel better temporarily, but it does not lead to anything psychically new. The opposites are not held together in tension but allowed to remain separated in their traditional moral corners. In this separation, the transcendent function cannot run its course; nothing new can develop between consciousness and the unconscious. On the other hand, allowing both yes and no to exist, holding the tension of a conflict without knowing the outcome, provokes a third, otherwise nonexistent possibility to come forward in the form of a unique image suited to the specific development of the self in a specific life. Understanding this image allows the transcendent function to be fulfilled, moving consciousness to a genuinely new state. When Pearl spontaneously encircled her devil-man in an egg shape, consciousness and the unconscious were meaningfully united in an image that never would have come into existence otherwise. Instead of rejecting the devil-man, she brought his image into her imagination and held the tension of his ambivalent presence. Even though she didn't want him to exist, relating to him kept consciousness and the unconscious together, allowing for the possibility that such a demon had a meaningful aim. In that tension, an image could arise in which the devil-man could show himself as an aspect of individuation.

Ascent of the Soul: Unio Mentalis and the First Coniunctio

Picture 7 of the *Rosarium Philosophorum* depicts the soul rising to join the spirit in the heavens (fig. 49); together soul and spirit form the first *coniunctio,* also called the *unio mentalis* (union of the mental aspects; in the philosophical egg images we observed, the miracle of this union was emphasized by the appearance of Sol and Luna, spiritual drive and reflective soul, together in partnership.) The union signals the beginning of the *albedo* stage, meaning that the black, rotting process in the tomb is coming to an end and some level of mental clarity is taking shape.

Jung explained that the *albedo* represents a "higher point of view where both conscious and unconscious are represented."[199] Here, Jung describes the psychological situation from a man's perspective:

---

[199] Jung, "The Psychology of the Transference," *CW*, vol. 16, par. 479.

Figure 49. Ascent of the Soul

In picture 7 of the *Rosarium, "Animæ extractio vel imprægnatio"* (extraction or impregnation of the soul), the soul, depicted by a homunculus, is separated from the body and rises to join the spirit in the heavens, taking on a new, more spiritual perspective. The soul and spirit combined is called the *unio mentalis*. From *Rosarium Philosophorum: Secunda pars alchimiae de lapide philosophico* (Frankfurt, 1550).

If after a long and thorough analysis and the withdrawal of projections, when the ego has successfully been separated from the unconscious, the anima will gradually cease to act as an autonomous personality and will become a function of relationship between conscious and unconscious.[200]

The same is true for a woman, where it is the animus that ceases to act autonomously. Whereas the anima becomes a function of relationship, the animus becomes a function of the quest for meaning.

Jung described the homunculus ("little human") in this *Rosarium* picture as being "on the way to becoming the *filius regius*, the undivided and hermaphroditic First Man, the Anthropos."[201] He symbolizes a psychic content freed from the unconscious and united with its symbolic meaning,

---

[200] Ibid., par. 504.

[201] Ibid., par. 481. My thanks to Alan Drymala for drawing my attention to this description, in personal communication.

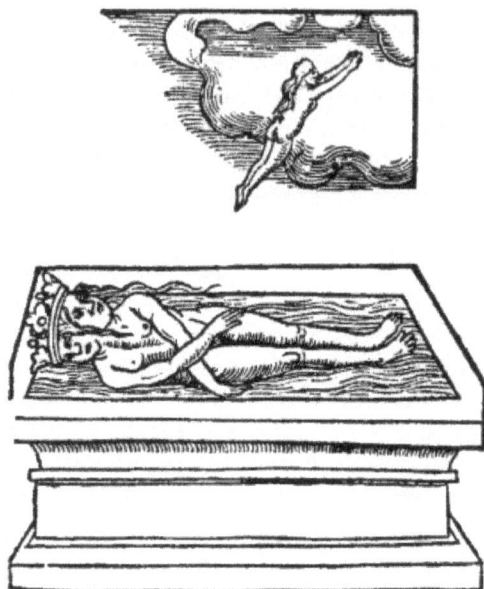

Figure 50. Fixation
In picture 4, "Fixatio," the soul figure rising to the spiritual realm in the second cycle of the *Rosarium Philosophorum* is feminine, expressing a woman's experience of the soul ascending and the subsequent fixation or suspension of life in the old way. From *Rosarium Philosophorum: Secunda pars alchimiae de lapide philosophico* (Frankfurt, 1550).

which becomes an aspect of the self and contributes to its substantiality (as we saw in the *retorta distillatio* explored in chapter 6). In this sense, the male homunculus represents the self *in potentia* in male psychology, a little version of the self building himself up in consciousness until eventually he can be realized as the immortal inner god-man.

In the second set of *Rosarium* pictures, which Jung mentioned in the essay but did not analyze, the little human is depicted as female (fig. 50).[202] Jung suggested that this set of pictures could represent a woman's experience of individuation.[203] In that case, we would say that the feminine

---

[202] A complete collection of the *Rosarium* cycles can be found in Smith, *The Rosary of the Philosophers*.

[203] Jung, "The Psychology of the Transference," *CW*, vol. 16, par. 520. Jung said, "The first series of pictures is followed by a second—less complete, but otherwise analogous—series, at the end of which there appears a masculine figure, the 'emperor,' and not, as

side of the self that has been hidden in the unconscious is on the way to becoming the First Woman, the immortal inner goddess-woman, building up a woman's experience of the feminine side of the self until it becomes a constant, felt reality in her life.

Uniting Upper and Lower

Although the *unio mentalis* may seem to suggest that what was low is becoming a "higher" reality and elevating all of life to a spiritual level, we must again be careful not to inflict our spiritual ideals onto this symbolism. The rising of the soul to the spirit doesn't imply that the goal of individuation is to live blissfully up in the heavenly realms or to leave earthly life and its urges behind. The following simple dream hints at how our traditional expectations of upper and lower levels of life can prohibit their becoming genuinely unified:

> *I am staying in a hotel that has two levels. The main floor is elegant, colorful, but a bit dark, even cramped in some corners. The upper floor is open, airy, light, and modern. I have always wondered if there could be much difference between floors in a hotel. Now I see that the difference can be quite dramatic. But I don't know how to choose where I want my room. Normally, I would pick the open, light-filled atmosphere. But I also love the rich tapestries, textures, color, and even the shadows on the lower level.*

---

in the first, an 'empress,' the 'daughter of the philosophers.' The accentuation of the feminine element in the *Rebis* . . . is consistent with a predominantly male psychology, whereas the addition of an 'emperor' in the second version is a concession to woman (or possibly to the male consciousness)." To clarify, although we see a hermaphrodite at the end of both cycles, the commentary that goes with them announces the birth of "a noble and rich queen" for the first, and "the king of all glory" in the second. The queen and king could represent the realization of the transpersonal anima for a man and the animus for a woman. It is also possible that the two cycles are not about male and female psychology per se, but about two cycles of transformation in the consciousness of a man or a woman. In the first cycle a relationship to the unconscious is realized, and thus a new queen is born. The second cycle would emphasize the difficult dissolution of the reign of solar consciousness before it is reborn in a new, royal relationship with the feminine— essentially a new god-image.

The upper, spiritual level of the hotel is airy, clear, and bright, but it lacks color, texture, softness, comfort, and the shadows that make light more appreciable. The dream was warning this dreamer about idealizing mental clarity or light at the expense of the richness of life on the lower, darker level. Even though we have the goal to bring unconscious contents to the spiritual or symbolic level, which we think of as an elevation, that doesn't mean we sacrifice the value of life lived with all of the colors and textures that come with ordinary life—with being decently or even joyfully unconscious, for this too has meaning. The dream suggests a both-and attitude, in which earthly life *is* the holy reality when imbued with its own symbolic meaning. As von Franz said, the eros that results from a union of opposites in the god-image heals humanity *in* its imperfections, not *of* its imperfections (p. 288).[204]

Receiving the Dew of Heaven

In the *Rosarium* picture 8, "Mundificatio" (purification), the body of the hermaphrodite is about to be saturated with rejuvenating dew from heaven (fig. 51). The dew is an image for the *aqua permanens,* the water of life that quickens and animates, preparing the body to return to life. The union of soul and spirit in the heavens has produced this eternal divine water, and now it can return to the body with its enlivening moisture.

The hermaphrodite in this picture is still in a state of suspension, indicating on the psychological level that the personality may not be purified of its old opinions enough to absorb the refreshing wisdom being offered from the symbolic realm. Egocentrality may not be sufficiently rotted away, making it possible for wisdom to be absorbed without being contaminated by pride or power (as we saw when Kat put her active imagination images up for sale). The fact that dew is present signals a growing receptivity for that wisdom, though not yet a full revival by way of it. An enormous tension exists in critical moments when a woman may still be in danger of the negative animus destroying an experience

---

[204] Von Franz, *Archetypal Dimensions of the Psyche*, 49.

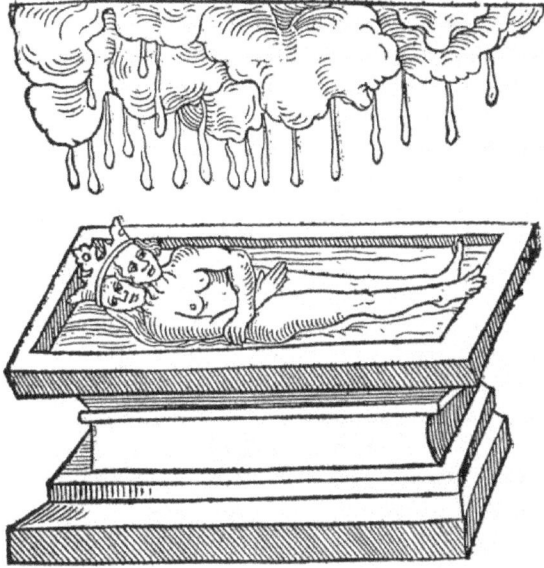

Figure 51. Washing or Purification

Picture 8 of the *Rosarium*, "Ablutio vel Mundificatio." Heavenly dew descends to quicken the mortified body. It may be possible for the personality to receive refreshing wisdom from the psychic realm, if it has become permeable enough to symbolic meaning. From *Rosarium Philosophorum: Secunda pars alchimiae de lapide philosophico* (Frankfurt, 1550).

of nourishment from the self, even though she has felt that nourishment before.

In the fairy tale, we have discussed how the ongoing murders of maidens can represent a paradoxical development in which an immature eros for the self dies over and over again and at the same time, a stronger eros builds itself up, finally reaching its fulfillment in the heroine. Her eros for the self is strong enough to choose the egg over obedience, and thus she redeems herself and her sisters. In a woman, this singular choice would indicate that after a long period of mortification, she has become conscious and humble enough to absorb the refreshing wisdom of the self instead of, for example, murdering eros for the sake of being right.

Jung explained that a psychological death to old motivations is a liminal state in which a person doesn't yet feel the rejuvenating quality of wisdom from the psyche, and this state of suspension can be experienced as a loss of soul. He said, "Nobody who ever had any wits is in danger of losing them in the process, though there are people who never knew till then what their wits are for. In such a situation, understanding acts like a life-saver."[205] We might have to watch ourselves for years, pitting one perspective against the other until in the fullness of time, a resolution penetrates us strongly enough to resolve the conflict. If the personality becomes receptive to the paradoxical wisdom of the moony, irrational, symbolic world, it can be refreshed. If not, the dew (like the sword in *Atalanta Fugiens*) acts as a poison against remaining identification with the old order, including the conscious, worldly certainty that is not whitened enough or has not yet developed enough of a lunar perspective to absorb the reality of the symbolic dimension. The divine water of the *mundificatio* washes and revives, kills and resurrects, depending on how receptive the individual is to a new point of view in which the opposites are meaningfully united. As mentioned in the previous chapter, the stone goes through repeated washings, soakings, and burnings until it becomes an absorbent, pure material that can be dyed by all the colors of the self. The psychological challenge is whether the personality can stand the tension long enough and transform humbly enough to absorb what the psyche has transformed.

As we have seen, a strengthened receptivity to the self may develop in the psyche and be expressed through dreams or creative images yet remain undetectable to the ego. But suddenly, as happened for Sandra and Sylvia, a woman may discover that she can finally absorb eros and wisdom that seemed elusive for so long. As if by magic, and yet with so much work behind her, she finally knows and feels that she is and always has been on her own sacred path. This ability to *feel* the healing tincture of the self strongly enough for it not to be destroyed by criticism indicates a more receptive attitude to the symbolic realm and a washing away of old critical patterns.

---

[205] Jung, "Psychology of the Transference," *CW*, vol. 16, par. 479.

Return of the Soul: Honey and the Second Coniunctio

In *Rosarium* picture 9, the homunculus that ascended in picture 7 (fig. 43) now descends, finally returning to the body that has been mortifying for so long, reanimating it in a new way (although the fully alive hermaphrodite isn't evident until the next picture). In the second *Rosarium* cycle, we again see a female version of the homunculus that is descending into the body. Psychologically, the body of the hermaphrodite at this stage symbolizes a personality that is genuinely enlivened by the paradoxical spirit-soul union that has taken place in the symbolic realm and which now returns to the personality (fig. 52).

If the *unio mentalis* corresponds to the *albedo* and mental clarity, this second *coniunctio* between the *unio mentalis* and the personality corresponds to the *rubedo,* or reddening, in which symbolic meaning finally gets into the blood and animates life in a new way. Immersing herself in honey, the heroine as an archetypal ego shows us a fully

Figure 52. Return of the Soul, in Masculine and Feminine Versions
On the left is "Animæ Iubilatio seu Ortus seu Sublimatio" (Of the rejoicing or rising or sublimation of the soul), picture 9 of the first cycle. On the right, "Revivification", picture 6 of the second cycle. The birds at the bottom of the left picture depict a new set of opposites coming into view and getting to know each other—a new iteration of drive energy and its potential to be contained. They indicate that the cycle of transformation between the opposites continues. From Rosarium Philosophorum: Secunda pars alchimiae de lapide philosophico (Frankfurt, 1550).

receptive attitude toward the eros of the self and its natural wisdom. In a woman or a man, this happens not only on the intellectual level but also as a numinous, sensory inundation of transpersonal eros. In the introduction, Elise's dream of the religious center with an altar girl and a related, animated young priest is another image that anticipates a union of new spirituality and new eros—a newly born royal pair that is the transhuman goal in any individuation process. In her own life, a woman genuinely feels in her bones that the archetypal meaning and wisdom of the self are directly related to her personally.

Bibliography

Abt, Theodor. *Book of the Explanation of Symbols: Kitāb Ḥall ar-Rumūz by Muḥammad ibn Umail*. Vol. IB, Corpus Alchemicum Arabicum. Zürich: Living Human Heritage Publications, 2009.

Abt, Theodor. *The Book of Pictures: Muṣḥaf aṣ-ṣuwar by Zosimos of Panopolis.* Supplement, Corpus Alchemicum Arabicum. Zürich: Living Human Heritage Publications, 2007.

Abt, Theodor. *Introduction to Picture Interpretation according to C. G. Jung.* Einsiedeln: Daimon Verlag, 2005.

Abt, Theodor, and Erik Hornung. *Knowledge of the Afterlife: The Egyptian Amduat—Quest for Immortality.* Zürich: Living Human Heritage Publications, 2003.

Allan, John. *Inscapes of the Child's World: Jungian Counseling in Schools and Clinics.* Thompson, CT: Spring Publications, 1988.

Bourgeault, Cynthia. *The Meaning of Mary Magdalene: Discovering the Woman at the Heart of Christianity.* Boston: Shambhala, 2010.

Chodorow, Nancy. *The Reproduction of Mothering: Psychoanalysis and the Sociology of Gender.* Berkeley: University of California Press, 1999.

Coles, Robert. *The Spiritual Life of Children.* Boston: Houghton Mifflin, 1990.

Crane, Thomas Frederick, ed. *Italian Popular Tales.* 1885. Reprinted: Outlook Verlag, 2018.

Dasent, George. Webbe, ed. *Popular Tales from the Norse.* Edinburg: Edmonston and Douglas, 1859.

de Jong, Helena Maria Elisabeth. *Michael Maier's Atalanta Fugiens.* York Beach, ME: Nicolas-Hays, 1969.

Edinger, Edward F. *Archetype of the Apocalypse: A Jungian Study of the Book of Revelation.* Chicago: Open Court, 1999.

Edinger, Edward F. *The Mysterium Lectures: A Journey through C. G. Jung's "Mysterium Coniunctionis."* Toronto: Inner City Books, 1995.

Foley, Helene P., ed. *The Homeric Hymn to Demeter: Translation, Commentary, and Interpretive Essays*. Princeton, NJ: Princeton University Press, 1993.

Fordham, Michael. *Children as Individuals*. London: Free Association Books, 1996.

Gregory the Great. "Homily 33." In Jacques-Paul Migne, *Patrologia Latina,* 76:1238. https://archive.org/details/patrologia-latina_1-221.

Grimm, Jacob, and Wilhelm Grimm. *Grimm's Complete Fairy Tales*. Garden City, NY: Nelson Doubleday, 1976.

Grimm, Jacob, and Wilhelm Grimm. *Grimm's Household Tales*. Translated by Margaret Hunt. Introduction by Andrew Lang. 2 vols. London: George Bell and Sons, 1884.

Grimm, Jacob, and Wilhelm Grimm. *Kinder- und Hausmärchen*. Berlin: Michael Holzinger, 2016.

Hannah, Barbara. *The Animus: The Spirit of Inner Truth in Women*. 2 vols. Wilmette, IL: Chiron Publications, 2011, 2018.

Harding, M. Esther. *The Parental Image: Its Injury and Reconstruction*. New York: C. G. Jung Foundation for Analytical Psychology, 1965; reprinted Toronto: Inner City Books, 2003.

Haskins, Susan. *Mary Magdalen: Myth and Meaning*. New York: Riverhead Books, 1993.

Herman, Judith Lewis. *Father-Daughter Incest*. Cambridge, MA: Harvard University Press, 1981.

Holroyd, Michael. *Lytton Strachey: A Critical Biography*. 2 vols. London: Heinemann, 1967.

Howe, Laurel. *War of the Ancient Dragon: Transformation of Violence in Sandplay*. Sheridan, WY: Fisher King Press, 2016.

Jansen, Katherine Ludwig. *The Making of the Magdalen: Preaching and Popular Devotion in the Later Middle Ages*. Princeton, NJ: Princeton University Press, 2000.

Jung, C. G. "Answer to Job" (1952). In *CW*, vol. 11. Princeton, NJ: Princeton University Press, 1969.

Jung, C. G. "Concerning Mandala Symbolism" (1950). In *CW*, vol. 9i. Princeton, NJ: Princeton University Press, 2nd ed., 1968.

Jung, C. G. "Concerning Rebirth" (1950). In *CW*, vol. 9i. Princeton, NJ: Princeton University Press, 1968.

Jung, C. G. *Memories, Dreams, Reflections.* New York: Random House, 1961.

Jung, C. G. *Mysterium Coniunctionis* (1955–56). *CW*, vol. 14. Princeton, NJ: Princeton University Press, 1970.

Jung, C. G. "On the Nature of the Psyche" (1954). In *CW*, vol. 8. Princeton, NJ: Princeton University Press, 1969.

Jung, C. G. "On the Psychology of the Unconscious" (1943). In CW, vol. 7. Princeton, NJ: Princeton University Press, 1966.

Jung, C. G. "Paracelsus as a Spiritual Phenomenon" (1942). In *CW*, vol. 13. Princeton, NJ: Princeton University Press, 1967.

Jung, C. G. "The Phenomenology of the Spirit in Fairytales" (1948). In *CW*, vol. 9i. Princeton, NJ: Princeton University Press, 2nd ed., 1968.

Jung, C. G. "The Philosophical Tree" (1954). In *CW*, vol. 13. Princeton, NJ: Princeton University Press, 1967.

Jung, C. G. "A Psychological Approach to the Dogma of the Trinity" (1948). In *CW*, vol. 11. Princeton, NJ: Princeton University Press, 1969.

Jung, C. G. "The Psychological Aspects of the Kore" (1951). In *CW*, vol. 9i. Princeton, NJ: Princeton University Press, 1968.

Jung, C. G. *Psychological Types* (1923). *CW*, vol. 6. Princeton, NJ: Princeton University Press, 1971.

Jung, C. G. *Psychology and Alchemy* (1944). *CW*, vol. 12. Princeton, NJ: Princeton University Press, 1953.

Jung, C. G. "The Psychology of the Transference" (1946). In *CW*, vol. 16. Princeton, NJ: Princeton University Press, 1966.

Jung, C. G. "The Relations between the Ego and the Unconscious" (1935). In *CW*, vol. 7. Princeton, NJ: Princeton University Press, 1966.

Jung, C. G. "The Spirit Mercurius" (1948). In *CW*, vol. 13. Princeton, NJ: Princeton University Press, 1967.

Jung, C. G. "A Study in the Process of Individuation" (1950). In *CW*, vol. 9i. Princeton, NJ: Princeton University Press, 2nd ed., 1968.

Jung, C. G. "Synchronicity: An Acausal Connecting Principle" (1952). In *CW*, vol. 8. Princeton, NJ: Princeton University Press, 1969.

Jung, C. G. "Transformation Symbolism in the Mass" (1954). In *CW*, vol. 11. Princeton, NJ: Princeton University Press, 1969.

Jung, C. G. *Visions: Notes of the Seminar Given in 1930-1934 by C.G. Jung.* Princeton, NJ: Princeton University Press, 1997.

Jung, C. G. "The Visions of Zosimos" (1954). In *CW*, vol. 13. Princeton, NJ: Princeton University Press, 1967.

Jung, Emma, and Marie-Louise von Franz. *The Grail Legend.* New York: Putnam, for the C. G. Jung Foundation for Analytical Psychology, 1970.

Kalff, Dora M. *Sandplay: Mirror of a Child's Psyche.* San Francisco: Browser Press, 1971.

Kalsched, Donald. *The Inner World of Trauma: Archetypal Defences of the Personal Spirit.* London: Routledge, 1996.

Kerényi, Carl. *Eleusis: Archetypal Image of Mother and Daughter.* Princeton, NJ: Princeton University Press, 1967.

King, Karen L. *The Gospel of Mary of Magdala: Jesus and the First Woman Apostle.* Santa Rosa, CA: Polebridge Press, 2003.

Kolodiejchuk, Brian, editor. *Mother Teresa, Come Be My Light: The Private Writings of the Saint of Calcutta.* New York: Doubleday, 2007.

Leonard, Linda Schierse. *The Wounded Woman: Healing the Father-Daughter Relationship.* Boston: Shambhala, 1982.

Luton, Frith. *Bees, Honey and the Hive: Circumambulating the Centre—A Jungian Exploration of the Symbolism and Psychology.* Toronto: Inner City Books, 2011.

Maier, Michael. *Atalanta Fugiens: An Edition of the Emblems, Fugues, and Epigrams.* Translated and edited by Joscelyn Godwin. Grand Rapids, MI: Phanes Press, 1989. Originally published 1617.

Miller, Alice. *The Drama of the Gifted Child: The Search for the True Self*, rev. ed. New York: Basic Books, 1997.

Neumann, Erich. *The Child: Structure and Dynamics of the Nascent Personality.* London: Routledge, 1973.

Neumann, Erich. *The Origins and History of Consciousness*. New York: Bollingen Foundation, 1954; reprinted Princeton, NJ: Princeton University Press, 2014.

Newton, Lara. *Brothers and Sisters: Discovering the Psychology of Companionship*. New Orleans: Spring Journal, 2007.

Oaklander, Violet. *Windows to Our Children: A Gestalt Therapy Approach to Children and Adolescents*. Moab, UT: Real People Press, 1978; reprinted Gouldsboro, Maine: Gestalt Journal Press, 2007.

Odajnyk, V. Walter. "The Archetypal Interpretation of Fairy Tales: Bluebeard." *Psychological Perspectives* 47, no. 2 (2004): 247–75.

Ogden, Pat, Kekuni Minton, and Clare Pain. *Trauma and the Body: A Sensorimotor Approach to Psychotherapy*. New York: W. W. Norton, 2006.

Olivelle, Patrick, trans. *Upaniṣads*. Oxford: Oxford University Press, 1996.

Pagels, Elaine. *The Gnostic Gospels*. New York: Random House, 1979.

Perera, Sylvia Brinton. *The Scapegoat Complex: Toward a Mythology of Shadow and Guilt*. Toronto: Inner City Books, 1996.

Pipher, Mary, and Sara Pipher Gilliam. *Reviving Ophelia: Saving the Selves of Adolescent Girls*, 25th anniversary edition. New York: Riverhead Books, 2019.

Punnett, Audrey, editor. *Jungian Child Analysis*. Sheridan, WY: Fisher King Press, 2018.

Read, John. *Prelude to Chemistry: An Outline of Alchemy, Its Literature and Relationships*. London: G. Bell and Sons, 1936.

Roberts, Alexander, James Donaldson, and Arthur Cleveland Coxe. *The Ante-Nicene Fathers: Translations of the Writings of the Fathers down to A.D. 325*. 10 vols. Grand Rapids, MI: W. B. Eerdmans, 1962. Originally published 1885.

Robinson, James M., ed. *The Nag Hammadi Library in English*, 4th rev. ed. Leiden: E. J. Brill, 1996.

Salaman, Clement, Dorine van Oyen, William D. Wharton, and Jean-Pierre Mahe, trans. *The Way of Hermes: New Translations of "The Corpus Hermeticum" and "The Definitions of Hermes Trismegistus to Asclepius."* Rochester, VT: Inner Traditions, 2000.

Schweizer, Andreas, and Regine Schweizer-Vüllers, eds. *Wisdom Has Built Her House: Psychological Aspects of the Feminine.* Einsiedeln, Switzerland: Daimon Verlag, 2019.

Shelley, Peter. *Frances Farmer: The Life and Films of a Troubled Star.* Jefferson, NC: McFarland, 2011.

Shirar, Lynda. *Dissociative Children: Bridging the Inner and Outer Worlds.* New York: W. W. Norton, 1996.

Simmons, Rachel. *Odd Girl Out: The Hidden Culture of Aggression in Girls,* rev. ed. New York: Houghton Mifflin, 2002; reprinted New York: Mariner Books, 2011.

Smith, Patrick, trans. *The Rosary of the Philosophers: Being the Rosarium Philosophorum.* Edmonds, WA: Holmes Publishing Group, 2007.

Swan-Foster, Nora. *Jungian Art Therapy: A Guide to Dreams, Images, and Analytical Psychology.* New York: Routledge, 2018.

Tatar, Maria, ed. *The Annotated Brothers Grimm.* New York: W. W. Norton, 2004.

Trungpa, Chögyam. *Mindfulness in Action: Making Friends with Yourself through Meditation and Everyday Awareness.* Boston: Shambhala, 2015.

Trungpa, Chögyam. *The Profound Treasury of the Ocean of Dharma.* 3 vols. Boston: Shambhala, 2013.

Uther, Hans-Jörg. *The Types of International Folktales: A Classification and Bibliography. Folklore Fellows Communications* 133, no. 284. Helsinki: Finnish Academy of Science and Letters, 2004.

von Franz, Marie-Louise. *Animus and Anima in Fairy Tales.* Toronto: Inner City Books, 2002.

von Franz, Marie-Louise. *Archetypal Dimensions of the Psyche.* Boston: Shambhala, 1997.

von Franz, Marie-Louise. *The Cat: A Tale of Feminine Redemption.* Toronto: Inner City Books, 1999.

von Franz, Marie-Louise. *Creation Myths.* Boston: Shambhala, 1999.

von Franz, Marie-Louise. *The Feminine in Fairy Tales.* Boston: Shambhala, 1972; rev. ed. 1993.

von Franz, Marie-Louise. *The Golden Ass of Apuleius: The Liberation of the Feminine in Man,* rev. ed. Boston: Shambhala, 1992.

von Franz, Marie-Louise. *The Interpretation of Fairy Tales*, rev. ed. Boston: Shambhala, 1996.

von Franz, Marie-Louise. *Number and Time: Reflections Leading toward a Unification of Depth Psychology and Physics*. Evanston, IL: Northwestern University Press, 1974.

von Franz, Marie-Louise. *On Dreams and Death: A Jungian Interpretation*. Chicago: Open Court, 1998.

von Franz, Marie-Louise. *Projection and Recollection in Jungian Psychology: Reflections of the Soul*. La Salle and London: Open Court, 1980.

von Franz, Marie-Louise. *Psyche and Matter*. Boston and London: Shambhala, 1992.

von Franz, Marie-Louise. *Shadow and Evil in Fairy Tales*. Boston: Shambhala, 1974.

von Franz, Marie-Louise, and Fraser Boa. *The Way of the Dream: Conversations on Jungian Dream Interpretation with Marie-Louise von Franz*. Boston: Shambhala, 1992.

Warner, Marina. *From the Beast to the Blonde: On Fairy Tales and Their Tellers*. New York: Farrar, Straus and Giroux, 1995.

Weinrib, Estelle L. *Images of the Self: The Sandplay Therapy Process*, 2nd ed. Cloverdale, CA: Temenos Press, 2004.

Wertenschlag-Birkhäuser, Eva. *Windows on Eternity: The Paintings of Peter Birkhäuser*. Einsiedeln: Daimon Verlag, 2008.

Wickes, Frances G. *The Inner World of Childhood: A Study in Analytical Psychology*. New York: D. Appleton, 1927.

Winnicott, D. W. "Ego Distortion in Terms of True and False Self" (1960). In *The Maturational Processes and the Facilitating Environment*, 140–52. London: Karnac Books, 1965; reprinted London: Routledge, 2018.

Zeller, Max. *The Dream: The Vision of the Night*. Los Angeles: Analytical Psychology Club of Los Angeles and the C. G. Jung Institute of Los Angeles, 1975. Reprinted: Sheridan, WY: Fisher King Press, 2015.

Zipes, Jack, trans. *Beautiful Angiola: The Great Treasury of Sicilian Folk and Fairy Tales Collected by Laura Gonzenbach*. New York: Routledge, 2004.

www.ingramcontent.com/pod-product-compliance
Lightning Source LLC
Chambersburg PA
CBHW051440270326
41932CB00024B/3371